How Sex Changed the Internet and the Internet Changed Sex

AN UNEXPECTED HISTORY

SAMANTHA COLE

Workman Publishing ■ New York

Library of Congress Cataloging-in-Publication Data is available.

ISBN 978-1-5235-1384-0

Cover design by Sarah Smith
Interior design by Sarah Smith and Rae Ann Spitzenberger

Photo credits can be found on pages 277–278.

Workman books are available at special discounts when purchased in bulk for premiums and sales promotions as well as for fundraising or educational use. Special editions or book excerpts can also be created to specification. For details, please contact specialmarkets@hbgusa.com.

Workman Publishing Co., Inc., a subsidiary of Hachette Book Group, Inc.
1290 Avenue of the Americas
New York, NY 10104

workman.com

WORKMAN is a registered trademark of Workman Publishing Co., Inc., a subsidiary of Hachette Book Group, Inc.

Printed in the USA on responsibly sourced paper.
First printing September 2022

10 9 8 7 6 5 4 3 2 1

For the workers, posters, players,
and survivors, my fellow members
in the "Now Online."

> "We exist in a world of pure
> communication, where looks
> don't matter and only the best
> writers get laid."
>
> **—legba, a player on LambdaMOO**

Some of my earliest experiences with writing creatively happened online, on message boards. As a homeschooled teenager growing up in the late nineties and early 2000s, I had the internet for a campus. On my message boards of choice, I gossiped about the week's intra-forum drama with other members, debated scripture with middle-aged theologians, befriended queer atheists, shared poetry and photography and bottomless pages of writing with people I knew only by their screen names. To me, their preferred font also served as their voice—a pink Comic Sans "sounded" a lot different than a dark green Times New Roman.

Writing was world-building and identity shaping. I crafted a parallel life on the other side of a static-charged monitor sitting in my parents' living room—and later, on a six-pound white-trimmed Dell laptop. The undercurrent of all these conversations about religion or poetry or politics was romance. All my constant digital scribing turned into my first meaningful relationships, my first loves and heartaches. My friends and I had never met, but we would whisper together in private messages about who had crushes on whom. My eyes would dart to the "now online" sidebar, a sea of usernames, scanning for theirs. We had proms and parties and asked each other to dance. Someone gave me a pixelated flower bouquet.

Now in my thirties, I spend hours each day glued to Twitter and Meta's Instagram, two monopolies that devoured—and then razed— the Geocities websites and bulletin boards I once considered my digital homes. Today's social media feeds are a mix of the worst people's unsolicited opinions about World War III, other people dunking on *those* people, and commands that I "don't scroll past!!!" crowdfunding requests for someone's sick cat. These are buttressed with a grab bag of news headlines involving personal, national, and global horrors against the most marginalized of society, photos of a celebrity chinchilla, and ten-second video clips of bouncing asses and boobs on beaches and beds. All of this is received in a kind of blur, algorithmically selected in the order I'm most likely to "engage" with it. We're *users* now, not members. And the products we're using are one another, our fellow "content creators." We pass around these little pixelated "bouquets" for the benefit of the companies running the platforms.

When you peer under the surface of all this consumerism and chaos, and back into the history of the internet, it becomes clear that the internet was built on sex, and sex has remained its through line no matter how hard some people try to deny it. A demand for sex built the shopping cart, the browser cookie, ad revenue models, payment processors, and the dynamic web page. The desire to explore and share our sexuality constructed the internet, piece by piece, as we know it today. And then technocratic billionaires betrayed the sexual for the sanitized and safe. We started labeling things "safe for work" and "*not* safe for work," a binary that's telling of who we allowed to call the shots. Sexuality is either unsafe or safe under a pretense of labor, depending on whether a boss is cool with it. Capitalists built walls around the "safe" parts of the internet to appease investors, advertisers, banks, and zealots—and pushed everyone who didn't comply to the margins.

But there's a catch: There is no adult side of the internet. The internet isn't a wall with sexy stuff on one face and "family friendly" on the other. It's a web. And the ways we knit that web together, from the very beginning in late 1970's chat systems to today, is a choice. They include how we defend or concede our dwindling rights to sexual expression online, how control of that web looks, how we choose who gets to decide and participate, and how those decisions shape our lives away from the keyboard and at what cost.

▪▪▪■■▪▪▪

The phrase "in real life" as a distinction from my already rich and captivating online worlds never made sense to me. Years before I sat down in front of an internet connection, the denizens of online social spaces had a word to address that dissonance: "meatspace." For them, the corporeal world was already an extraneous one; the "real" interactions happened online. What sat in the computer chair was just flesh.

For a long time "meatspace" was an inside joke among tech nerds and geeks, a way to wink at the idea that the only thing separating the digital realm from the physical was a sack of wet bones, brain matter, and synapses. It was also a kind of dig: Bodies were just animated meat and anyone who took the "real world" too seriously was an ignorant sheep. As the internet went mainstream over the years, "in real life," or IRL, became the bloodless replacement for "meatspace."

In my late teens, the main forum where I spent most of my time changed owners. Things quickly took a turn for the worse. Terms of use got stricter, who was allowed to participate became narrower, and the digital walls closed in on users. My little friend group started to splinter off. We moved to separate chat platforms, then microblogging sites like Tumblr. Every move weakened our ties. It was my first time I realized that the homes we build on the internet—places I thought would be constant, infinite—were temporary.

As I came across new tidbits or abandoned web pages in my research for this book, I couldn't shake the notion that none of what I saw was stable. From early 80's Usenet forums to the most current social media accounts, there were no guarantees they would still be there when I returned. YouTube play-throughs of erotic video games had already disappeared by the time I reached them, taken down for violating the platform's terms of service against sexual content. Nineties porn websites that were hand-coded with care and the hottest new live-cams or chat programs were gone, their owners having let the domain registrations lapse long ago. Links to news articles about early online sex work return 404 errors after newspapers folded, merged, or were acquired and shuttered, their URLs crumbling behind them.

What remains are writings carefully preserved through something of an internet oral history, kept by the people who were there. One of them was Carmen Hermosillo. Under the nom de plume "humdog" she wrote critically, lovingly, and prophetically about the virtual worlds she inhabited and how they made her feel: "many times in cyberspace, i felt it necessary to say that i was human," she wrote. "once, i was told that i existed primarily as a voice in somebody's head."

Hermosillo's virtual and physical worlds were inexorably intertwined. She wasn't living apart from the systems she interrogated. She committed herself fully to dalliances, love affairs, and heartbreak online, to the point of full immersion and at the expense of her IRL self. Those close to her, her friends online, suggested she slow down, take a break from the internet for a while. In 2008, after the particularly devastating end to a relationship formed in the virtual world of *Second Life*, she deleted nine of her profiles and personas across many platforms and was allegedly found dead in her apartment days later.

People bring their whole selves to online communal spaces, including their sexuality. Often, it's painful and complex. Even in pre-internet, text-based worlds, virtual residents were wary of the commodification of self that these new cultures set into motion. "i have seen many people spill their guts on-line, and i did so myself until, at last, i began to see that i had commodified myself," humdog wrote. Now, near-nakedness on Instagram or TikTok can either make you viral or get you banned, depending on the fickleness of the algorithm that day.

The things that happen online matter in "meatspace." When dating websites connect the right people, whole lives can change, the directions of entire families' stories and ancestries are altered. When people first pointed webcams at their sex lives, they invented a new industry—and more than twenty-five years later, a way for more people to take ownership of their erotic labor or talk on Zoom with an isolated friend. Internet forums built for spreading hate and revenge don't stay online; they reach out into the world to hurt people. When discriminatory laws push sex workers off the platforms they use to survive, they suffer in real life, and their digitally inflicted hardships serve as a bellwether for what's to come for the rest of us. Our communities narrow, online and off; our many parallel worlds get smaller.

It's not a different society or another species living and working online between the pixels. It's us. The internet has changed sexuality, love, porn, and our own erotic tastes in more ways than we'll ever fully realize. And sex has shaped the internet into what it is today— although those in power would prefer that it be erased from the internet altogether. This is a history of control: how we had it, grappled for it, lost it, and how we can learn from the past to get it back.

And it's a history that's still being written as I type this.

The revolution will be digitized

CHAPTER 1

The Internet Was Built on Sex

"many times in cyberspace,
i felt it necessary to
say that i was human.
once, i was told that
i existed primarily
as a voice in
somebody's head."

—Carmen Hermosillo, 1994

The first node in the modern internet's predecessor, ARPANET, was a Sigma 7 computer that ran the "SEX" operating system, programmer's shorthand for "set X." That 32-bit computer was the size of a washing machine and sat in the University of California, Los Angeles's, Boelter Hall, room 3420. The walls were, and still are, avocado green.

On the night of October 29, 1969, Charley Kline, a UCLA graduate student programmer, sat at that Sigma 7. He was on the phone with Stanford Research Institute (SRI) programmer Bill Duvall, stationed at another Teletype terminal about 350 miles north in Menlo Park. Until then, access to information or computing power was limited to one of a few machines scattered across the country—to use one, you had to travel to it and log on in person. The Advanced Research Projects Agency, or ARPA, wanted to change that. They would network the computers together over telephone lines—something major technology companies of the time said couldn't be done.

Letter by letter, Kline started to peck out "LOG," hoping Duvall could see it on his system. If they could make it to G, the computer would recognize it as a login attempt, and return the I, N. Their conversation went something like this:

> > Kline: "Did you get the L?"
> > Duvall: "I got the L!"
> > Kline: "Did you get the O?"
> > Duvall: "I got the O."
> > Kline: "Did you get the G?"
> > Duvall: "The system just crashed!"

Vacuum tube array from early mainframe computer

The first phrase to travel across computers was "Lo."

They debugged and tried again an hour later, this time successfully completing the sequence. The UCLA node running SEX and the

SRI system were the first two computers to form a network—the first long-distance "connection."

There was nothing technically sexy about these systems. That early operating system's name was either a coincidence or a nerdy joke between computer scientists. But it unwittingly foreshadowed a founding truth that courses through the entire history of the internet: One of the most basic drives humans have is sex. And sexuality is inextricably woven into the fabric of the internet—its architecture, protocols, standards, and business dealings—whether the people using these systems realize it or not. It's a truth that's part of the internet's history regardless of how hard Silicon Valley monopolies and their investors try to erase it.

■■■■■■■

A year before anyone beheld that first "Lo," Douglas Engelbart prepared to give his biggest presentation yet. As the head of the Augmentation Research Center at Stanford Research Institute, he was scheduled to speak on the first day of the 1968 Fall Joint Computer Conference— an unseasonably warm Monday for December in San Francisco. The description for his talk wasn't exactly titillating. Attendees were in for a "computer-based, interactive, multi-console display system."

But those attending the conference would have heard rumors about what Engelbart and his team—a group that dropped acid under test conditions, for research—were up to in their Menlo Park headquarters.

Sitting on stage in front of a thousand or so audience members, Engelbart started with an apology for staying seated at a terminal instead of standing at

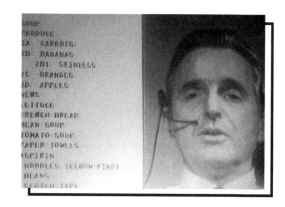

Douglas Engelbart in the midst of the "Mother of All Demos"

a podium. He also noted the unusual format of his presentation: a twenty-foot projection screen behind him on stage, beaming live two-way video (via leased microwave link lines from his computer workstation keyboard and mouse setup) to the lab team, working on an SDS-940 computer, thirty miles away.

This setup, he'd recall decades later during a 1986 talk, was expensive to pull off—and he was spending NASA and ARPA sponsorship money to do it. The whole thing was a big risk. "If this had flopped, we would have sort of gotten into trouble," he said.

It didn't flop. Engelbart showed the world, for the first time, the beginnings of his team's vision for computers working to augment the potential of human minds. What he and his colleagues presented that day became known to history as the "Mother of All Demos," demonstrating the capabilities of interactive computing that would define how we use computers for the next fifty years and beyond. They probably couldn't have imagined future generations would put this interactivity to use in finding love and sex on their computer screens.

Graphical User Interface (GUI)
Before computers had windows, icons, and cursors, you'd navigate from program to program through text commands. The invention of GUIs in the sixties, and their popularization with Apple home computers in the eighties, made using computers more accessible to people without programming or command-line knowledge.

The setup was primitive. He used a peripheral mouse—a chunk of wired, wooden block sitting on a wheel—to point and click around on a screen, for a level of human-computer interactivity that was unprecedented. Tiling between windows, using hypertext to link, video conferencing, and collaborative document editing were all shown, for the first time, in the ninety-minute talk. At the demo's close, the audience gave a standing ovation. Engelbart remembers the feeling as akin to Moses parting the Red Sea.

Throughout the sixties, computers were largely regarded as computational machines only; they sent humans to the moon and calculated war strategies, but they weren't considered a conduit for creativity or innovation for the average person. Engelbart's neat haircut and crisp shirt and tie belied a controversial belief system that ran counter to, and quickly outpaced, those modalities: He thought humans could work together with machines toward rapid, unprecedented ingenuity. In a paper published before the demo, Engelbart wrote that things like the peripheral mouse and interactive pages would go beyond simple gimmicks to a "way of life" that allowed for "human feel for a situation" to coexist with powerful computing methods.

All of this history so far predates the internet, but only barely. As director of DARPA, J.C.R. Licklider, a psychologist and computer scientist, pushed for the formation of the ARPANET project. Engelbart used the same SDS-940 computer in his demo that Duvall sat in front of to receive the "lo."

"We are as gods"

The internet as we know it today evolved from these early systems, but most of those working on it didn't see its potential beyond research labs. Years before the first email, Licklider was one of the few who saw the internet's future as not only a communication tool, but also a creative one. "In a few years, men will be able to communicate more effectively through a machine than face to face," he said in 1968. "When minds interact, new ideas emerge."

One of the earliest ways people found to interact through the internet was in bulletin board systems (BBS).

Legend has it that the first bulletin board system was the brainchild of necessity—and like many good legends, this one began in a storm. In mid-January 1978, Chicago was in the grips of the most brutal winter it'd seen in any year before or since. A bored thirty-three-year-old IBM employee named Ward Christensen called his computer club friend Randy Suess from his snowed-in home in the suburbs with an idea.

Punch cards
Up until the seventies and even into the eighties, computers were programmed using punch (or "punched") cards, slips of paper that held one line of code each.

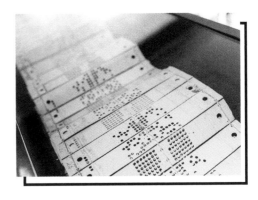

Punch cards were the "programming language" for early computers.

He wanted to make a computerized version of the index-card-and-pushpin cork board they used at club meetings for things like parts requests and carpools. Stuck at home, they missed the simple connection that board provided.

Snow was still on the ground by the time Christensen and Suess's "Computerized Bulletin Board System" went live for the first time a month later, when transportation systems finally thawed enough for them to visit each other and get the thing online.

For the first time, home computer owners (and the relatively few people who also owned modems at the time) could communicate with one another. People weren't yet "users" but "callers," dialing in from a computer running BBS software, connected to a telephone line and a modem. Callers would log on by dialing the address of whatever BBS they wanted to enter. By dialing in to a server—which was actually just another person's home modem—callers could log in to simple, text-based systems. One caller, one modem, one computer. It was the simplest representation of what the internet would someday become, a tadpole in the primordial soup of online life.

BBS: Bulletin Board Systems
Pre-internet programs for connecting to email and forums through telephone modem lines.

That early style of BBS was too much like a corkboard to foster fluid conversations; it was great for finding interesting people and places near you with which to connect away from the keyboard or trade knowledge, but it didn't leave room for a social life to unfold entirely online. CommuniTree, one of the first bulletin board systems, was created in 1978 as a social experiment on the system, which until then was populated by hard-core microcomputing hobbyists who could navigate the complex command codes required to talk to one another on BBS. Topics started at the tree's roots, or conferences, and grew like branches as more people added to the conversation. The message that greeted visitors to its first conference borrowed from the print publication *Whole Earth Catalog*'s statement of purpose: "We are as gods and we might as well get good at it." Instead of hardware and software, people got online to talk about spirituality, religion, enlightened matters of human nature—anything but computer processing.

It proved that the internet could be used for more than hacking and hardware, and that a real community of anarcho-socialist flower children could spring up inside of a machine built by the Department of Defense. But CommuniTree was too pure to live, choked out by what would soon become the world's biggest computer company: Apple.

Apple started providing public schools with personal computers in the mid-eighties, as part of a deal cut with the federal government. The kids who figured out how to use the modems on those computers found CommuniTree—and bombarded the sapling with expletives and messages that would still be considered not safe for work. Systems operators tried to keep the noise at bay by hiding messages, but all that text sent from bored and belligerent grade schoolers still ate up precious disk space. Eventually the disks became overwhelmed, and the tree died. "The barbarian hordes mowed us down," one CommuniTree resident said.

But that was not the end of all BBS. Many more formed and flourished—and a ton of them were much more sexy than post-Enlightenment discourse.

The Whole Earth 'Lectronic Link, or The WELL, was the first large-scale social BBS. Started by *Whole Earth Catalog* founder Stewart Brand and physician Larry Brilliant in San Francisco in 1985, it was the natural successor to CommuniTree's lofty dreams: a "watering hole for articulate and playful thinkers from all walks of life."

To most internet users today, BBS is remembered—if it's recalled at all—as a blip in the history of online life. But the BBS era represents almost twenty years of computing history, from the late seventies to the mid-nineties, as hundreds of thousands of users built virtual

After a long military career, active duty in Vietnam, two divorces, crises of faith, and feats of activism, Sister Mary Elizabeth Clark was leading a pastoral life of service when a trip to rural Missouri to help tend a local herd of cattle led her to meet a young man with AIDS. The man was isolated by his bigoted community and wasting away under the secrecy of his condition. "In that area, if anyone found out someone had AIDS, chances are their farms would have been burned," she said. "He had nowhere to go to find out about the disease."

He didn't have a private phone line, but he did have a home computer, and Sister Mary Elizabeth had an idea: an online service for people like that young man, who didn't have access to safe and private medical help, but could log on to a bulletin board system. UC Irvine student Jamie Jemison was already running the AIDS Education Global Information Service, or AEGIS, but it was floundering; Sister Mary Elizabeth took it over in 1990, inspired by her meeting with the young man in Missouri, and turned it into a BBS that saw more than 300 visitors an hour at its peak. In 1999 it saw 25 million hits per month. She spent eighteen hours a day keeping the board updated with information from the latest journal articles and medical studies. The information she provided was lifesaving for some; doctors as well as patients logged on to read the latest on experimental treatments.

It was a one-woman online journal with no precedent. "This is strictly an act of love," she said.

Sister Mary Elizabeth Clark would move from typewriter to keyboard to start an early BBS that provided information for those suffering from AIDS.

homes within them. Some historians estimate that more than 106,400 individual BBSes ran at the peak of its popularity, with the biggest welcoming tens of thousands of callers.

"It's Just So Human . . . So Basic"

As BBS populations grew, they were the first to grapple with censorship of free speech rights. Some installed profanity filters to automatically censor bawdy language in public chats. One early BBS, The KEEP, declared in its rule document: "NO SUCH THING AS FREEDOM OF SPEECH HERE." Everyone was encouraged to speak freely, but not at the expense of others' enjoyment of the system:

> There is currently no profanity filter installed on The KEEP. However, if foul language becomes a problem here, it CAN be re-installed. We here at The KEEP have nothing against adult language from the mouths of adults when used discriminately. Unfortunately, some people aren't so discriminating. We would like to foster a friendly, family atmosphere here, where any person of any persuasion or age would feel welcome.

On the WELL, the more taboo conferences were some of the most popular. San Francisco minister David Hawkins started the Sexuality conference in 1985, and it was a hit: One topic titled "Is the Sexual Revolution Dead?" got more than one hundred responses in a week.

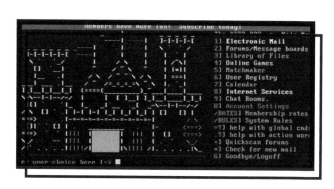

The landing page for "The Keep," an early, influential BBS that wrestled with free speech issues

Many BBS system operators devoted their online worlds to porn. With names like SleazeNet, ThrobNet, and Pleasure Dome, these sites let callers know what they were getting into when they dialed in. Accessing a BBS was an intensive process, usually involving a series of questions about your location, age, and interests. Sometimes, gaining membership involved picking up the phone to speak directly to the system operator, or SysOp.

Pleasure Dome, a BBS run by Virginia Beach resident David Taylor in the mid-nineties, joined BBS Direct, a company that set up local-access phone numbers in a hundred cities so that people could call it without worry about burning through long-distance charges while they scrolled. Taylor sold subscriptions to the Dome for $30 a month or $40 a year. Women got in free. Taylor told the local newspaper—which published a curious look at Pleasure Dome and the growing adult BBS culture sweeping the nation in 1994—that he vetted new subscribers (and their age and gender, subjectively) by calling them on their landline and hearing their voice.

> "I have a quaint view that makes me think that discussing the ability to write 'fuck' or worrying about the ability to look at pictures of sexual acts constitutes The Least Of Our Problems surrounding freedom of expression,"
>
> –The WELL denizen Carmen Hermosillo, 1994—a statement that seems nearly prophetic today, as we grapple with Facebook censorship and Instagram "shadowbanning" anything even mildly sexual in nature

Around the same time, sexy CD-ROM games and galleries were getting popular among porn collectors and first-time PC owners who wanted to test out their new toys. Program disks like *Penthouse Select-a-Pet* and *Virtual Sex Shoot* games and galleries held pornographic images that could be easily saved and sent over email, arranged for delivering in BBS. Porn piracy started almost as soon as porn hit the internet.

While pirated porn was taking over, much of what happened on BBS communities prioritized sharing banter over sharing files and was driven by genuine connections. A lot of the little dramas that played

THE MINITEL PINK

The Minitel is the piece of technology time forgot. Launched as an experiment in France in 1980, the country's telecom agency tried to replace phone books with these little terminals, which consisted of a small keyboard and CRT monitor, meant for setting up in the home study. The French government gave the hardware away to anyone who wanted it, but only allowed registered newspapers to make services for the Minitel. To access anything more than phone book information, you'd need to pay. Between its rollout in 1980 and its death in 2012, it generated hundreds of millions of dollars.

It had plenty of practical applications, with message boards, AIM-like chat, and travel booking services, but the most popular were adult, including dating and porn. On *Messageries Roses*, or "pink messages," operators posed as women ready to flirt.

Lonely souls would log on to a Minitel dating service and post ads much like newspaper personals—and in France, details often focused on what you wore as a way of expressing what you were like.

It was the "meeting of minds without impediments of appearance" that drew American audiences to the online world, the *New York Times* wrote in a 1995 article about the Minitel. But French internet denizens went about things differently, where people logged on and described what they were wearing in flirty detail: "The naked get dressed in order to titillate their audience, and clothes, intended to conceal what is intimate and private, reveal the soul."

A Minitel machine, Paris, France, 1986

out among users happened in public view of anyone else who happened to dial in. Like being at a party where sparks start to fly between friends, one could easily eavesdrop on people flirting between the written lines, over messages about the Grateful Dead or Star Trek, drugs or politics or favorite bars.

Stacy Horn started the EchoNYC BBS in 1989 as a hobby project, where she could talk to the most brilliant and interesting thinkers in New York. "East Coast Hang Out" was meant to be just that: a forum whose constituents loved this online community as much as their own cities. The idea came to her as an NYU graduate student spending her days working in Mobil's telecommunications department; she'd pitched a similar internal troubleshooting-chat concept to her corporate bosses but it never caught on because employees were too afraid of their mistakes being exposed.

At the same time, her nights spent among other students in the Interactive Telecommunications Program energized her—and when the assignment came to call into The WELL's burgeoning online community across the country, she was mesmerized. In what felt like clairvoyance, someone in The WELL said they'd heard she was starting an East Coast version of their community. The thought had never crossed Horn's mind, but she knew she had to do it the moment she heard it. She left her job at Mobil and threw herself into building Echo full time.

Almost immediately, her foray into online community building became hard work. She had to train newcomers to use computers and navigate Echo in real-life classes held in her apartment. This was on top of troubleshooting the server and keeping it running, plus mediating interpersonal online problems and meting out judgment calls as a one-woman moderation

> "It's delicious. It's just so human, and just so basic, to want to be in the presence of falling in love. And even if it's just sexual attraction, that's exciting, too."
>
> —**Stacey Horn,** EchoNYC BBS founder

team. Trolling wasn't much of an issue—joining Echo required calling Horn and mailing her a check for $19.95 a month. But she was moderating an intimate, intense group of people who often dated within the Echoid pool; spats, harassment, and general jerkishness sometimes required Lord Horn, as Echoids called her, to act unilaterally.

Echo is still active today—but now it lives on a cloud-based server instead of inside her apartment, and only about a hundred people still participate, mostly old friends from the old days. At its peak, two thousand people were on Echo, there to talk about society, art, movies, TV, and just about anything you'd overhear in a New York coffee shop. Including sex.

NSFW
"Not Safe for Work," digital shorthand that whatever possesses this label could be sexual, graphic, or otherwise awkward to have to explain to your boss if you're caught looking at it.

Occasionally, when Echoids would date among themselves and then break up, the sight of one another's online chats about everyday mundanity became too much. They'd sometimes ask Horn to delete their account because it was too painful to keep logging on. Leaving a relationship and losing a friend group paralleled as painfully on Echo as it would if it'd happened in their face-to-face lives.

In virtual worlds, those basic human experiences of love, jealousy, heartbreak, and healing are just as real as they are in "real life." The thrumming potential of the internet as a place to bring your entire self (and in many cases, much more than you'd bring to a flesh-and-blood interaction) was so vibrant that it threw into question the entire notion of what constitutes the real and the virtual, the imagined and the valid. In these relatively spartan online spaces, it might seem like denizens had more control over their experiences there than they did in the flesh-world; after all, it was just text lines on a screen, no messy complications like pheromones, facial expressions, or vocal subtleties, and they could pull the plug at any moment. But as more people came online, the less predictable—and more deliciously chaotic—the internet became.

CHAPTER 2

Cyber-Utopia, Censorship, and Tinysex

"People can communicate mind to mind.
There is no race. There are no genders.
There is no age. There are no infirmities.
There are only minds. Utopia? No, the internet."

—1997 television commercial
for MCI, an internet service provider

As more people bought personal computers, internet service providers started selling more than access to the internet. They started trying to sell a real place, somewhere you could visit. It wasn't quite heaven inside your PC, but it was about as close as you could get: a world of people ready to accept you for who you are, without snap judgments getting in the way.

We know better now.

Between the mid-eighties and the early nineties, life online had an optimistic glow. Techno-utopians settled virtual worlds in hopes that on the faceless internet, people would not only self-correct centuries of racism, sexism, and discrimination, but would also be free to experience more authentic encounters of every kind—including sexual. It was a naive idea, like most big beginnings.

Those early dreamers used Multi-User Domains (MUDs) and BBS to their imaginary capacity, describing themselves as otherworldly creatures or multiple personalities, or bending genders and sexualities to their fullest, weirdest potentials. But many more logged on to those spaces and described themselves as stereotypically hot, fit, tall blondes with blue eyes and flowing hair. When given the chance to become anything, they became Fabio and Pamela.

Cybersex

Like modern-day sexting, cybersex (sometimes "cybering") can mean typing out sexual fantasies to another person, but also encompassed settings like erotic video chatting and multiplayer virtual reality. Cybersex as a term has mostly fallen out of fashion.

These virtual worlds seeded how we use the internet today. Players had full control over how people see them, including as sexual mates. "On the Internet, nobody knows you're a dog," went the now-famous 1993 *New Yorker* cartoon caption. And it was true. You could be a strikeout in person, but a knockout online.

Some spaces offered relative anonymity and fluidity. In a role-playing group online, you can be a lady-frog avatar in medieval England or a lothario or a god of ancient origin—while other communities demanded that members identify themselves as they do IRL (in real life). In those spaces, usually more close-knit BBSes like Echo and The WELL, holding accountability for your own words was as important as the freedom to speak them. Callers took romantic advances more seriously when a real person was attached. Babies were born because their parents met on BBS—some people *exist* thanks to these early online worlds. Friends attended funerals for people they never met in person but knew intimately through MUDing.

Away from Keyboard (AFK)
An acronym to let fellow players know you're stepping away to tend to physical needs.

But instead of mold-breaking virtual freedom, what happened was the reinforcement of prejudices and personal biases, as people carried them from the AFK (away from keyboard) world to the online one.

"It sounds so naive now, doesn't it?" Stacy Horn said. "It was a shock to me, too, the extent of how much it *wasn't* a utopia."

YKINMKBYKIOK: Sex on Usenet

As BBS was gaining traction with a certain techy crowd, Tom Truscott and Jim Ellis, two Duke University students, were working on Usenet. First launched in 1980, Usenet was—and still is—a computerized corkboard of messages and responses. But like BBS, the advent of the World Wide Web stole a huge chunk of those users away. Unlike BBS, Usenet is decentralized and relies on local servers. Instead of dialing in to a central computer and modem, people post to their local news server, which forwards it to a network of other servers, so that every server has the same copy and people from all over can chime in on the same topics.

'On the Internet, nobody knows you're a dog.'

Keenly observed in the *New Yorker*, 1993

If early BBS was a sophisticated parlor of the intelligentsia, Usenet in its heyday was a rowdy cafeteria. People spent a *lot* of time debating proper behavior on newsgroups. Brawling missives sent to fellow users landed in between nuanced discourse on every topic under the sun, from euthanasia to wine to suicide to computer science.

> **"Usenet is like a herd of performing elephants with diarrhea—massive, difficult to redirect, awe-inspiring, entertaining, and a source of mind-boggling amounts of excrement when you least expect it."**
>
> —**Gene Spafford,** one of the first on Usenet, in 1992

A 1984 thread debating whether there should be a women's-only space[1] on Usenet (and whether forbidding men from participating in one part of Usenet constituted discrimination) is illustrative of the time, and tone, that people often brought to the space:

> net.women.only is the last vestige reminding us what a******s men are
> with their itchy rmgroup fingers, and their dominant attitudes to control
> everything! Back off! It still serves for women to request to be
> included. Their replies are answered by mail, not by news. Get it?
> Please go play in net.women,
> and stay out of net.women.ONLY ONLY, get it? Geesh!!

When it started, every conversation on Usenet fell under seven major categories: comp.*, misc.*, news.*, rec.*, sci.*, soc.*, and talk.*. In April 1988, Brian Reid—one of the members of the Usenet "backbone cabal"—together with Gordon Moffett and John Gilmore, added another hierarchy, alt.*, as a place for free speech to thrive. An inside joke was

---

1 Debates about women-only online spaces weren't unique to Usenet, and raged in just about every mass medium at the time. Anita Borg, founder of the mailing list Systers, wrote in 1993: "It is not the reluctance of women nor our participation in forums like Systers that limits communication and joint problem-solving with men. It is the sexism in our society, our field and our consciousness that limits us all."

COMING OUT ONLINE: "EARLY AND OFTEN"

In 1983, Reverend Jerry Falwell declared AIDS a "gay plague." People weren't even referring to it as AIDS yet, with phrases like "gay cancer" and "community-acquired immune dysfunction" still in the public's vocabulary. Harvey Milk, California's first openly gay elected official, had been assassinated just three years prior. The World Health Organization still deemed homosexuality an illness. It was the year Ronald Reagan's communications director, Pat Buchanan, called AIDS "nature's revenge on gay men." And the year soc.motss was born.

Short for "members of the same sex," soc.motss (first named net.motss) was an international Usenet group founded by programmer Steve Dyer, a place for net-savvy LGBTQIA+ people to gather and talk about anything at all. It was a forum "to foster discussion on a wide variety of topics, such as health problems, parenting, relationships, clearances, job security and many others," he wrote in the group's first post. For many people, those discussions meant they could be openly gay in a way they couldn't be away from their keyboards. They sought suggestions ("Does anyone have any recommendations on books written for the families of gay people?"), solidarity ("When i first posted to net.motss it took me all of 1 minute . . . to decide 'not to care' if co-workers, etc saw my postings"), straightforward advice ("Do come out. Early and often"), and current events. Mostly, they found a community that didn't yet exist offline at the same scale. Estimates place the audience for their musings at around 83,000 people.

Within a decade, Usenet faded away but the people of soc.motss didn't. They've held an in-person conference every year since 1988 (except for ones on Zoom in 2020 through 2022, due to the Covid-19 pandemic).

that "alt" stood for "anarchists, lunatics, and terrorists." It was christened with alt.sex, alt.drugs, and, appropriately, alt.rock-n-roll.

But the birth of alt.* was, much like housekeeping in Usenet tended to be, arduous. In a 1993 interview, Reid said he started alt.sex when Gene Spafford, an admin, refused to create soc.sex—even after a successful vote to bring the new newsgroup into existence. In interviews about the alt.* project, Reid reasoned that if the other groups had been more inviting and inclusive, alt.* might not have taken off like it did.

There was ample opportunity on Usenet to post something embarrassing that could be unearthed decades later by some archivist or nosy author. Alt.sex*[2] spawned hundreds of discursive groups, many as inside jokes or irony: alt.sex.aliens, alt.sex.reptiles, alt.sex.fetish .potato.salad.and.beer, to name a few. Even outside of the alt.* hierarchy, users held yearslong conversations about sexuality; on rec.scuba, one discussion about whether it's possible to have sex during scuba dives (complete with asides and cautionary tales about Vaseline and Spare Air) went on from August 1997 until January 2020.

> **Spivak pronouns**
> Gender-neutral pronouns used in MUDs and MOOs (see page 24): e, em, eir, eirs, and emself designate nonbinary, gender-fluid, or simply unknown genders of players.

The most famous of the sexually explicit newsgroups was the BDSM newsgroup alt.sex .bondage, established in 1991. It had more than 200,000 readers as of 1996 and was the second-largest after alt. sex. Regulars called it asb.

The group pioneered many of the internet etiquette principles we still use today, especially in sexually charged spaces. Due to its sensitive content and descriptions of the goings-on of people's personal lives (or at least, the personal fantasies they lived out in their heads), asb was an early adopter of "blind" or "anonymous" posts, which masked the sender's server address. The community also used "Spivak" gender pronouns, addressing unknown-gendered or gender-fluid users as "e," "em," and "eir." The group followed a strict

---

2 An asterisk at the end of a hierarchy name suggests that there are many more subgroups within it.

ACRONYMS ABOUND

As in the rest of the internet, acronyms served as a clumsy shorthand for the sex-positive culture of asb.

YKINOK: Your Kink Is Not OK

YKINMK: Your Kink Is Not My Kink

YKINMKBYKIOK: Your Kink Is Not My Kink But Your Kink Is Okay

TPE: Total (or True) Power Exchange, used in BDSM contexts

HNG: Horny Net Geek, someone who sends too much unsolicited (and usually unrequited) spam

CHDW: A Clueless Het-Dom Wannabe (pronounced "chudwah"), a straight male dom who is faking his way through it

virtual consent credo. "This newsgroup worships at the altar of consent, and if you don't . . . keep an eye peeled for police officers," a user called "Big Al" wrote in the welcome message to asb. "The exception to this rule is that if you're nonconsensual in fantasy and keep it that way, it's okay."

Both BBS and Usenet fell out of favor when paid internet access services like America Online and MCI came about, and graphical user interfaces democratized the technical task of getting connected. The hurdles of command line interfaces were too high for most casual users, and the work of maintaining large servers was too burdensome for owners. But even as they went the way of the stone tablet, the sexual sides of Usenet hierarchies and BBSes set into motion events that would shift the way the internet would operate forever.

The Rimm Job

Conversations online hummed along more or less undisturbed by outside scrutiny for fifteen years, until a *Time* magazine cover story rocked the cradle of the internet.

On the magazine's July 3, 1995, cover, an illustrated child looks at a computer screen, an expression of horror on their screen-lit face.

"CYBERPORN. EXCLUSIVE: A new study shows how pervasive and wild it really is. Can we protect our kids—and free speech?"

The story relayed the findings of a new study about online pornography, published in the *Georgetown Law Journal* by a purported "research team" at Carnegie Mellon University. The only person on that team (if there was a team at all) was Martin Rimm, a computer engineering undergrad in his thirties. Rimm titled his study "Marketing Pornography on the Information Superhighway." He gave the news of its publication exclusively to *Time* reporter Philip Elmer-DeWitt, who whittled Rimm's eighty-five-page summary of findings down to pop-magazine newsstand size, proclaiming it "significant not only for what it tells us about what's happening on the computer networks but also for what it tells us about ourselves."

In his law-journal article, Rimm seemed to claim to have found and downloaded nearly a million images from explicit BBS servers, and that much of it was porn. The takeaway from the report and the *Time* story was that a shocking 83.5 percent of all images on Usenet were pornographic. And not just garden-variety porn, but some of the most vile variety: pedophilia and bestiality, which got the most focus in Rimm's report.

The July 3, 1995, *Time* magazine cover story presaged the breathless fear around sex and sexuality on the internet.

Almost immediately, internet research scholars alighted on the *Time* story and study with full, flaming rigor. Mike Godwin, staff counsel for the Electronic Frontier Foundation at the time, learned that the report itself was held hostage under mysterious embargo terms in the journal's offices. He had already caught wind of the study the year prior, when Rimm scandalized the CMU administration into blocking access to sex-related groups on campus. Rimm had asked Godwin to endorse the study as legitimate, but refused to show him the full text of his findings; Godwin declined.

With the help of a friend who was attending the law school, Godwin got access to the office on a weekend; he and his friend photocopied the study, and then sent the photocopies by Federal Express mail to scholars and researchers in his personal network. As the photocopies made their way to those prospective fact-checkers, Godwin also began typing up selected passages of the law-journal article and posting them to The WELL so that the academics and journalists there could get a taste of what was methodologically and rhetorically questionable about it. Godwin, who met his first wife on an Austin, Texas–based BBS more than a decade earlier, knew that internet forums would be important to the future of American discourse, and he was deeply invested in protecting internet freedoms before most of the country even came online.

Once it faced unofficial peer review—a trial by WELLfire—the law-journal article was revealed to be full of shoddy research practices and unsupported claims. Godwin's suspicions were already on alert after Rimm's refusal to show his work a year prior, and he knew that research papers submitted to law journals don't face the same academic peer-review process as scientific journals. Rimm admitted that his own findings were impossible to replicate—which Godwin took to be evidence of intentional fraud.

If anyone at *Time* had looked into Rimm's history beyond the illusion of prestige that came with being associated with Carnegie Mellon and Georgetown, they might have noticed a pattern of hucksterism. Years before, Rimm wrote a *New York Times* op-ed about the danger of casinos near his Atlantic City high school in 1981 while working as an editor of his school newspaper, then embarked on a Gonzo undercover investigation in which he impersonated a sheik to get into casinos. The story was credited with helping raise the gambling age in New Jersey from eighteen to twenty-one. His self-published book, *An American Playground*, was a love letter to Donald Trump–style grifterism; another self-published work by Rimm, *The Pornographer's Handbook: How to Exploit Women, Dupe Men, & Make Lots of Money*, has an

ISBN, but no trace of the book's actual text exists today. Some critics speculated that Rimm tried to use the absurd title as a Trojan horse to convince pornographers into letting him into their servers for the study.

The research in Rimm's study was unforgivably flawed. He seemed to draw his conclusions mainly from a narrow subset of BBS and Usenet groups—and his data-collection efforts were highly suspect, since he didn't make them transparent in the paper or in interviews after. Researchers who analyzed the study believe he may have only been looking at the Amateur Action BBS run by Robert and Carleen Thomas, a California couple whose 1994 federal jury conviction for transmitting images of bestiality, incest, and extreme BDSM pornography across state lines drew national headlines.

Regardless of where Rimm's reportage came from, it was clear that he was only looking at a small slice—a percent of a percent—of sexual content online, most of it only reachable via a BBS phone line. Rimm also wasn't looking directly at the porn he claimed to analyze. Based on his own scant methodology and the work he was building on following the CMU censorship kerfuffle, he had only collected the text *descriptions* of images from adult BBS files, and then assumed that the descriptions were accurate to the content. In many cases, they weren't: for example, a file labeled "tied-up bitch" could be a joke image of a female dog on a leash. Philip Elmer-DeWitt, who'd worked at *Time* for sixteen years by the time he wrote the "Cyberporn"

Multi-User Domains (MUD) and MUD Object Oriented (MOO)

MUD and MOO were real-time, pre-web chat rooms where people gathered for elaborate role-playing games or to just hang out and try on a new persona. The "D" in MUD originally stood for dungeon but would eventually be replaced by the much more safe-for-work domain, dialogue, or dimensions, as more MUD-makers tried to shake the nerdier, kinkier image of these early communities. Object-oriented versions were programmed to include set pieces that players could interact with—spotting a barstool in the MOO's description of the imaginary room and typing "sit" to pull up a seat, for example.

story, said in later confessional pieces that he'd been "too green" to say no to the temptation of a cover story with one source and no outside experts. But the credibility he lent Rimm's report transferred to the highest-profile conversation about censorship and pornography online at the time.

Shortly after *Time*'s infamous cyberporn issue was published, Senator Charles Grassley of Iowa waved a copy of the magazine around on the Senate floor. Grassley demanded the story—not the *study*, but the article about it—be entered into the Congressional Record. He used it to bolster his argument that the internet was rife with sexual dangers any minor could stumble into and online pornographers needed to be stopped. For the children. Congress was in the middle of debating the Communications Decency Act (CDA), an amendment to the 1996 Telecommunications Act and a piece of legislation that aimed to limit how pornographic and obscene materials could be disseminated digitally. Grassley, along with CDA author Senator Jim Exon of Nebraska, argued that internet service providers, including BBS owners like the Thomases, should be held liable for any content transmitted that could be interpreted as "obscene, lewd, lascivious, filthy, or indecent." Rimm's report, which implied that most of the internet consisted of porn, was a godsend to their case.

Cyberporn panic wasn't totally new at the time. Almost as soon as people started bringing machines home and connecting them to the internet in increasing numbers, the national conversation occasionally turned to how these clunky portals cropping up in computer dens could open new, scary, and potentially dangerous worlds for children. But Rimm's report was the first time legislators and the religious right began to gain the momentum they needed to try to wipe what they saw as morally repugnant uses of the "information superhighway" off the road completely.

Meanwhile, people in Multi-User Domains were building whole societies online and grappling with profound questions of autonomy, community censorship, and moderation—and sexual assault of the disembodied kind.

"THE CLITORAL HOODS"

In October 1994, Carnegie Mellon University undergraduate Marty Rimm emailed the president of CMU to relay a message that might as well have been kompromat: The university's computers were hosting obscene content, as nodes connected to the internet. This wasn't a matter of pearl-clutching impropriety. By simply doing CMU administration the backhanded favor of making them aware of it, Rimm had opened them up to liability under federal law.

Instead of trying to weed out the offending content—a move that would have been labor-intensive and Sisyphean—the administration announced that all of the biggest adult hierarchies would be removed from its systems, including alt.binaries.pictures.erotica.*, alt.binaries.pictures.tasteless, alt.sex.*, and rec.arts.erotica. The assault on alt.sex*, especially, struck a hard blow to students and faculty who used non-pornographic forums like alt.sex.safe and alt.sex.fat for education and support.

The student body was incensed. On alt.censorship, staff and students decried the decision as fascist. Protests and talks were held on campus, with faculty support. At a "Freedom in Cyberspace" rally where both sides presented their cases, CMU vice provost for education Erwin Steinberg said the newsgroups "contained images of 'forcible sex with women, children, animals and the like,' reducing consenting adults to voiceless chattel."

The most fervent objectors to this sex panic were a group who deemed themselves the "Clitoral Hoods." The Hoods were a direct-action group of anti-censorship, sex-positive feminist students and faculty that made it their daily work to make CMU administration regret—or at least reconsider—restricting access to these groups. They made fliers with a cartoon Ariel from *The Little Mermaid* masturbating, and cheeky slogans like "Oh, Erwin, protect us again!"

"The strategy used by CMU is an ancient one: Blame the woman; she spoiled our fun," Donna Riley, then a PhD student at CMU who helped lead the Hoods, wrote. "As usual, women are the objects for discussion, the subject of the images to be banned, the subject of male protection and the object of blame and scorn."

Sex in the MUD

He is awake and looks alert.

If you type the @look command at someone in a MUD, that was the standard response you'd see automatically displayed back at you—a simple, gamified statement that was common in MUDs. They were rudimentary chat systems by today's standards, but they allowed a few features that BBS didn't, including real-time conversation. Instead of submitting your post and waiting hours or days, you had instantaneous interactions. And because they'd evolved from games, most MUDs allowed for as much creativity and character development as a player wanted to inject into their interactions. MUD worlds were hosted on single mainframes, usually housed in a university or large institution but accessed from any computer terminal around the world, as long as it was connected to ARPANET.

Roy Trubshaw and Richard Bartle met as students at the University of Essex in the late seventies, introduced by mutual friends who thought the computer whizzes would get along. Bartle, a first-generation student who learned to code on computers donated by BP to his local high school, was at the top of his math and computer science classes. At the time, Trubshaw was working on the first proof-of-concept for Multi-User Dungeons. Dungeons & Dragons was wildly popular, and at-home coders replicated D&D-style storytelling gameplay to their own text-based games on computers, in the form of single-player "dungeon crawler" adventure games. Trubshaw named his connected "dungeon" after the variant for adventure game *Zork.*

An entry page to MUD2, as seen running on Wireplay, a 90's dialup multiplayer gaming network.

Bartle and Trubshaw launched *MUD1* in 1978 as a place to be their true selves, and for the hundreds of thousands of people who would eventually replicate, build on, and grow what they'd made, it would become exactly that. But sex didn't factor into their dreams for *MUD1*—they just wanted to make a better world than the one they were living in. And the only place they held that kind of power was online.

"Being computer scientists, we were social outcasts. None of us expected to get a romantic partner, ever, so we resigned ourselves to this fact of life and never even discussed it," Bartle said. "We'd no more have hit on each other than we'd have hit on our own siblings . . . We didn't know how to behave in the presence of people who were prospective romantic partners, but knew ourselves to be so totally outgunned that it wasn't worth the pain of having our heart crushed."

Often, that power to change reality began with the pronouns players would use, which were sometimes different from those they used in real life. One of the first questions players answered before they could join *MUD1* was "What sex do you wish to be?" Technically, Bartle became the first gender-bending MUD user when he signed on as female to demonstrate the game's role-playing capabilities. But he believes that the first user to role-play as a woman who was secretly a man also happened to be one of *MUD1*'s most popular and charismatic denizens.

"Sue the Witch" played in the MUD all night, most nights, and was the most proficient at using the system and playing the game, second only to the creators themselves. She rose in the ranks to arch-wizard, a player-class with all the permissions, technical capabilities, and authority of a system administrator. *MUD1* had hundreds of "mortals," or baseline players, along with various character levels like necromancer and sorcerer, a few dozen wizards (a rank that could be earned through points, and assigned new powers over mortals), and at the top, arch-wizards: an invitation-only class that consisted of a handful of power players.

Sue had a lot of social leverage, and not just because she was good at the game. She wielded her power as an arch-wizard wisely, commanding respect while maintaining comaraderie with her friends in the MUD. Under the byline "undergraduate Susan Thomas," she wrote an article for PC World in August 1984 that put MUD1 on the map, drawing in a fresh influx of character-players to their world.

But Sue seemed to be painfully shy in real life, and when the gang would meet up in person at computing conferences and trade shows, she refused to come over to say hello. She'd send photos from the shows, sometimes showing herself in them, but always with a new hairstyle or makeup look.

As Bartle tells it, Sue may have been a social recluse in real life, but that didn't stop her from romancing another brilliant MUD player. Seventeen-year-old Mik,[3] a video game design savant, fell for Sue—hard. He wrote her letters, and she'd mail him back cursive-scrawled pages spanning into the triple digits, whole manuscripts of missives about her life and thoughts. Even though they had never met in person, young Mik proposed marriage—and Sue said she'd have to think about it. The next day, she announced that she'd accepted a job in Norway, then abruptly logged off forever.

> ### Internet vs. WWW
> The internet was developed in the late sixties as a government defense program for connecting computers and their data across distances. The World Wide Web didn't come along until 1989, and runs on top of the internet, making up the browsers, websites, and platforms we know today.

With her home address from all of those letters, a confused and heartbroken Mik drove a merry band of MUD friends to her house and knocked. A woman answered the door. It wasn't his beloved Sue, but Sue's wife. It turned out Sue was actually a man named Steve, who'd just gone to jail for defrauding the Department of Transportation.

Later, Steve called Bartle looking for absolution. Confronted with the question "What sex do you wish to be?" when he first signed up for MUD1, Steve explained that he had decided to see what it might be like to play as a woman; "Sue" was born, and it snowballed from there.

---

3 Mik's real name is unknown to the author, and closely guarded by Bartle.

The revelation of Sue as Steve rocked the MUD1 community for a while, but it was far from the only MUD gender-swap drama to unfold. Players would frequently choose genders opposite of their own and then catch feelings for others who were also gender-bending in-game; untangling the resulting romantic mess was usually complicated and dramatic. But because wizards had the power to issue a "snoop" command on anyone's private chats, in-world intimacy wasn't very prevalent; if people wanted to take it to that level, they'd need to get on the phone and use their voices, meet in person (which was easier than on today's internet, since MUDs were relatively local and long-distance calling into one would rack up your phone bill), or write old-fashioned pen-and-paper letters.

Sometimes sex scandals did crawl into the public spaces of multiuser worlds, however. Those micro-dramas had the power to send a whole community into upheaval.

"The control is the thing"

When an evil, oleaginous-faced clown in a semen-stained jester costume forced another person to violently, sexually abuse herself in the middle of a party, everyone who was there that night was traumatized. Everything about the internet that was still to come may have shifted in that moment, too.

It didn't matter that it happened in "virtual reality," as they called it at the time. To those who were there, it was very real.

This was the text-based world of LambdaMOO, and it consisted of scrolling descriptions of worlds, inhabitants, and their actions within. MUDs and their more user-customizable cousins, MUD Object Oriented (MOO) games, were, like every other technology to this point, created for entirely unsexy and mostly scholarly reasons. Their primary occupants were middle-class university students, career technologists, and tech enthusiasts. Despite MUD1's founders' aversion to romance, MUDs as an internet phenomenon were kept alive at least in part thanks to their sexual intrigue. They're remembered today by the types of legends passed down about their digital lives, like the one journalist Julian Dibbell described in his essay "A Rape in Cyberspace," published in the *Village Voice* in 1993.

MUDs and MOOs were already a well-established part of the conversation and controversy about online life by then. Most were adventure games, predecessors of today's massively multiplayer online role-playing games, or MMORPGs, like *World of Warcraft*. But *LambdaMOO* was one of the few purely social games, more analogous to games like *Second Life* today. Pavel Curtis, a researcher at Xerox PARC in Palo Alto, started *LambdaMOO* in 1990 and modeled it after a sprawling mansion, but there were lots of MOO social communities thriving on this nascent internet at the time—mostly college students and techies with access to the hardware and knowledge to access them.

In the well-populated *LambdaMOO*, the cyberclown "Mr. Bungle" made his attack.

The Mr. Bungle player used a clever little code-tool called the "voodoo" command to pretend he'd taken control of other characters. On everyone's computer screens in the virtual living room that night appeared line after line of horrifying sexual crimes against other players:

> exu eats his/her own pubic hair.
> As if against her will, Moondreamer jabs a steak knife up her ass, causing immense joy.
> You hear Mr._Bungle laughing evilly in the distance.

This being a role-playing game with objects that could act on other players, one of the room's stunned onlookers eventually silenced Bungle with a command that muted his actions. But in the aftermath, the *LambdaMOO* residents whose otherwise peaceful world Bungle violated were left with the question of what to do with this criminal.

BDSM
The acronym for Bondage and discipline, Dominance and submission, Sadism and Masochism. The first recorded use of the acronym was in alt.sex.bondage in 1991.

Pavel Curtis, creator of *LambdaMOO*, 1994

The player behind Bungle turned out to be an NYU student, but their account of the incident has never been documented. However, their actions inspired the people of *LambdaMOO* to install a political system of petitions and ballots; before, only the wizard class of players had almost total control to intervene when things needed fixing, but post-Bungle, the people decided they needed a way to mete out punishments or vote on other important changes to their world. Their first democratically reached decision was to issue the @toad command on Bungle, banning the evil clown from their world forever. After petitions were made and ballots were counted, a wizard stepped in and toaded the clown.

Later, following more bad behavior from a more embedded player (a local if there ever could be one in this virtual reality, who'd developed platonic and romantic relationships in the MOO), someone proposed that the whole system was too liberally run and needed a serious muzzling. Purely petition-based law wasn't working, they said, and needed to be disbanded in favor of an elected committee who would hear cases, submit issues to vote, and establish rules of conduct, including banned words and obscenities to mute. Today we would consider this a platform's Terms and Conditions.

That debate took up the issues that the Bungle incident left hanging: Who has control over who in these virtual worlds?

Dibbell's *Village Voice* essay unintentionally reinforced an idea that people outside of virtual communities already had about MUDs and those who sat hunched over keyboards—that they were perverts, social outcasts, unable to have real sex, and so turned to the virtual equivalent of erotica or phone sex. "One-handed typing" became a tongue-in-cheek nod to netsexual dalliance. Chasing the appeal of tinysex—another nomenclature for cybersex, named for the "tiny" worlds built in MUDs—almost destroyed Dibbell's relationship with his real-life girlfriend. But the way Dibbell described netsex was as a totally different, sublime, and unique experience that was not at all masturbatory and definitively *not* pornography.

It was around then that online infidelity became a topic of wider debate for the first time in history, even if it was only a hypothetical thought experiment for most people. Would it be cheating if your boyfriend went online as a woman and typed out his sex fantasies? What if he and another player talked on the phone sometimes? Where is the line? The answer, of course, would be different for everyone.

Sociologist Sherry Turkle was one of the first researchers to take this virtual world as seriously as those participating did, and infidelity was a hot topic among her interview subjects. In *Life on the Screen*, Turkle's 1995 book, she interviewed people about their netsex anxieties.

"In some ways, I'd have an easier time understanding why he would want to have an affair in real life," one of Turkle's interviewees, who caught her boyfriend hiding a MUD love affair, said. "At least there, I could say to myself, 'Well, it is for someone with a better body, or just for the novelty' . . . In MUDing, he is saying that he wants that feeling of intimacy with someone else, the 'just talk' part of an encounter with a woman, and to me that comes closer to what is most important about sex."

In the end, the most interesting thing about Dibbell's time in *LambdaMOO* wasn't his witnessing a "cyber-rape"—it was his own, firsthand participation in netsex that came weeks later. What he experienced mirrors what Turkle's interviewees reported—wrestling with the underlying question of what is "real."

Media theorist Sherry Turkle

After weeks of mulling, hemming and hawing, and trying to hold his away-from-keyboard (AFK) relationship together, he stumbled into the private, virtual bedroom of another MOO resident and spent the night in her digital embrace.

Later, he grappled with whether what he did could be considered authentic "cybersex," even if he never touched himself as he sat in his computer chair. He wrote:

> I just knew. My body knew. That even though its eyes had seen no one, and its ears heard no one, and its hands touched no one—still it had been held, and closely, by another body, and it had held that body closely in return.

People who became embedded deeply enough in MUDs and BBS found themselves starting to contemplate the boundaries between "real life" and "VR" and what fundamentally makes a person, a person. If you could log on and start describing yourself from scratch, as another gender, race, species, or something altogether alien, was that "you"? Would the experiences you had in that virtual body belong to you? Where does your mind end and your self begin?

Cybersex or netsex
The terms people used in the eighties and nineties for sexual connections that took place online, whether it was typing out fantasies to each other or mutual masturbation. Today we'd consider it "sexting" or "erotica."

"In real life, the control is the thing," one MUD player told Turkle. "I know that it is very scary for me to be a woman. I like making my body disappear. In real life, that is. On MUDs, too. On the MUD, I'm sort of a woman, but I'm not someone you would want to see sexually."

This freedom of self-creativity meant endless possibilities for cybersex: One might be a six-foot-five-inch hulking male bodybuilder character in one server, and then change to a vivacious blonde in the next. This shifting happened in every way, shape, gender, and form possible. This was a boon for queer players, who could safely meet online, especially if they weren't open about their sexuality in real life.

All of this creative freedom was a double-edged sword. Unbridled ability to be whoever you want, in a world limited only by imagination and breadth of one's vocabulary, meant it was easy to get carried away by strong emotions. Players' feelings of loyalty, love, and betrayal were no less strong here than away from their computers. While some people felt that they had more control over gender expression and sexuality online, *losing* control was also part of the allure.

It's said that life online moves faster than life in the meatspace. Thrown into an emotional sensory deprivation tank with only text across a screen to serve as guides, players in early virtual communities were forced to bond quickly to the social whole, or break away from it.

"The MUD quickens things," said one of Turkle's interviewees, who'd met someone he thought was his soul mate online—until he spent a week with her in person. "It quickens things so much."

Graphic Images

THE INTERNET OPENS ITS EYES

"There is a strange poignancy about
a pornographic woman who knows she is
'just a piece of ass in a software
package,' yet who asserts a desire
for pleasure nonetheless."

–Linda Williams, *Hard Core* (1989)

Normally cropped to the shoulder, this centerfold picture of
Lena Sjööblom from *Playboy*'s November 1972 issue become the
de facto standard used to advance digital imaging technology
for decades, reaching iconic status along the way. It would be
the only time Ms. Sjööblom posed naked for the camera.

I n the middle of the November 1972 issue of *Playboy*, Lena's[1] lapis blue eyes peek out above the folded middle page until the entire spread unfurls, her legs dangling out toward the ground. She stands nude in front of a floor-length mirror across two glossy pages, her bare backside lit in dreamy, boudoir-bejeweled peach and aqua tones as she clutches a long pink boa, covering her front. She's glancing over her shoulder, wearing a floppy, purple-feathered hat that looks like it was pulled out of a theater trunk. The entire image is almost unplaceable in time, absent of pop references—it could be a scene from a backstage dressing room in 1920 or 2020.

For more than half a century, Lena inadvertently influenced an entire field, changing how we used computers, and how we lived. Her Miss November photoshoot helped make the technology possible for collectors to view a picture of her *Playboy* issue on an eBay listing on their computer screens. For decades, hers was the standard test image that all other digital images would be tuned to.

If there's one truth underpinning how we see and share images online today, it's this: Wherever there were computing breakthroughs, there were nudes. Lena's became the most famous, but others came before her.

The first Playmate to appear in research for computing technologies predated Lena by a decade. In 1961, Lawrence G. Roberts, a lead architect for ARPANET, used 6-bit grayscale scanned photos of model Teddi Smith from the July 1960 issue of *Playboy* to help demonstrate a new technique called image dithering in his MIT master's thesis.

In 1966, Bell Laboratories computer engineer Ken Knowlton and cognitive neuroscience researcher Leon Harmon created the first ASCII

ASCII
An acronym for the American Standard Code for Information Interchange, a system for representing 128 English characters as numbers in order to digitally represent text.

Image dithering
A method of "mixing" colors by placing pixels strategically close to one another, developed when systems had limited palettes.

---

1 For her *Playboy* appearance, Lena spelled her name with two n's to make it easier for an American audience to pronounce.

nude, partially as a prank on their colleague Ed David. They pieced together a twelve-foot-wide mosaic of dancer and choreographer Deborah Hay, in naked repose on his wall. It was reassembled from a black-and-white photo using the tiny electronic symbols for transistors and resistors that were present in their daily work. Known later as *Studies on Perception I*, the nude wasn't only a slapdash prank; engineers at Bell and artists including Hay were collaborating on works that would demonstrate bitmap mosaic representations using computers. But it's safe to say that this particular example ended up on David's wall as a joke.

In their embarrassment at the gargantuan nude on display in the building, Bell Labs' public relations department told them, "You may circulate this thing, but be sure that you do NOT associate the name of Bell Labs with it," as Knowlton recalled. But another one of Bell's artist-collaborators, Robert Rauschenberg, displayed it during a gallery event held at the lab. From there it ended up printed in the *New York Times* on October 11, 1967, for a story about the avant-garde

> **"[Bell Labs'] revised statement was: You may indeed distribute and display it, but be sure that you let people know that it was produced at Bell Telephone Laboratories, Inc."**
>
> **—Ken Knowlton,** Bell Labs computer engineer who helped create the first piece of ASCII porn

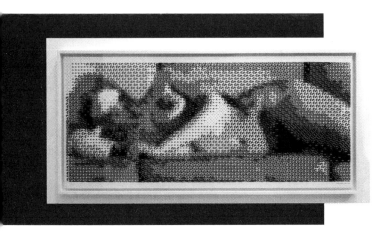

Ken Knowlton's bitmapped nude from his *Studies on Perception* went from prank to art.

art-and-science reception. Suddenly, the imaging experiment–turned–prank was "Art" with a capital "A."

Nudity, especially the naked feminine body, has always been something that those in charge have banished to the basement until it becomes useful to their purposes. But it's always there: Like the source code of all computing creation, eroticism is embedded everywhere in the background of how we experience the internet.

> **Bitmap**
> An image represented using tiny dots on a matrix.

Tuned to Lena

In 1972, Lena Sjööblom took a modeling gig with *Playboy*, posed for a nude photo, got the paycheck, and moved on with her life.

The twenty-one-year-old Swede was new to the States and living with her first husband in Chicago when he suggested she sign up with a local modeling agency to bring home extra cash. She'd done some fashion modeling—jewelry and clothing catalogs—and eventually, through a connection with a photographer, became *Playboy*'s Miss November centerfold.

It was the first and last time Lena posed nude. She turned down a personal invitation from Hugh Hefner to visit his mansion. She took more gigs with Kodak, posing for "Shirley Cards" (named for the first model to pose for one, a white, brunette Kodak employee named Shirley Page) that helped technicians calibrate the lighting and color balances on film. Her friends thought the *Playboy* anecdote was a fun bit of trivia, but for Lena that photo was in the past.

But for the rest of the world, Lena was changing the internet.

A few months after that issue of *Playboy* hit stands, at the University of Southern California's Signal and Image Processing Institute, electrical engineer Alexander Sawchuk and his team were working on image-processing algorithms for computers. They used "test images"—a specific set of photos shared across imaging labs, so that each lab was working from the same standard—to put their image compression algorithms through their paces. The team's work would eventually contribute to the development of the JPEG file format, one of the most common image formats we still use today.

None of the historical retellings of Lena's story seems to include (or wants to reveal) who, exactly, brought the *Playboy* to work that day. But most accounts agree that when they needed a new image to scan into a Hewlett-Packard 2100 minicomputer,[2] the November 1972 issue of *Playboy* was chosen for convenience. They were bored with the old test images and wanted a photo with a human face, interesting textures, and a glossy finish to test the limits of the technology. The centerfold was perfect.

They cut Lena's photo out of the magazine from her shoulders up, effectively making the photo safe for work. Some have attributed the crop job to taste or tact; more likely, it was a technical matter. The top 5.12 inches of the page fit into the Muirhead wirephoto scanner, making a 512 x 512 pixel image.

The image suited their purposes so well, they gave the scans to other researchers working on similar image processing tasks, and it eventually traveled so widely that it was accepted as a standard across the industry. There were other test images in use at the time, but Lena became the established standard that labs around the country could agree on. Part of her enduring legacy is propelled by controversy. Over the course of two decades, Lena's image spread quietly and uncontrollably before *Playboy* even noticed. By the time the publisher *did* notice, when the trade magazine *Optical Engineering* put Lena on its July cover in 1991, it was too late for them to try to reel her back in—the publisher gave permission for educational and research purposes instead.

Compression
Converting an image to a smaller file size, ideally without losing quality.

But copyright violation wasn't the cause for contention. With the tech world's dot-com explosion offering promising futures for all at

---

2 The HP 2100 minicomputer was only "mini" by seventies processor standards: It weighed around 100 pounds and was two feet deep by about a foot tall, according to a sales pamphlet.

the same time, women were world-building, moderating, and hosting BBS servers, MUDs, and their own websites right there with the old boys' club. But women still weren't seen as equal competitors and colleagues with their male counterparts in the computing workforce. The Lena test image, some argued, was just another artifact of the carelessly patriarchal thinking that had ruled the last thirty years. Some demanded the image be retired.

Editor-in-chief of industry journal *IEEE Transactions on Image Processing* David Munson Jr. wrote an open letter addressing those complaints in 1996. His verdict was not to censor uses of Lena, but if there were other, equally useful options available, researchers should opt for those instead. "In cases where another image will serve your purpose equally well, why not use that other image?" Munson wrote. The issue appeared settled.

For years, Lena herself had no idea any of this was happening. She was living quietly in Sweden, unaware of the ruckus her photoshoot had stirred among computer geeks in the US. It wasn't until she was invited to the Fiftieth Annual Conference of the Society for Imaging Science and Technology in 1997 that she understood the scope at which her image was being used, let alone as the gold standard for more than twenty years. She'd never even accessed the internet until then.

The conference was a surreal experience for Lena, mainly because all these people, mostly white male engineers, had never considered her real, physical existence before. They were meeting the *Weird Science* woman of their academia days, a set of pixels and colors they'd studied closely but never saw as part of a whole human.

"It was strange to have all these people come up to me and say, oh, you're a real person."

—**Lena Sjööblom**, in *Losing Lena*, a 2019 documentary about her *Playboy* image's legacy

The attitudes of experimentation on women's bodies and images push women out of the industry before they have a chance to start. In 2015, Maddie Zug, a senior at the Thomas Jefferson High School for Science and Technology, wrote an op-ed to the *Washington Post* about her experience

Unbeknownst to Sjööblom, her image was scanned and reproduced countless times around the world by those trying to advance image digitization technology.

as one of a handful of female peers assigned to use the Lena image for a coding project. The teacher warned them not to look up the image. Of course, the first thing everyone in that computer lab did was search for the original and pull up the whole centerfold on their screens.

"At the time I was 16 and struggling to believe that I belonged in a male-dominated computer science class," Zug wrote. "I tried to tune out the boys' sexual comments. Why is an advanced science, technology, engineering and mathematics school using a *Playboy* centerfold in its classrooms?"

Today, female technology students still have many of the same complaints as they have from the beginning: Gender wage gaps, male-skewed advancement opportunities, and sexist attitudes still thrive in tech. Having to sit through a computing class where a story about a huddle of men and their unaware Playmate is the week's lesson is salt in the wound.

Though now in her seventies and a grandmother, Lena seems to hold few strong opinions on the use of her image. Though the test image still haunts our modern machines, like a nostalgic nod, current image processing researchers occasionally use her in their papers. But in recent years, several journals and institutions announced they would outright ban submissions that featured Lena, including the Optical Society, the Society for Industrial and Applied Mathematics, and the entire family of around 150 *Nature* journals.

For some in the image processing world, Lena has simply outlasted her usefulness. In his 2018 farewell letter as editor-in-chief of *IEEE Transactions*, Scott Acton urged his colleagues to think outside the old standbys. The Lena crop contains around 260,000 pixels—pretty good for her time. An image from the iPhone 11, released in 2019, contains more than 12,000,000.

Five years after Lena's Miss November issue, the Apple II would become the first graphics-capable personal computer to enter American homes. Before image processing reached the masses, however, people made do with what they had: text, assembled into mosaic.

ASCII pr0n

It's like watching people have sex in the digital rain of *The Matrix*: Linda Lovelace drips and bobs in greenish symbols across a black screen. Vuk Ćosić's 1998 project, *Deep ASCII*, is a full-length rendering of the 1972 classic porno *Deep Throat*, done entirely in text characters.

For as long as people have been able to string letters together to form words, we've used those letters to create art. Poets were creating shapes from their text as early as ancient Greece, with Simmias of Rhodes arranging prose in the shape of eggs and angels wings. Islamic calligraphy's intricate script adorns courtyards and mosques, not as mere written words but as artwork telling a story of high praise.

Before computer graphics capabilities became standard issue in home machines like the Apple II and Commodore 64, people got creative with how they sent visual smut. Arranging slashes, dots, and lines into nipples and legs was a creative way to get porn across the internet before image processing. But text-based nudes and pinups

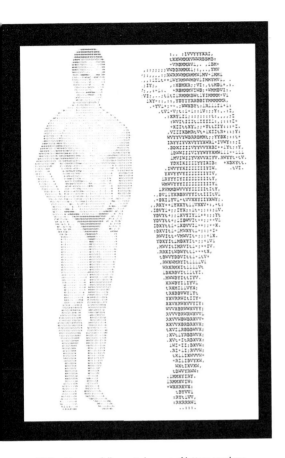

ASCII art is a carefully created canvas of letters, numbers, and keyboard symbols, made in a variety of subtle styles.

weren't crude digital cave drawings. They were often intricate, realistic representations of the real thing.

Some historians credit ASCII porn as being the first form of pornography sent across the internet. ASCII—pronounced "ass-key—art arrived with the need for standardized telegraphic codes in the early sixties.

Being made up of text instead of image files, ASCII artworks loaded quickly on the page and didn't require decoding like a download of an image file might. It was simple, and anyone could do a crude ASCII of boobs[3] or stick-figure pinups—but it took a patient artist to craft something in realistic detail, line by line, like weaving on the loom of a keyboard.

In the hacker culture of the early internet, ASCII (including PETSCII and ANSI, see page 46) and RTTY (short for Radioteletype) have a long history of subverting artistic norms. Warez hackers used the form to tag their pirated software with title screens acting as walls of graffiti. Artists signed off their messages and art pieces with their initials, tiny call signs for the digital art world. The ones who were there back then never dropped the habit; ASCII artists still sign off emails with

3 (.Y.)

three little letters, or sometimes an ObAscii—Obligatory ASCII.

Nowadays, the process of making ASCII-rendered videos like Ćosić's *Deep Throat* homage can be automated to be a lot less painstaking. The form mostly died when graphics cards and download speeds got faster, and downloading a photo no longer took all day.

ASCII pr0n (as it's often stylized, in homage to 1337 hacker slang) was mostly a fun pastime for forum junkies. It was shared around on BBSes, Usenet, and between people swapping physical hard drives, CDs, and floppy disks, also known as the "sneakernet."

1337

Pronounced "leet," 1337 is a style of internet slang popular with hackers (or haxx0rz), originating with BBS culture in the eighties and nineties. 1337 is short for "elite," as in elite hackers or gamers. Spelling words out with numbers and characters helped get around obscenity filters that banned words like "a$$" or pr0n. People still use a version of this today, with words like "seggs" and "corn" standing in for "sex" and "porn."

Seedy ROMs

When the khaki-wearing techies pulled the plug—literally disconnected the electricity—from the adult expo booths at Comdex '94, Fay Sharp considered it an act of war.

"We always believed in freedom of choice . . . and this industry needs a show!" said Sharp, one of the adult software distributors kicked out of the Computer Dealer's Exhibition, or Comdex, a giant annual computer-industry trade show.

From 1979 to 2003, tens of thousands of computer geeks descended on Las Vegas every November (and at spin-off events around the world throughout the year) to see what new, major technologies might debut at Comdex. The first year introduced the revolutionary innovations of spreadsheets and Ethernet, and by 1992 the show advanced to futuristic leaps like IBM's unveiling of its speech-command software. In 1993, the *New York Times* noted adult-themed multimedia CD-ROMs

Teletext, another textmode art medium, was serious about porn. Technically, teletext didn't make use of the internet, but its existence is intertwined with internet history. Invented in the early seventies, this broadcast television information service first launched in the UK as a public information service. ANSI (an acronym for the American National Standards Institute that became the homonym for this art style) was a more vibrant, blocky style of textmode display than ASCII, with 256 characters instead of 128. Viewers could page through text and ANSI-created graphics and see news reports, the weather, and advertisements on their TV set.

Like a visit to the red-light district on your TV, "after hours" teletext programming was neon and scandalous, advertising phone sex hotlines and X-rated videos. German and Austrian teletext broadcasters especially embraced the smutty teletext page. "Dauergeile stute!!!" "Extra grosse videos und fotos," "Ich hab eine große Oberweite," the pages implored, next to detailed ANSI breasts, thongs, and torsos.

as among the newcomers, described in a cartoonish scene of gawking groups of men waving wads of cash and trying to get a look at one of the half-dozen adult exhibitors presenting wares including LA *Strippers: Bikes & Babes & Rock 'n' Roll* on disk.

Warez
Cracked software (w4r3z in leetspeak)— programs that have been pirated with anti-piracy protections disabled, making them easy to share online.

The showdown in '94 between the adult exhibitors and Jason Chudnofsky, chief executive of Softbank Comdex Inc., came at the urging of tech giants like Intel and Microsoft, who didn't want porn games and busty women standing so close to their very serious hardware. "Comdex is a place where people show creative new products for the betterment of the industry," Chudnofsky said. "This is not appropriate." He moved them to the basement beneath Comdex proper, and that was the breaking point for Sharp. That, and the fact that they'd cut their power supply quite literally.

"There's a demand for adult material and no one is going to keep us from doing this," said Sharp. "The show should go on." She started AdultDex the following year, down the street at the Sahara.

Like the ASCII nude, with Bell Labs trying to separate its research from its squeaky-clean reputation, Silicon Valley giants were vigilant about keeping adult entertainment at arm's length—while profiting directly from the advancements made by said entertainment.

Along with scanned images from porn magazines, CD-ROMs were the stuff that adult alt.binaries and alt.sex.pictures BBSes thrived on.[4] These forums were a space for ripped binary files shared over the internet, encoded on upload and decoded when downloaded. Pornographic images on disk were the sparks that lit the wildfire of internet porn.

Sharp claimed that CD-ROM producers made $260 million in 1994 off titles like *Virtual Valerie*, *Samurai Pervert*, and *Porno Poker*. These galleries and games cost between $4 and $80 and were stocked in mainstream video and record stores in the X-rated sections. Renting them was a popular option.

---

4 Some have described alt.sex.pictures as containing "gigabytes of copyright violations."

AdultDex attendee, circa 1995

CD-ROMs loaded with porn on curated disk and interactive games were a main draw of AdultDex, and many attendees were there to see what was new in the world of image galleries and games. A copy of *Virtual Sex Shoot*, the photographer role-playing game by Digital Playground, went for $56 at the time (more than $100 in 2022 money). And to play that game, you'd need one of Intel's machines, which cost several hundred dollars. People were spending a lot of money on porn you could put on your PC. But many more of the minds at AdultDex were ahead of their time, showcasing tech that wouldn't become popularized for commercial use for another decade or more. Digital Sexsations exhibited an early teledildonics device (see page 149), a lighter-size piece of hardware that you attached to the back of a computer; it claimed to control sex toys in real time over internet chat. Sexy Servers, a sex-friendly web-hosting firm, networked mainstream connections for its real-time video conferencing software—at a moment when real-time video was unheard of for most of the internet-connected world. Others sold "turnkey Adult websites" for as much as $5,000 to pornographers who wanted to mimic the success of webmasters like Danni Ashe, a former stripper who made millions of dollars running her own adult website. Webmasters, many of them sex workers themselves, shared tips of the trade.

"People who develop CD-ROM software should be overjoyed that we're here, because we're helping sell CD-ROM drives," Lawrence Miller, a partner at sex game maker New Machine Publishing, told the *Baltimore Sun*.

Software makers were *not* overjoyed. Yet AdultDex went on, running during the same dates as Comdex as a separate event, with as many as fifty exhibitors. Attendees to Comdex could get into AdultDex by showing their badges and paying a $20 tack-on fee. An estimated

> **"Just as a few years ago people who wanted to do golf simulations were going out and spending several thousands of dollars on a computer for a $39 program, more people are doing that now so they can use adult programs."**
>
> —**Mark Brown,** an adult CD-ROM magazine publisher

20,000 to 30,000 people came out every year after that, mostly wayward Comdex sons. Chudnofsky himself admitted that Comdex would lose $500,000 because of banning adult material. The mainstream may have cast them aside, but triple-X techies showed that they belonged in the future of computing as much as the next Intel executive.

You can almost smell the cigarette ash ground into the thick, gem-toned carpet through the photos of the second annual 1996 AdultDex: Men in polo shirts and cheap brown suits standing too close to tanned women in bikinis and leather, or leaning their five-o'clock shadows on their breasts. One thing that's never changed throughout decades of Las Vegas porn conferences: In this gin-scented setting, men and women do seem like separate species.

Some attendees crouch over bulky beige computer monitors set up in between the slots to see copies of PC games like *Private Investigator*, where you play P.I. Dick Slammer on a side-scrolling mission to screw your way to catching the senator cheating—and win his jilted wife as the prize.

The admission money that adult offerings brought to Comdex before it was banned was only part of the allure. It also drew media attention.

Ripped files

Binary files store data in the form of bytes, which computers can read and display using a viewer program. These were useful on BBS forums, because binary files could store non-text data (like images and audio) that were "ripped," or saved and reshared, to boards without permission from the CD-ROM maker. In BBSes, one would only know which files to download based on their descriptions or file names, and just hope the files delivered as promised.

"Booth babes," the Vegas tech conference equivalent of Vanna White, were at Comdex before they were popularized at its successor, the Consumer Electronics Show, or CES. The Device Girls, a hit act at the 1999 Comdex, parodied the Spice Girls—and made lasting impressions on several tech reporters in attendance.

Booth babes were allowed to stay at Comdex to dance and entertain attendees, even after game makers and their CD-ROMs were kicked out.

In 1997, after the adult crew was evicted from Comdex, the media's gaze got AdultDex's Sharp into a spot of trouble with the law; as she told it to *Billboard*, some reporters in attendance made a fuss about live, nude performances. Las Vegas vice officers handed out seven citations for "lewd and dissolute conduct" (exposing their breasts) and two more for "performing a live sex act" (women touching one another), but Vegas casinos are licensed for toplessness, so the cops retracted everything and apologized.

Sharp was exasperated, if not just pissed off. But this time, she seemed a little excited for the attention given to her cause. "We were on CNN, the local TV; we have even had an editorial in the newspaper that

The National Semiconductor booth featured the "Device Girls," a play on the Spice Girls, at Comdex in fall 1999.

was favorable," she told *Billboard*. "It's giving us the kind of publicity we could never buy. It's showing adult interactive is very much in the mainstream."

AdultDex fizzled out in 2003, its founders moving on to run other, less popular events for webmasters. Comdex also dissolved the following year, for varying reasons. In 1998, the AVN Adult Entertainment Expo formed similarly as a split from CES's stiflingly Safe For Work rules (CES banned its own booth babes in 2020). Even though it didn't survive, AdultDex left its mark. It helped prove that there was a real demand for the tech world to make room for sexual content, and forced organizers and companies to confront them as real, living, and extremely savvy businesspeople, far from the basement-dwelling parodies of porn peddlers left over from the seventies and eighties. People bought computers and CD-ROM drives to access their work. Microsoft, IBM, and Apple were mass-producing the gears of home computing, but sex was what made them turn.

Webmasters of Their Own Domains

"I predict the Internet
will soon go spectacularly
supernova and in 1996
catastrophically collapse."

—Robert Metcalfe,
the inventor of Ethernet, in 1995

t took about an hour and a half, including two bus transfers, for Jen Peterson and Dave Miller to haul their hulking 75-megahertz computer tower, monitor, and modem back to their North Baltimore apartment from the nearest Sears in spring 1995.

"I had just gotten a shiny new Sears card and Dave convinced me that we should go buy a computer with it," Jen said. "I wasn't really into computers, but I was into Dave, so I said sure."

The journey was "every bit as epic a trip as Frodo and his posse took," Dave said—and almost as world-altering, for them and the grand scheme of the yet-uncharted future of the internet. "Jen n Dave" was one of the earliest amateur adult sites on the World Wide Web.

The couple had met three years earlier, right after Jen graduated high school, and moved in together a year later. They bought that big machine plus a dial-up internet connection, and almost immediately, a new world opened to them: groups of people around the country on Usenet, sharing their sexploits in storytelling and photos for the whole web to see. Jen and Dave were already dabbling with taking their own nudes on film as part of their personal sex life; they'd ship

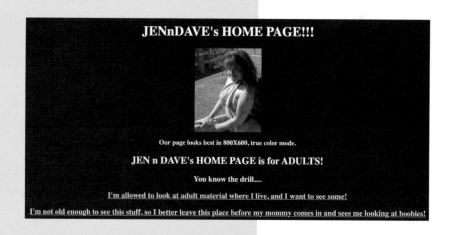

A version of the original landing page for Jen n Dave's site

the rolls off to the liberal-minded Seattle Filmworks for processing.[1] They jumped into BBS forums and spent the summer riding out a historic heat wave busily scanning and posting their own mounting stack of film and prints to those groups.

By October, the pair had garnered something of a fan club, and decided to dedicate their own little corner of the web to their images. They set up jen-dave.com, and resisted charging for access at first, staying afloat with visitor donations. It was more fun that way.

But in February, after the passage of the Communications Decency Act of 1996, they and hundreds of other adult sites set up credit card memberships as an age verification method—and fans of Jen and Dave's exploits could see their entire archive in one place, for a credit card payment of $10 every three months.

They made $20,000 in their first three weeks.

For the first few years, the biggest problems successful adult webmasters had were keeping up with the demand for new content, paying a newly astronomical internet bill, and not downing servers with the influx of traffic in the process. Charging for access kept the lights on, but was also a convenient way to throttle some of the bandwidth demands of their 25,000 visitors a day. Jen and Dave's internet service provider at the time, Concentric Internet Services, offered "unlimited" server space and traffic capabilities, Dave said. The traffic to their site pushed the limits on that claim until, after a series of tense emails between Dave and customer service, he claims that the ISP changed its policies to get rid of falsely advertised "unlimited" offerings altogether—something Dave remembers today with a sense of stubborn pride.

They didn't want to start requiring memberships, but all of these factors forced them into an accidentally lucrative amateur pornography career.

Until the 2000s, spending money online for most people was a question of *whether* you would, not how much you would. Once you had

---

1 Many processing studios would ban customers who sent in explicit film and refuse to return the negatives. "It was funny that we didn't always get all the prints back, especially the ones that featured my ass prominently, but we did at least get the digital copies," Jen said.

the hardware set up and the technical knowledge for getting online, you could connect to the pre-web internet for free. Some BBS communities required users to pay for subscriptions to offset the administrators' own time and expense, but there were still newsgroups and multiuser games to be joined and played without cost. Anyone, theoretically, could develop their own plot of virtual land.

Soon enough, that digital wilderness was bought up by big companies in narrowing competition. By the mid-eighties, there were three major players on the ISP field, each with their distinct operational ethos: CompuServe, Prodigy, and AOL. There were others (including many of the big BBS system administrators that went on to start their own ISPs), but these three pulled ahead of the rest because they understood something fundamental about the nascent internet. Getting online offered something watching TV or reading a newspaper couldn't: interactive connections to other people, conversations and cultural moments you weren't privy to unless you were there, online. Many people accessed MUDs and chat servers using these services.

That was still pre–World Wide Web. Tim Berners-Lee wouldn't invent it until 1989, after years' worth of micro-dramas, heartbreaks, and scandals broke out and dissolved in forums and chat rooms. The money being made and spent online at that time was primarily through subscription-based servers. With the advent of the web, the scene exploded like a piñata full of money. Suddenly, anyone with a little HTML experience or willingness to learn had a shot at bringing hundreds of thousands of visitors to their sites a month and—with some advertising and networking finesse—the chance to convert those visitors to cash.

Those heady days developed and popularized many of the financial technologies we now use and find indispensable: affiliate linking programs, site subscriptions, members-only content, online credit card transactions, and advertising models.

The Rise of the "Nerds with Big Breasts"

In a 1999 photo for the local alt-weekly newspaper, Caity McPherson stands triumphant next to the Microsoft campus sign in Mountain View, California, pulling open a light green blouse to reveal a lacy lavender bra to the camera. She looks like the Clark Kent of sexual power, in defiance of the companies that would both make the adult industry possible *and* try to crush it in the new millennium.

Like thousands of other would-be dot-com moguls of the nineties, McPherson, formerly an HR manager at a semiconductor company (and a peep-show dancer before that), carved out a niche for herself in the wide world of web porn. Xerox, Yahoo!, Lycos, Sun Microsystems—in the late nineties, no technology giant was safe from her Tech Sign Girls, a clan of barely clad women who would scurry onto company property while McPherson held the camera, strip in front of rush-hour traffic, and pose alongside these self-serious household names. Then she'd post the photos online for waiting fans.

McPherson was one of many pornographers rushing to homestead on the net. Many of them were strippers and performers moving their

Caity McPherson, a "Tech Sign Girl," posing in 1999. McPherson was an early pioneer in building online audiences in creative ways.

fan clubs and clientele online for the first time, like neon OPEN signs welcoming the first shoppers to the internet. Others, like Jen and Dave, were just exhibitionists with a side hustle that turned into more.

Thousands of names and sites sprung up and dissolved in those years, but out of the gold-rush frenzy of digital porn rose two names now famous for striking it rich as webmistresses: Danni Ashe and Beth Mansfield.

The women represented two sides of the classic male-fantasy coin: Danni was an ex-stripper turned HTML-coding "nerd with big breasts," as she's famously quoted saying, and Beth was a mom and accountant living quietly in Tacoma, Washington—a girl next door who happened to run a wildly successful site for hard-core porn.

Their enterprises represented two of the most popular approaches to online adult businesses: direct-to-consumer content for sale, and link directories.

Danni's Hard Drive launched in 1995 and within a few years was a one-stop shop for Ashe and her friends' nudes, video clips, columns by models, and interactive videos where members could tell models what they wanted through a chat room. By building her own website down to the code, Ashe ensured that every content and business decision was under her own control.

Like Jen and Dave and many more amateur pornographers, she started her online career in response to a thriving Usenet fan base. After years working as a stripper and model, Ashe found her own images, posted without her permission, all over Usenet forums; instead of dismissing the posters as voyeurs or thieves, she started talking with them. They encouraged her to start her own venture, and she launched Danni's Hard Drive in 1995. DHD was the free site side; "Hotbox" was the members-only area.

Danni's Hard Drive was meticulously curated by its founder, Danni Ashe, an influential early webmaster who showed a different side of porn, one not created by, and for, men.

Danni's insistence on editorial and pictorial control over what went on Hard Drive set it apart from much of the porn already online. She, and the independent models-turned-webmasters after her, invited the viewer in; none of it was stolen, it was all there because they wanted to show it to you. She carefully curated columnists, models, and photo galleries.

It was all distinct from a lot of the hyperaggressive, macho porn out there. Danni herself never shot any content with men and never posted images of herself with anything—even a sex toy—inside her.

RSS feeds

Short for "rich site summary" or "really simple syndication," RSS feeds are aggregated lists of updates from a particular website, like a news outlet or blog.

Danni's Hard Drive was one of the thousands of web pages featured on Beth Mansfield's Persian Kitty, a link directory of adult websites. Before search engines indexed every site on the web, and long before RSS feeds or social media started tailoring every piece of content to an individual's specific preferences, directories were how one got around the 'net.

Yahoo! was a link directory at first, albeit a huge, well-funded and -staffed one. In the mid-nineties, it was the first stop for people looking for websites in specific categories—under adult picture gallery sites, for example, you could narrow your search down to BDSM, Amateur, Anal, Vintage, Nude Celebrities, and so many more. A lot of early webmasters, adult and otherwise, tinkered with link sites for the fun of it. Setting up a really good hobbyist shrine to your favorite finds around the web, from the Grateful Dead to NSYNC to Nintendo, was a way to set yourself apart from the rest.

Mansfield started Persian Kitty in 1995 as a simple list of sites sorted into categories such as free or paid, gay, lesbian, phone sex, and adult BBS servers. Each hot-pink link came with a short description of the amount of content within and the cost of membership, if applicable. In 1999, PK listed around four thousand links. At its peak, it was getting more than half a million visitors a day.

Running a link directory this size was tedious work. Webmasters had to keep the site updated with new content to keep visitors coming

The financial fate of link directories' survival rested in affiliate links and banner advertising, revenue streams pioneered by porn that've become commonplace on most websites today, from the biggest news outlets to baking bloggers. The goal of a link directory was to be the first place internet surfers visited before hopping around the rest of the web. If you could place an advertisement with a well-known, highly trafficked site like PK—or Ron Levi's Cyberotica .com or any number of other high-quality link pages—the odds were good that a small percentage of their hundreds of thousands of viewers would end up on your site.

For banner ads, each click-through translated to a few cents (some sites charged two cents per click, others as much as twenty-five cents) that the advertiser paid to the host site. Banner ads for porn were often explicit in an attempt to get the visitor a taste of what lay inside, including animated elements like sparkles or flashing Vegas-type billboard text dangling before web surfers like shiny fishing lures. The trade-off for hosting a banner ad was that they slowed your site down. Most people using the internet in the mid-nineties were accessing it with a 56k dial-up modem; it would take days to download a single gigabyte file back then (compared to a few seconds today). When you're competing with dozens of other sites, every second counts.

back and continuously check each of the links hosted to make sure they were still working. As so many people started their own sites in bids to play the adult web lotto of fame, sites were constantly dying and popping back up. Mansfield claimed to spend six hours a day maintaining the site, vetting linked sites personally.

By 1998, Mansfield claimed she was netting $93,750 a month annually. She said she was getting buyout offers in the millions every week, but always turned them down.

Women like Ashe and Mansfield were so popular, so revered as examples of how to make it online, that people didn't just flock to the net attempting to replicate their success in the adult internet industry, but they also tried to mimic the intrigue of being in their shoes.

The internet started to flood with sites claiming to be run by "real amateurs" posting their own photos. The reality was that many—some estimates landed around 95 percent—were actually run by entrepreneur web developers with little connection to the content they posted. Like gender-benders in MUDs, men pretending to be female porn stars online could get ahead of the competition if they did it convincingly enough.

The true amateur webmasters were becoming outnumbered. Brittany Halford started her website while she was attending university in Canada around 1997 and claimed in 2000 that she and one other person—Asia Carrera—were the only authentic webmaster-amateurs on the net at the time. The true number of models who were also uploading their own nudes and porn to their own sites was probably closer to the hundreds, but that still would have been a tiny fraction of the more than 17 million sites on the web at the time. (For comparison, there were 1.8 billion websites as of December 2020, increasing by the minute.)

Link directories
Websites with the sole purpose of sending visitors to other websites, usually organized in some way—by popularity that week, interests, subscription cost, etc.

By the end of the nineties, authentic amateur models were so rare that it became a sign of exclusivity, a selling point for attracting new subscribers.

"I was one of the original amateur models on the net and have been doing this for close to 4 years. I am here to stay," Halford's homepage, brittspage.com, read in 1999. "My page is owned by me. I built it, run it and maintain it. If you have been jerked around by other adult sites (heck, I have been too!!) then welcome to a true amateur page that is run with honesty and integrity."[2]

Carrera's site, Asia Carrera's XXX Buttkicking Homepage, is still online and has kept relatively the same aesthetic and general

---

2 Halford may have run an honest website, but she may not have been above a cyber-hustle. In August 2000, Halford tried to register the domain name "creampies.com" and then attempted to sell it to the owners of the already registered creampie.com for $125,000. She lost that case, which was deemed domain-squatting.

layout since she launched it in 1996: black and purple rain wallpaper, animated green electric squiggles, neon image highlights, and beating-heart GIFs. Along with Carrera's erotic offerings—$10 a month for unlimited membership access to video clips and photos—she used to offer advice on how to start one's own web page, just like hers. So many people were ripping off her designs down to the purple rain wallpaper, she wrote, she might as well dedicate a page to links on how to use Photoshop, make GIFs, and set up their own domain.

The visitors that these independent sites attracted were only a fraction of the audience big enterprise magazines like *Playboy* commanded when they came online. *Playboy*'s website, which launched in 1994, saw more than 4.3 million visitors a month by the end of 1997. It made money the same ways independent models and webmasters did, through ad revenue and memberships.

For a decade prior, print magazines like *Playboy*, *Penthouse*, and *Hustler* had been competing over aesthetics. Hugh Hefner's vision for a more discerning men's magazine—less peep show, more parlor—drove *Playboy*'s initial success. But when others started publishing more and more hard-core photos, Hefner's vision wavered. On the internet, the pressure to push everything to the limits of shock value was even more intense: Instead of sitting alongside a handful of magazines on a newsstand, every website was in competition with every other website on the planet. And if one site cut its prices, it undercut hundreds of others.

Asia Carrera's Buttkicking Homepage is still live today, and in the exact same form as shown here, a throwback to the early days of web design.

Chargebacks and Cheap Thrills

As we've already seen, the nascent internet was far from a technological utopia, and the same goes for the world of early porn websites. They often replicated the same imbalances, stigmas, and injustices that the print and video porn industries struggled with, problems repeated in the digital realm by capitalists looking for a windfall.

RICHARD GORDON'S BET ON PORN

In 1979, FBI agents entered a Washington, DC, apartment, opened a closet door, and found Richard Gordon tucked inside, seemingly hiding from a plethora of white-collar crimes. As evinced by tickets on the Concorde to Paris laying nearby, the insurance and financial-planning salesman appeared to be trying to skip out on federal investigations into accusations of mail fraud, stolen checks, and lying to banks.

Like many hotshots of the dot-com era, Gordon was a smooth serial entrepreneur with a grifter's lean. In spite of his run-in with the feds (and a couple years in jail), by the nineties he was running multiple ventures, including magazines and an interior decorating company. But his most notable contribution to the online age was Electronic Card Systems, which later became CreditCards.com, a company that pioneered e-commerce online—and he did it by catering to adult websites. "At that time, if you had anything to do with internet porn, you called Electronic Card Systems," a former employee said.

Years before sites like eBay and Amazon became the faces of online purchases, Gordon's companies were figuring out how to make online credit card transactions. He set up credit card transactions for Dial Talk International, a large Japanese network of adult websites. One of his biggest clients in the US was Clublove.com, the website that distributed Pamela Anderson and Tommy Lee's stolen sex tape in 1998.

Gordon eventually moved on to credit card processing for Brave New World, which designed websites for the American Bible Society—which dropped him promptly after learning about his pornographic past.

As more and more entrepreneurs logged on, the tactics for getting people to your site became shadier. One of the many things adult webmasters excelled at was quick adaptation to whatever would make users happy—and if not happy, at least blissfully unaware of the machinations that kept the virtual porn flowing. The ones willing to push the limits of how far they could screw the customer ended up screwing themselves, and everyone else, in the process.

Search indexes
Search engines like Google, Yahoo!, or Ask Jeeves refer to search indexes to pull up results. Web crawlers—simple programs that "crawl" websites—scan through web pages to assemble the text and media on a page into a search index.

Advertising on the web was still very new in the mid-nineties, and a lot of sites tried to draw an analogy between the magazine and newspaper ads of print to the internet with the aforementioned banner ads. But that advertising was based on "visitors," as in those "You are the 985th visitor to this page!" counters that used to appear on websites. They were counting the number of "hits," or requests from one visitor's browser to the website's server. Some counters inflated those numbers by including images in hit counts, so that every graphic that loaded on the page was a hit, and the web page itself was a hit.

The adult industry's attempts to tell the difference between individual visitors and server requests helped create the data-collection industry as we know it today. Through IP addresses and other pieces of individual data, server logs showed where in the world a visitor was coming from, what site brought them there, what broken links they encountered along the way, and how much time they spent on each page. These were the building blocks of targeted advertising and algorithmically generated, hyper-personalized online content.

But most web hosts wouldn't give complete access to this information to webmasters, and the visitor counters could be easily faked if the site owner themselves placed it on the page and manipulated the numbers. Expensive server log analysis programs were an option, but every cent counted when you were running a site in close competition with hundreds of others all over the world. In early 1996, Ron Levi, the owner of one of the biggest porn operations, Cyberotica, developed what some claim was the first third-party traffic counter, called XXX Counter, which site administrators couldn't manipulate.

When one webmaster bent the truth, others in the industry suffered. In 1998, Persian Kitty's Beth Mansfield was getting twenty to twenty-five emails a week from pissed-off porn customers. But they weren't mad at *her*. They were pleading for her help in canceling their memberships to Xpics, an adult gallery photo clearinghouse. The site, founded in 1996 by porn entrepreneurs Mario Carmona and Brian Shuster, promised "100 percent free" trial memberships to try out its adult galleries, simply by giving Xpics a credit card number, under the pretense of age verification. After the trial ended, memberships were $9.95 per month.

Affiliate links

Links that are selling something, provided by the seller who can track how many times it's clicked and where the clicks come from. When someone clicks an affiliate link—usually a URL for a buyable product or other business's website—the owner of the website where the link was hosted gets paid some agreed-upon amount by that business.

The trials were nearly impossible for subscribers to end before the charges started, sometimes as soon as hours after signing up. Once you logged in, you could never leave—it was a Hotel California of online porn. Some reports say they were making close to $10 million a month by ripping people off.

Print magazine subscriptions were offering slippery free trial subscriptions way before adult sites, and today membership companies like Amazon use complicated, multistep dark patterns[3] to trap users

---

3 User experience designer Harry Brignull coined the term *dark patterns* in 2010. According to him, they are "tricks used in websites and apps that make you do things that you didn't mean to, like buying or signing up for something." As of this writing, Amazon's membership cancellation process involves five pages of options other than canceling.

into staying subscribed forever. But the stakes were higher for adult sites, already under scrutiny by financial institutions as "vice" commerce and forging new paths for purchases online. Shady subscription schemes, banks that seemed hesitant to take on sex-working clients, and consumers who were skittish about making online purchases for the first time, not to mention told by society to be ashamed to buy sexual experiences—all of this created a perfect set of dominos for discrimination.

At its peak, Carmona and Shuster's network of sites, which included not only xpics.com but also sexmuseum.com, assawards.com, and more, were reportedly raking in millions. Xpics was the nineteenth most visited website on the internet (not just the adult internet, but the whole internet) in May 1998, beating out four-year-old Amazon.com. Webmasters would sign up to partner with Xpics, put a banner ad (or two, maybe three) for Xpics on their site, then get a check from the company based on how many people clicked through it.

At the time, most banner advertising offered three to five cents per ad click, and clicks were only counted every twelve hours. Xpics offered eighteen cents per click, every six hours. Websites that ran Xpics banners and had decent traffic could offer free content (which brought in more traffic) and pay their bills with those ads alone, with checks from Xpics amounting into the thousands every month. Webmasters flocked to the program, which created an ecosystem of sites dependent on Xpics to stay afloat through its advertising program.

Third-party payment processors
Companies that work as a middleman between online merchants and banks. Paypal, Square, and Stripe are third-party payment processors that are popular today.

As more webmasters and consumers started getting vocal about the site's malpractice, Xpics' rip-off stopped being a secret. Some reports alluded to Visa also pulling services from the site and filing Better Business Bureau complaints. When Xpics pulled the plug on the banner ad campaign in 1998 amid rumors of fraud, they left those sites to flounder.

In 2000, the whole scheme caught up with them: The Federal Trade Commission determined that Carmona and Shuster were improperly billing people and forced them to issue refunds.

Plenty of websites still run these sorts of schemes today, just on a slightly less egregious scale—it's usually possible to cancel a membership through the third-party biller you used to sign up. But you'll need to remember the email address you used, the credit card number, and the website for that biller itself, which isn't always obvious when you're signing up or after you've left that page.

> "Everybody looks at porn. If more people admitted it, they'd be able to go to their credit card company and say, 'Hey, I'm being ripped off.'"
>
> —**Jane Duvall**, webmaster of Jane's Net Sex Guide, to *Wired* in 1998

Chargebacks—claims filed by consumers to their credit card companies that charges were fraudulent, even if they weren't—plagued the industry, and still do. This happened in part because of subscription trial scams like Xpics and partly because it was easy for buyers to cry fraud to their banks and get their money back once they'd seen their fill of a site. It was their word against webmasters, and banks already hated porn.

To fill the void left by mainstream financial systems ditching porn, third-party billers rose to popularity: CCBill, iBill, and Paycom. These third-party processors come with steep processing fees. As of 2022, CCBill's "Adult Plan" charges 10.8 to 14 percent per transaction.

Grifts like the one Xpics was running can only succeed in a society that's ashamed to buy porn.

Admitting It's Over: Indie Webmasters on the Decline

Jen-dave.com moved to CCBill in the late nineties after trying out a few different payment processors. They never made Ashe-level millions, but for a few years they were making between $60,000 and nearly $100,000 a year from the site. They quit their day jobs and worked on the site full time.

The shift from community-driven passion project to their entire livelihood started to wear on Dave— in part because of the hundreds of emails their former Usenet friends

Jen, of Jen n Dave, 2020

and fans sent through the site: *You're a sellout, you're an awful person. You planned this from the start.* He hid the hate mail from Jen, but it ate him up; he didn't want to compete with the thousands of other amateur sites out there. Talking today about the money they made two decades ago still makes him anxious.

While Jen took over the main responsibilities for keeping the site running, including HTML coding, that anti-capitalist spiritual conflict turned into a full crisis of conscience for Dave. When he finally revealed the burden of criticism he'd been carrying, years into the site's lifetime, Jen told him something he never forgot.

"If someone asks you what's the first thing you'd do if you won the lottery, and your answer is 'quit my job,' you have the wrong job," Dave recalls Jen saying as they stood outside a self-help seminar, smoking a cigarette on a break. "That dazed me."

Dave stepped even farther away from the site's day-to-day management, allowing Jen to revive it. They started experimenting with the latest technologies, like a primitive webcam that posted a new shot of a room in their apartment, usually empty or with Jen at the computer, every thirty seconds. By 2000, she'd raised the price of memberships to $14.95 a month, and offered CD-ROM package deals of hundreds of images and dozens of videos for collectors for $34.95, with a three-month subscription to the site thrown in. They went to parties thrown by other adult webmasters and hosted their own events for free (where there was no sex "until there was," according to Jen). They kept banner ads to a minimum and attempted to run a site that could be a model for industry ethics. They believed that just because you're posting dirty, doesn't mean you have to play dirty.

"We tried to lay a *good* foundation for that shit and helped fight the assholes who invented pop-up ads that couldn't be closed and recur billing," Dave said. "We lost, but we tried."

By 2012, when a journalist for the *Baltimore Sun* visited their apartment to profile their cyberadventures, jen-dave.com's popularity was rapidly waning. The birth of their twins, among other growing-up milestones, took priority. And the internet landscape was radically different from when they started: Massive porn conglomerates were gobbling up competition, stolen porn was a Google search away at all times, and algorithms were feeding people exactly what they wanted.

The most difficult part of their journey, for Dave, was "admitting that it was over," he said. "At some point I realized there would be no more parties and that I'd have to go back to having a day job and that would be all." Jen still runs her own website, JenPM, but they shuttered the original site—leaving only a love letter to their fans left up on the homepage.

> "I said, 'Look, what would we do if we hit the lottery tomorrow and never had to worry about money again? We'd make the site free again, right? So, what's the problem if this is how we pay our bills, while we have fun with it? Screw those people who want to call us greedy.'"
>
> **—Jen,** recounting a conversation she had with Dave

"I was never a truly moral or ethical person until I got into porn," Dave told the *Sun* reporter. "In the process of doing something I really loved, then being called a sellout, and coming to terms with that, and working with truly wonderful people, I started looking at the big picture, trying to experience life with the rest of humankind."

A Brief History of Online Dating

"Dear Dating Service, please give that wonderful, groovy computer a big kiss on his marvelous electronic brain for me. That last date was gorgeous."

–Dating service client Sally, published 1968

n 1727, the *Manchester Weekly Journal* ran a personal advertisement written by Helen Morrison that declared her intentions to seek a husband. Men had been placing newspaper personals for more than thirty years by then, advertising their assets and readiness to take a wife. But this was the first time a woman had the audacity to run one for herself.

Morrison's ad shocked the *Journal*'s readership so much that they decided she must be made an example of, lest her gall become contagious among single women. After a public outcry, the mayor committed her to an asylum for four weeks.

Nearly two and a half centuries later, in sixties London, Joan Ball founded St. James Computer Dating Service—the first computer-assisted dating company. As a young woman, she was wrongfully committed to a mental hospital for standing up to her mother's abuse. Despite tooth-and-nail success, Ball is largely excluded from online dating history. The punishment for women who stray from the social norms was, and often still is, to put them away and try to make the world forget.

> **"Nudes pls? Sorry just going through a dark time right now Love is rough But also so beautiful Just a tit?"**
>
> –@beam_me_up_softboi on Instagram, 2021

In 1965, a year after Ball, Harvard undergrad math major Jeffrey Tarr founded the world's second computer dating company. Tarr's primary motivation was to meet more women outside the limited campus pool. His company, Operation Match, ended up raking in $270,000 in profits in its first year—equivalent to more than $2.2 million today.

The first online dating network arrived decades later in 1984, with the Matchmaker Electronic Pen-Pal Network. Started on bulletin board systems, Matchmaker grew to fourteen boards across as many major cities around the US.

On its heels, sites like Match.com and OkCupid promised not just proximal and hobby-based love, but also something closer to

New dating craze sweeps the campus

boy...
girl...
...computer

An early article about Operation Match in *Look* magazine, 1966

Operation Match: a computer that knows you and has a mate waiting.

In 2005, only about 44 percent of people in the US thought online dating was a good way to meet someone, and more than a quarter felt that online dating was only for the desperate. Now, the majority of people don't feel strongly about online dating either way—perhaps a sign that internet-facilitated relationships are just part of life now, as common as meeting at work or a bar.

As the online dating scene exploded into the late-2000s, more people discovered what those who used BBS or MUDs had known for decades: that virtual love was no less powerful than meetings in person. In fact, it was often more so.

"Online relationships are vulnerable to a 'boom and bust' phenomenon: when people reveal more about themselves earlier than they would in [face-to-face] interactions, relationships can get quite intense quite quickly," wrote sexuality researchers Alvin Cooper and Leda Sportolari in 1997. "Such an accelerated process of revelation may increase the chance that the relationship will feel exhilarating at first, and become quickly eroticized, but then not be able to be sustained because the underlying trust and true knowledge of the other are not there to support it."

"The Great God Computer"

Before he became the oddball mustachioed *Today Show* film and book critic, Gene Shalit was a reporter. And in the history of computerized dating, Shalit's visit to Harvard to interview student-entrepreneurs working on the hot new dating-craze technology of 1966 put the fledgling industry on the map. His breathless write-up for *Look* magazine sent the reader spinning:

A nationwide dating spree is on. Thousands of boys and girls who've never met plan weekends together, for now that punch-card dating's here, can flings be far behind? And oh, it's so right, baby. The Great God Computer has sent the word. Fate. Destiny. Go-go-go.

"Nationwide" was more like "Greater Boston Area–wide," but the mood was right: a niche but awestruck public, mostly of the educated middle class, was eager to throw money at whatever promised to grease social wheels in a novel way.

It's telling the way male techies of a certain era—the late sixties into the nineties—liked to refer to computing "godlike," as if they themselves were gods. Most of them certainly ran their sites like they were all-powerful. Jon Boede at Matchmaker .com insisted on staying global SysOp for the Matchmaker BBS network, while local admin ran boards in the fourteen major cities where they operated.

> "We call him God. He's the guy who created it all."
>
> **–Bobby Dominguez,** local BBS admin for a Tampa, Florida, Matchmaker group, quoted in the *Tampa Bay Times* referring to Jon Boede, Matchmaker.com founder

This hubris sometimes came with the whiff of Greek tragedy. David Dewan, founder of a company called Contact that was a contemporary to Operation Match, as well as Gary Kremen, the first founder of Match.com, both lost their girlfriends to their own service after suggesting they sign up and see if their algorithms would pair them together. Ross Williams, who founded Singles365, met a woman through the site and used his power as creator to block other men's messages from her inbox. They dated for four years and then broke up, though Williams didn't see it as related to the site, or his manipulation of it.

For the most part, these men made their fortunes by making everyone's worlds in their own image. Kremen's first Match questionnaire was a bunch of criteria he, personally, thought was important in a date: data points of education, sense of humor, and occupation. Neil Warren's eHarmony criteria reflected his own religious beliefs—including the notion that women should always be shorter than men, and that men are most compatible with a wider range of women younger than themselves.

David Dewan founded Contact, an early dating service that employed algorithms to match people.

The Operation Match system of the late sixties, however, was low-tech for a God Computer. Students would fill out a two-part, seventy-five-question pamphlet, one for your own answers about your lifestyle and beliefs and the other describing your ideal mate. Answers to questions like "Do you believe in a god that answers prayer?" and detailed scenarios about their approaches to blind dates or crossword puzzles would supposedly be compared with the answers of thousands of other respondents. Fold up the pamphlet, mail it back, and the Operation Match guys would convert it to punch cards on an IBM 7090 computer[1] between the hours of two a.m. and four a.m.—the time when it was cheapest to rent the machine. They'd sort the cards by a few important criteria like location, religion, age, and height, and the rest were basically matched at random, Tarr said in a documentary.

The literal and metaphorical machinations of matches were almost beside the point. It was the mysticism of the computer that provided the real sparks. "It had a legitimacy that maybe your buddy Tom or your girlfriend Sarah would not have in saying 'this is the perfect girl or the perfect guy for you,'" Operation Match VP and fellow Harvard alum David Crump said. The narrowed selection, the excuse to call up a consenting stranger, and the hours of conversation that

---

1 The 7090 required a whole room to itself, and the one Operation Match used was housed in the Avco service bureau in Wilmington, Massachusetts. When it wasn't churning out dates, that model machine was doing rocket science: Four IBM 7090 systems were incorporated in the Air Force's Ballistic Missile Warning System in the sixties, and NASA used the model to send Mercury and Gemini mission astronauts to orbit.

followed, trying to figure out what the computer must have seen in you to match you—those were the real secret ingredients.

Trust in relinquishing romantic control to a vague computer algorithm is a phenomenon that hasn't changed much, even as the realm of virtual dating evolved way, way beyond punch cards. In a 2016 study, researchers built on the basis of self-determination theory—the dialectic approach that outlines people's needs for autonomy, competence, and connection to others—to examine how online daters feel about choice and control. "Offline, daters often seek validation of their choice of romantic partner from members of their social network," they wrote. "In the case of online dating, validation may come in the form of an algorithmic recommendation, which allows online daters to feel more satisfied with their initial choices." In this sense, the computer supplants the advice of real humans who've known you for years.

"The Great God Computer must know something we don't," Tarr told author Dan Slater for his book on the history of online dating, _A Million First Dates_. "The idea that we were matching based on compatibility was purely a marketing thing. It was always more art than science."

"Every journalist just assumed we were making better matches," Tarr explained to Slater. "And we were happy to perpetuate that thinking."

An IBM 7090 helped process punch cards for Operation Match's early computer dating service.

In spite of all the excitement about computer-facilitated love, Operation Match entered the world just a few decades too early to really catch on. Online dating wouldn't take off until people could date from the privacy of their own homes and control their own selections and questionnaires (or at least, have the illusion of control and wide selection).

And Tarr may have been in it to get girls, but—like another famous Harvard student who'd start "FaceMash" (see sidebar, page 76) in his dorm nearly forty years later—he was still something of a visionary. While Operation Match gained popularity, he told Shalit he dreamed of expanding the service to installations of "hundreds of special typewriters," strewn around campus for students to type in their requirements for a date that night, "all linked to a centralized 'mother computer'" that would return compatible names of others who were free for a date that night. Sounds a lot like the dating apps of right now.

"I met, I liked, I married"

By the time Ball heard about Operation Match, she'd been running her own computer dating company, the St. James Computer Dating Service, in London for four years, since 1964. In 1965, St. James merged with another marriage bureau and became Com-Pat, or Computer Dating Services Ltd.

The London *Times* ran a short "Report on Computer Romance" in 1966, about the "first couple" to marry as a result of computer dating. Susie and Leon filled out Com-Pat questionnaires after seeing advertisements in the paper; in a twist, the pair didn't speak the same language.

"What the calculating brain did not take into account as it sifted through thousands of permutations for likely matches, was that Leon has limited English and Susie speaks hardly a word of Italian," one article said. "'It doesn't seem to matter,' said Susie (blonde, placid, optimistic, according to the computer). 'We are extremely happy and I am helping Leon with his English.' Leon replied, 'I met, I liked, I married.'"

In December 1968, Ball sat with a gaggle of her employees in the Com-Pat offices and flipped through the latest issue of *News of the World*, looking for an article in which she'd been quoted. Like everything else in her life, Ball getting interviewed for the piece was against the odds. For years she struggled to place advertisements anywhere, meeting endless rejections from publications too nervous to promote anything remotely sexual. Her office landlord took the name of her business off the front door directory so often she stopped putting it back up.

Ball's company was barely staying afloat when she saw an advertisement for Dateline, another UK-based computer dating service, plastered across the London tube: "Could you be sitting next to the new man in your life?" The founder of Dateline, John Patterson, started the company in 1966, after watching the success of Operation Match in the States.

Exasperated and enraged, Ball called several newspapers, desperate for any kind of publicity. Her next appointment with the matching mainframe was coming up—and she was short on clients to feed it.

Finally, the tabloid *News of the World* bit. The resulting article also profiled Operation Match and Dateline, and flooded Ball with new business: By Christmas, two thousand people sent applications to Com-Pat, hoping the computer could find their match. That write-up brought more press attention, and more clients. When satisfied customers called the office to thank Ball, she'd beg them to tell their stories to the press, but they often said they were too worried about their

FACEMASH

Mark Zuckerberg's hot-or-not-style game, called "FaceMash," displayed images of female Harvard students side by side and asked the player to choose who was more attractive—an idea that came to him while drunk and annoyed at being rejected by a woman. "I'm a little intoxicated, not gonna lie," Zuckerberg wrote in his personal blog. "The Kirkland [dorm] facebook is open on my desktop and some of these people have pretty horrendous facebook pics. I almost want to put some of these faces next to pictures of farm animals and have people vote on which is more attractive."

reputation or their jobs to go public with how they had met their new lovers. Even as thousands of people around the UK found happiness through computerized matchmaking, introducing your partner as having come out of a computer program was still taboo.

Even with small wins like these, Com-Pat couldn't stay afloat in a market that wouldn't fully accept it. After years of trying to drum up advertising through word of mouth from happy clients, the company floundered. Ball eventually sold Com-Pat to Dateline's John Patterson, for £5,000. The only condition was that he pay the £7,000 of debt the company carried. The sale crushed her.

With the advantage of being a slick businessman and having the UK computer dating market now primed by Ball's Com-Pat, Patterson developed Dateline into a more sexually forward service that was "adventure" focused. Later, he started a separate, even more explicit service, according to technology historian Mar Hicks. "That service asked users how sexually experienced they required their partners to be, along with which specific sex acts customers had engaged in previously, and which ones they wished to perform in the future," Hicks wrote. According to Hicks, Patterson ran into trouble after selling lists of women who were "ready to go" to men without the women's knowledge or consent.

Dateline was ultimately prolific but not particularly successful for its clients, if the definition of online dating success is a happily-ever-after. Patterson estimated that the company matched more than forty thousand prospective couples a year, but only around two thousand of them ended up married.

Despite their groundbreaking and innovative work in computer dating, neither Patterson nor Ball found their happily-ever-afters. Patterson was found dead in a bath by his ex-wife at fifty-one, following years of struggling with alcoholism and failed relationships.

Ball never married. She and her partner in work and life, Kenneth, drifted apart amid their drive to constantly put the business and their clients first. When Ball later read letters from Kenneth about their breakup, she realized too late that they'd simply miscommunicated their feelings all along.

Light the Match: The Online Dating Boom

In the grand scheme of sex online, there are few areas where the internet's impact is as profound as it is in dating. The ability to find sexual partners from a device in your hand while sitting at a bar or on your couch, by casting a net as wide as the world, represented a seismic shift in how relationships happen.

And all of this was already happening on pre- and proto-internet systems like Usenet, BBS, and chat programs, such as CompuServe's CB Simulator. Rush Limbaugh famously met his third wife through CB Simulator, but so did many other average people—and the first online weddings happened over the service. One couple in 1983 "broadcast" their vows live to all their friends in virtual attendance, followed by a text-based reception. But it wasn't until the introduction of the World Wide Web that algorithmic matchmaking became a sought-after industry.

Like almost every dating site founder mentioned so far, Andrew Conru started Web Personals as a student who cited the mostly male engineering departments as the reason he couldn't get laid. Launched in 1994, Web Personals is widely credited as the first online personals site. Conru was a classic dot-com bubble entrepreneur—he also founded software management company W3 and Adknowledge. These companies worked on some of the earliest technologies for shopping online, user registrations, and advertising networks. Also, he invented the online shopping cart.

Conru was the first to develop technology that gave sites the ability to track users from page to page—all as part of his work on Web Personals.

Web Personals, founded by Andrew Conru in 1994, was one of the first online dating websites.

"While we take it for granted today that websites change dynamically based on who you were, in the early days, websites were just static pages, everyone saw the same thing," he told *Vice*.

More than 120,000 people signed up for Web Personals in the single year he owned it. Conru sold the site in 1995 for $100,000. He wasn't done with online dating, however—he founded FriendFinder.com the following year. Just days after that launch, after seeing how many people posted nudes and kink-heavy content to FriendFinder, he started Adult FriendFinder as a separate, racier site.

As of 2016 Conru was still single, something even he found ironic.

Technically, Matchmaker came before Web Personals—but it came *after* Web Personals in the race to the web. Gregory Scott Smith founded Matchmaker in 1986 as a BBS service and ran its server off a single Apple II computer in Houston, Texas. As membership grew, Smith ported the system to a Radio Shack TRS-80 running six modems and expanded it to San Antonio, then San Jose, California. It expanded again in 1987 when Matchmaker's programmer, Jon Boede, opened the system up for franchising. Wherever someone wanted to set up a local clone of the Matchmaker BBS, they could.

> ### Algorithmic matching
> Most modern dating apps use algorithms to make matches, but they all do it differently. Tinder mainly uses your location and whether you've used the app recently, while OkCupid relies on "match percentages" calculated based on answers to quizzes and preferences.

One of the biggest franchises, Christie's Matchmaker, had more than four thousand individual members and twenty boards by 1995.

Like the computerized dating services of the sixties, visitors to a Matchmaker BBS filled out a questionnaire about themselves and their preferences. They were sorted by location and demographics using those questionnaires, then matched with people who had similar responses.

When the World Wide Web started siphoning people off BBS, Matchmaker made the jump, too, moving to a .com address in 1996. In 1998, it had 2 million members, with 31,000 new ones joining every week—ballooning to 4 million by 2000. Search engine company Lycos acquired Matchmaker.com in 2000 for $44.5 million cash. From there, it did the typical dot-com start-up shuffle; it was bought by another company, then another, until finally it shut down when a parent company did, in 2016.

Things started changing even more rapidly in the early 2000s, when sites like Match, eHarmony, and Plenty of Fish entered the field and started competing with one another. Between 2000 and 2010, at least eighteen new dating sites launched. Most used the questionnaire matching approach: Users were paired with people who answered similarly to them or were most likely to be compatible. The problems they were working to solve—loneliness, sexual desire, a need for romantic connection—are ancient ones, but the ways each went about solving them were different.

Match.com founder Gary Kremen's inspiration for online dating was born of necessity. He was paying $2.99 per minute dialing 900-number services when he got the idea for an online database for love that would be more anonymous and less expensive than hours on the phone.

Kremen saw the future of the internet and how it would revolutionize and digitize everything we do—including relationships—and bet on the widest spread possible. As part of a new internet classifieds company, he registered several basic URLs that represented the sections of the classified pages, including jobs.com, housing.com, autos.com, and match.com. They were relatively cheap back then. In 1994, angel investors and venture capitalists gave Kremen $1.5 million in funding to build out the online classifieds sector, and Match.com went live in April 1995.

Right after launching Match.com and predicting the lucrative online sex industry, he quickly registered Sex.com—only to have it stolen by elaborate domain registration fraud and turned into an advertising-heavy site that received up to 25 million hits a day. After a five-year legal battle he got it back, and in 2006, he sold Sex.com for $13 million, making it the most expensive domain sale up to that point in history.

Perhaps because it started from such a personal place, Match.com was, according to him, his baby. It was the project he'd go to bat for against his investors, who found it too salacious for the rest of their portfolios, opting to drop it in favor of focusing on cars and houses. In 1998 the board voted to sell Match.com—and Kremen threw a raging fit. Today, Match Group is a $22 billion conglomerate and owns many of the biggest online dating companies in the world.

While Kremen was enduring his blow-up and bow-out of the industry, clinical psychologist Neil Clark Warren was building the beginnings of what would become eHarmony. His 1993 book, *Finding the Love of Your Life*, was the culmination of his master's degree in divinity and his work as a professor, then dean, at Fuller Theological Seminary's graduate school of psychology. But his obsession with stable nuclear family units came from a childhood where his parents stayed together despite being deeply incompatible. The book became a website, and the website became the dating service eHarmony.

eHarmony's "29 Dimensions of Compatibility" gave its system a scientific-sounding flair, but the reality, at least at first, was more Holy Spirit than science. In trying to attract a marriage-or-bust user base, Warren, an evangelical Christian, coded conservative limits into the app. The algorithm would only match taller men with shorter women, and rejected outright anyone who was divorced. Weeding out those who Warren saw as a risk to his happy-family marriage-oriented goal

"I screamed and screamed and screamed. I hit someone I think, I was so angry. I said: 'I think this is the one, let's forget the other classifieds, we've got traction here, we've got real income, it's growing like this every day. Let's back the successful horse.' But the old-timers were embarrassed by dating."

—**Gary Kremen,** founder of Match.com quoted in the book *Sex.com*, when he learned his site would be sold against his wishes by investors curved the odds that users would find success with his system and live happily ever after—making his system more of a success. His criteria changed as society got more progressive, however; eHarmony was forced to start a separate website for gay couples in 2007, after a discrimination lawsuit.

Warren stayed bitter about it. "I think this issue of same-sex marriage within the next five to fifteen years will be no issue anymore," Warren told Yahoo! Finance in 2013. "We've made too much of it. I'm tired of it. It has really damaged our company." In 2016, he backtracked. "We've suffered from the contentiousness of that topic," he told CNN. "We didn't want to pretend to be experts on gay and lesbian couples. We're not anti-gay at all . . . It's a different match."

While eHarmony turned potential members away at the door, Match.com looked for ways to include as many people as possible. Queer communities relied on the internet to connect, to find common spaces to escape the isolation of heteronormativity in a white cis man's world, and they'd been doing it since the Usenet days.

They didn't need eHarmony. Grindr and Scruff were some of the earliest smartphone dating apps, paving the way for Tinder, Bumble, and Hinge—at this point, household names in millennial and Gen Z lives.

"A thirty-year-old woman would be matched with men between twenty-seven and forty, while a thirty-year-old man would be matched with women between twenty-three and thirty-three. People who had been married four or more times were rejected, as were gays and lesbians, as were people whose responses to the questionnaire failed eHarmony's 'dysthymia scale,' indicating depression."

—**Dan Slater,** writing about eHarmony's early practices, in his book *A Million First Dates*

"You Have 1 New Match": Dating Apps Go Mobile

The arrival of smartphones and apps in the mid-2000s shifted the game once again. With the power of hyper-accurate GPS in our pockets, dating within a local pool became even easier. And with the industry booming, the next generation of dating apps was less often dorky dorm projects and more lab-created start-up ventures.

Dopamine hit
Notifications on our phones and computers cause our brains to release dopamine, the "feel good" chemical. It's the same one that makes us come back to a delicious meal or great sex over and over—or likes, retweets, and dating matches.

Tinder launched in 2012 as an experiment within start-up incubator Hatch Labs. It was predicated on a similar idea as Operation Match: Most people are more likely to approach someone if they know the other person is open to romantic advances. A GQ profile of the founders and their Los Angeles–based company describes an office setting like something out of a start-up bro parody: flannel shirts, sneakers, Nerf gun darts, leather upholstery, and fast cars. But it's not Silicon Valley culture they're exporting; rather, it's a matter-of-fact confidence that would better fit in with pick-up artists than math majors.

On Tinder you see a face, you like it immediately (or you don't), and you swipe (right for yes, left for no). If someone else swipes right, it opens a chat channel between you in the app. From there, it's up to you.

Smartphones are incredibly addictive in part due to muscle memory and the dopamine hits that come with notifications. Tinder keeps users rapt because its makers gamified these physical reactions to digital content. "We always saw Tinder, the interface, as a game. What you're doing, the motion, the reaction," cofounder Sean Rad told *Time* magazine. They modeled the match interface after a deck of cards, they said, where you either hold the top card or flick it away to the discard pile.

There are no questionnaires on Tinder, only short bios, a handful of photos for each user, and endless swiping sessions based on proximity. Bumble, an app designed to upend the traditional "men make the first move" belief, works similarly, the catch being that only women are allowed to initiate conversations.

Whitney Wolfe Herd, Tinder's former vice president of marketing, launched Bumble in 2014. She started the company just one year after leaving the company and suing them for sexual harassment, alleging that Tinder cofounder Justin Mateen publicly called her a "whore" and his fellow founders dismissed her complaints. She was removed from the founding team because a woman's presence at that level would "make the company seem like a joke," Mateen allegedly said, among a series of other verbal abuses.

Bumble solves Match's problem of finding more women to invite to the party by putting the control in their hands to begin with. Men use the app because more women are on it.

Wolfe's is the rare perspective in online-dating founders that doesn't see tech as the solution to our love-unlucky society. What she does see is the trend of women being pushed away from tech roles through experiences similar to her own. "This isn't necessarily a tech problem, this is a society problem," she told *Time*. "I don't think it's been socially acceptable for women to drop out of college and start a tech company."

Algorithms: The Hands of Fate

Online dating hasn't just shifted our methods of meeting up—it's allowed advertisers to manipulate our behaviors in real ways.

There was perhaps no richer or more accurate portrayal of what users thought of themselves, wanted, dreamed of, or lived like than a dating profile: Through answering guided questions that promise to help you find your soulmate, millions of people willingly plugging their most intimate preferences ("Which pubic hair style do you prefer for a partner?") and most mundane ("How do you feel about cooking with a partner?") into a database. They're compared against others—neatly alongside demographics like age, gender, height, body type, and location—to provide a gold mine of data points to advertisers. And most online daters are under thirty, making their data even more valuable.

But advertising isn't most dating sites' bread and butter. Most rely on paid subscriptions. Advertisers don't like to touch anything sexual—it's not "brand-safe"—and questions about things like pubes certainly fall into that category.

"Yes, we know whether you smoke and how many hours a week you play video games. We know everything," OkCupid founder Sam Yagan told Slater. "But when it comes to businesses like ours, businesses that have historically carried a stigma, advertisers are risk averse." Even if dating sites have a hard time attracting advertisers to their sites, some have no issue doing it the other way around, selling scads of ostensibly anonymized user data to marketing firms.

"For a lot of folks, dating is about lifestyle changes," advertising executive Jeff Greenfield told *Consumer Reports*. "That's a great opportunity for curated ad experiences" for things like books and travel. It doesn't stop when you delete the apps, either; no longer swiping every night could mean yet another lifestyle change, in the form of an exclusive relationship. Then it's time for jewelry ads.

Studies have shown that targeted advertising, as well as software design that targets users to come

Algorithms are just lines of code that set up a series of if/then commands.

back to their products, has real effects on the things people do and the choices they make online and off. Facebook, for example, employs this style of advertising to manipulate users into seeking out more and more fringe content, the type that draws on attributes such as "recently single," "into kink," or "is depressed."

Even the founders of these sites know that technology can't truly fix online dating, because interpersonal relationships are messier than any algorithm can sort—yet. It's possible, in fact, that constant iteration and innovation and disruption on something so fundamentally human is actually making it worse. Nearly half of US adults believe dating is harder now than it was ten years ago. But 48 percent of eighteen- to twenty-nine-year-olds and 38 percent of thirty- to forty-nine-year-olds say they've tried online dating at some point.

"I wager that most people who use OkCupid don't like [online dating] because most people don't like dating," OkCupid cofounder Christian Rudder told students at a Northeastern University event. "Dating itself is horrible and dating apps are never going to fix that."

Web tracking

Website operators have many ways to track what visitors do on their sites, from seeing that person's location data to analyzing what they click and how much time they spend on a page. Advertisers build whole profiles of people based on their activity around the web.

Sixty years after the first "dating computer," countless apps, software iterations, and marketing gimmicks still haven't managed to optimize the experience of finding human connection—let alone make the process less miserable. Like couples who met through the randomized Great God Computer, online dating today still feels like drawing names out of a hat and hoping who you get is a decent person.

More people than ever are questioning the constraints of institutions like marriage, monogamy, and procreation, but most Americans still believe in the idea of a "fate" or "the one"—another person who enters your life and completes it—and more than ever rely on the destiny prescribed by an algorithm. Fed by our own whims and wants, the great algorithm behind the curtain attempts to push us toward that fate by taking stock of our

"I can have dick delivered to my door faster than a pizza," Steve, an executive in Atlanta, told *Slate* in 1999. Queer people generated so much revenue for America Online's chat rooms—not AIM, but its predecessor—that former AOL CEO Steve Case is on the record as saying, "Thank God for the gays and lesbians." Because AOL took a live-and-let-live approach to what users did on the service, chat rooms were a meeting point for a lot of people who were marginalized by the rest of the "IRL" world. Online, they could be seen on their own terms—by other people who shared similar backgrounds and identities. AOL management officially sanctioned a "Gay and Lesbian Community Forum" section of the system, including daily AIDS reports from the Centers for Disease Control as well as PG-rated pinup photos and discussions about every aspect of life, sexual or not.

On AOL, cruising could start online and finish offline. Gay men especially flocked to these spaces, where chat rooms like #gaymuscle formed under the pretense of a hobby (here, bodybuilding), but conversations carried sexually charged subtext.

Being able to screen sexual partners before meeting, and have those conversations in a safe, distanced place—especially if it was outside of a dangerously unaccepting home community—meant safer sexual experiences for everyone. "This is the first time a closeted person can participate fully in the lesbian and gay community without fearing losing their job, their home, and their family," LGBTQIA+ media company PlanetOut founder Tom Reilly said in 2002.

But San Francisco's summer of 1999 put the #SFM4M (men for men) chat room in the public eye, when a syphilis outbreak was traced back to that AOL chat room. The *Journal of the American Medical Association* reported that "gay men who had syphilis in San Francisco were eight to nine times more likely to have met a recent partner in the AOL chat rooms than elsewhere," according to CNET. Eight men from the chat were infected, but had arranged to have sex with ninety-nine others, total.

preferences and reflecting them back at us: "people you may know" lists on Facebook and Instagram, suggested accounts on Twitter, networks of users like us, connected by some web of personal data we can't see.

The yearning to take control of one's fate, one swipe at a time, is strong. Tinder, Bumble, and Hinge each have a "Boost" feature—Tinder's and Hinge's expose your profile to more people, and Bumble's extends the time you have to respond to matches. *Maybe the next swipe will be the one. Maybe if I hold a puppy in my profile picture, I'll get more matches.* But how much sway could we really have over systems that influence everything from our favorite brand of toothpaste to the next concert we'll attend—to the next person whose digital path we'll cross?

Dollars
&
Sense

Porn 2.0
AND THE CAMGIRL REVOLUTION

"I would rather be a cyborg than a goddess."

—Donna Haraway

FEEL SO LONELY," said the card Jennifer Ringley held up to her computer's silent webcam. She flashed the message to a half-million viewers around the world who logged on to see her do nothing, in snapshots of her bedroom every few minutes.

It was the late nineties and the student from suburban Pennsylvania was in the process of establishing herself as the first "camgirl." Her viewers watched her come of age in her dorm room: bored, studying, masturbating, playing with her cat, making out with her boyfriend, exploring her sexuality under the watchful eyes of a global audience.

This was the era of MTV's *The Real World*, which debuted in 1992 as the unscripted, sexually charged result of throwing seven twenty-somethings into a swanky apartment on the Lower East Side and broadcasting their every move around the country. Exhibitionism was becoming less about Madonna nude in a coffee table book and more everyday life on display. Around 527,000 people tuned in for each weekly episode of the first season of *The Real World*. Ringley's webcam drew that many viewers every day. People tuned in to reality TV for the same reason they logged on to watch grainy webcam footage online: because they hoped to see something sexual, something scandalous.

The invention of the webcam started a ripple that, a decade later, would completely upend how the entire internet operates. Commercially, it shifted the power from studios to individuals. Socially, fans were able to speak directly to their favorite stars for a level of intimacy they'd never experienced from the internet before. For workers, it shifted some to a safer, more stable model of making money on their own terms. Whether they were personalities like Ringley, lifecasters

Jennifer Ringley, an early lifecaster, sent a message felt by many.

turned YouTube celebrities, or porn performers, one device—a goofy little bauble of an eyeball perched on top of a computer monitor—flipped the viewers' gaze back at them.

These changes were especially prominent in the adult industry. For all of pornography's history until the nineties, the majority of films were made by men, for men. There were exceptions: Candida Royalle founded Femme Productions in 1984 and remained the pre-eminent voice for women- and couples-centric porn for years; Susie Bright's *On Our Backs* magazine published lesbian erotica for lesbians (as opposed to the kind made for men). But for the most part, the disembodied dick and cum shot reigned.

The internet-connected webcam changed all that.

The internet's explosion fueled the rise of independent porn performers who could be directors, videographers, producers, actors, marketers, and full owners of their own work. And all it took was a laptop, a webcam, and an internet connection. "If you're the middle guy who has been eating off this industry for twenty years, it's a big change," Todd Blatt, a failing porn producer who was selling off his Ferraris, said to the *New York Times* in 2013. "The girls don't need anybody."

Livestreaming
Broadcasting video over the internet in real time.

Lifecasting
Livestreaming your daily life. The most hard-core purist lifecasters (like Jennifer Ringley) left the camera on 24/7 without censorship or curation, but less dedicated streamers chose to turn the camera on and off during intimate moments.

"No Better Place to Hide Than in the Open"

When Ringley saw a webcam for sale in her college bookstore, she had to have it.

She wanted to experiment with taking and uploading photos to her personal website. At the time, a few sites were experimenting with "live" cams—usually still images that auto-refreshed at regular

For seven years, Ringley's webcam took (and published) an image every few minutes.

intervals every few seconds or minutes. The Amazing FishCam,[1] a video feed started in 1994 of a forty-gallon aquarium in Mountain View, California, refreshed every three or four seconds. This tiny window into someone else's space, even if it was just some tropical fish, was captivating.

One of Ringley's friends joked that with her new webcam, she could be the human version of the FishCam, a creature on display in the bowl of her dorm room. She set up her camera in 1996 and started with only a few dozen friends watching. For a short time it was a staged show she'd put on for her tiny audience, but it quickly shifted to a twenty-four-hour surveillance feed of Ringley's room—an idea that interested her much more for its uncensored, unfiltered authenticity.

It wasn't really streaming video in the sense we know it today. It was just a camera shutter timer and upload sequence that Ringley

---

1 FishCam was the (literal) pet project of Netscape founding engineer Lou Montulli, who used it as a test bed for many of the internet protocols we now use every day: Animated GIFs, image uploading, and dynamic HTML pages are just some of the technologies developed through testing and viewer feedback of the FishCam.

coded to be automated: Every minute, the code told the camera to snap a photo, and every two minutes, it uploaded that photo to her site, boudoir.org (which she later renamed jennicam.org).

"The concept of the cam is to show whatever is going on naturally. Essentially, the cam has been there long enough that now I ignore it," she wrote on the site's FAQ page.

Turning the camera around or covering it up every time she needed to change clothes or have a guy over would make the thing a too-constant presence. For the experiment to work, she had to forget about it. It needed to melt into the background of her life.

Murmurs of livestreaming as the thrilling technological future were already starting. But no one had yet to train a webcam on total mundanity; Ringley was the first lifecaster to turn on her round 320 x 240 pixel Connectix QuickCam and point it at her cramped dorm room to capture whatever might happen, at all hours.

Other lifecasters predated her, but they streamed with a little more self-censorship. Steve Mann, then a professor at the University of Toronto, was the first lifecaster to document and upload his existence moment-by-moment from 1994 to 1996. Mann is a mad scientist of augmented reality: Long before Google Glass introduced the public to the idea of wearing camera-equipped AR glasses in our daily lives, his "Wearable Wireless Webcam" consisted of a camera strapped to a helmet and an antenna that transmitted whatever he was looking at to a website. But Mann wasn't a purist about his lifecasting experiment: He took the helmet off during intimate moments and was actually quite concerned about personal privacy in this new age of individual surveillance.

> "So whatever you're seeing isn't staged or faked, and while I don't claim to be the most interesting person in the world, there's something compelling about real life that staging it wouldn't bring to the medium."
>
> **—Jennifer Ringley,** of JenniCam, an early livestreaming sensation

The general public was getting to know internet-streaming video, but it was a one-way mirror. The audience couldn't talk back—until CU-SeeMe. Developed in the early nineties, the software was ten years ahead of its time. Skype wouldn't come out until 2003, but CU-SeeMe was the same concept: a chat interface combined with real-time video.

Developed as one of the first free softwares for video conferencing, Cornell University's CU-SeeMe was released to the public in April 1993 as a tool for schools. What made CU-SeeMe special was its democratizing mission, baked into the system by developer Tim Dorcey. "While others worked to advance the state of the art in video compression, high-speed networking, and other low-level technologies necessary to support high-quality video conferencing, we hoped to facilitate the accumulation of experience that would provide impetus for those efforts and guide their direction," he wrote in a 1995 whitepaper on the project. It didn't have to be the best available. He just wanted people to use it.

People did use it, for porn. Webmasters set up mirrors of the software that used the program without taxing the CU-SeeMe server load itself, explicitly for adult livestreaming. In 2000, those included sites like "Backdoor," "Adult XXX Amateur Club," "Biker Bar," and many more. Most of these sites required voyeurs to keep their webcams on if they wanted to

Dynamic HTML
First introduced in 1997, dynamic HTML meant that web pages could be animated and interactive after the page fully loaded.

Animated GIFs
Short for graphics interchange format, animated GIFs are still image frames assembled like a flipbook, usually playing on a loop.

CU-SeeMe was early livestreaming tech that portended things to come.

watch, making the experience much more intimate than the typical one-sided webcam show or clip site.

Ringley, however, wasn't trying to join the adult industry one snapshot at a time. "This site is not pornography," her FAQ page said. "Yes, it contains nudity from time to time. Real life contains nudity. Yes, it contains sexual material from time to time. Real life contains sexual material. However, this is not a site about nudity and sexual material. It is a site about real life." Mostly, she was just a young woman coming of age—something that's infinitely fascinating in our society and seen as fair game for endless scrutiny.

At its peak, JenniCam was getting millions of hits a day. And she was inspiring others to do the same. Ana Clara Voog started streaming as anacam in August 1997. Like Ringley, she'd stream 24/7, via a new image uploaded to her website every three to five minutes. But her motivations were different. Voog was focused on artistic expression and social experimentation.

Image uploading
Moving a file (like a photo from a digital camera, or a document from a thumb drive) from one device to another.

Video compression
Encoding a video file so that it takes up less space. This was important in the early days of the internet, when bandwidth was limited and internet speeds were much slower than today. It's also why everything from back then looks grainy or low-quality.

"The anacam project was a long-chain event I constructed in order to help me make sense of the world," she said in 2018. "I have an eccentric and resilient way of dealing with my suffering, for the most part. I turn it into art."

Like Ringley, Voog was adamant that what she was making wasn't pornographic—if viewers caught her in the nude that was part of the experiment, but it wasn't the whole point.

Both women also made the distinction between what people saw, and who they were. "I didn't care if people knew personal things about me or looked at my naked body. These things are transitory," Voog wrote. "It's a photo of my body not my actual body and

I control the output and the gaze, I reasoned. I was determined to live a transparent life. 'No better place to hide than in the open,' they say."

Sex was part of the stream because it was part of her life, and Voog did it all on camera, from conception of her first child to birth in front of her online audience. She posted baby updates to her LiveJournal twice after giving birth in 2007, where viewers commented with encouragement. "I saw you in the birthing tub this morning, and by the time I came back you had already given birth to her :)," one wrote. "Thank you for sharing this with us."

Sometimes, the webcams' watchful eyes caught too much. In 2000, Ringley's camera, and all of her viewers, caught her having an affair with her neighbor and fellow camgirl's fiancé. The internet erupted in hatred for Ringley, but also fascination for the futuristic scandal. The *Washington Post* called Ringley a "redheaded little minx" and "amoral man-trapper." But she kept streaming for three more years until 2003, when she announced her site would shut down for good. The experiment in radical self-exposure had gone from capturing carefree young adulthood to the routine of a grown-up with a day job, leaving the cam sitting to stare at nothing for most of the day.

She has since disappeared from online life altogether. She doesn't have any social media profiles connected to her old name, and married a man with a generic last name, making it a lot harder to find a trace of her today.

As with any sexual exploration that happened in view of the internet, plenty of people—mostly men—lined up to give their opinions and pathologize these women's behavior. Something, after all, must be *wrong* with them, they reasoned, for them to want to put themselves on display 24/7. Leo Hindery Jr., the head of Tele-Communications, Inc., brought up Ringley's site as an example of the "stunningly immoral" potential of the internet, in a speech to Roman Catholic bishops in 1998: "It may sound pathetic, but people actually relate to Jenni; they feel they know her personally—so much so that men worldwide regard Jenni as their 'virtual' girlfriend," Hindery said. He likened the internet to the "electronic pew" of the corrupt.

"I find comments like those to be very typical of someone who has never actually seen my site," Ringley later retorted.

The word "exhibitionist" was thrown around a lot. "Psychologically [lifecasting] could be harmful. Like any behavior you can take that to an extreme, you could post details, it could get out of hand, it could also affect your relationships with others, especially if the others are aware and disapprove," psychologist John Grohol said in 2007.

> "why is everything that is naked all of a sudden porn? i know so many have asked that boring question before. and i've never been confronted with it so vividly. but here I am."
>
> **–Lifecaster Ana Voog,** from her online diary, Septermber 17, 1997

The *Baltimore Sun* called Ringley an "exhibitionist pioneer," and the founder of a fan club site devoted to her claimed that she told him the label fits—"For Jennifer, of course, she has told me, and I don't take it as a big secret, that she is an exhibitionist," he said. Yet she never used that word for herself publicly in the many interviews and appearances she gave during the height of JenniCam.

Voog kept streaming—twelve years from start to finish—long after Ringley's show ended. She was also called an exhibitionist, but denies exhibitionism had anything to do with it.

In 2007, Justin Kan, a twenty-three-year-old in San Francisco, strapped a camera to a hat à la Steve Mann. He streamed his life to the internet nearly uninterrupted—everywhere except in the bathroom—for Justin.tv. The audience wasn't just

The Fish Cam was just a live feed of a fish tank, but was wildly popular in the (very early) heyday of live streaming.

passively watching him; a chat system allowed them to talk to him and other viewers during the broadcast. A decade after *The Real World: New York* and JenniCam, it wasn't a novel idea, but it did capture the same unquenchable voyeurism that people had for watching other people's lives. And the one thing everyone demanded, that they were watching and waiting for: When would Justin have sex?

After a few weeks of luckless dates, Kan finally went back to a woman's apartment. His audience held its breath. Just moments before things got heavy, he turned the camera-hat around backward, then took it off completely. His producers (there were several people working behind the scenes of Justin.tv) scrambled to overlay fake noises and a placeholder image over the stream, while thousands of people watched live.

High-speed network
Broadband internet (accessed through a coaxial or fiber-optic cable, or radio signals, aka Wi-Fi) started to overtake dial-up (over a phone line) around 2004. Because broadband is always on and not limited to the relatively low capacity of a phone modem, it's much faster.

Annalee Newitz, writing for *Wired* in 2007, one month after the stream's launch, summed up this frenetic horniness:

> Justin, you are so socially-conscious! But why get girls to do the dirty work for you when you've got such a sweet body and are slutting around town right now? Nobody cares if there's some dumb NYC chick getting laid—we've seen that a million times before. We want to see Web 2.0 entrepreneurs getting it on. That's novelty! That's entertainment! That's good from a business perspective, and you know what? It's good for society too.

Over the next few months and years, Justin.tv grew into something much larger than a dude with a camera on a baseball cap. It was always meant to be a Silicon Valley tech company, not a plucky streamer's project. By April, the team secured $50,000 in seed money from start-up incubator Y Combinator. Shortly after, the site was opened up to anyone who wanted to stream, and partitioned into section categories: People & Lifecasting, Sports, Music & Radio, Gaming, News

LONELYGIRL15

On June 16, 2006, the world got its first look at sixteen-year-old Bree when she uploaded "First Blog / Dorkiness Prevails" to YouTube. In the ninety-five-second clip of her in her bedroom, the soft-spoken teen rests her chin on her knee and lists off a few names of other YouTubers she admires, before awkwardly making faces and rolling her tongue to the tune of Gnarls Barkley's "Crazy."

On the other side of the webcam, twenty-five-year-old Mesh Flinders and Miles Beckett, twenty-seven, sat watching her antics. This was Flinders's own bedroom, transformed into a teenage girl's room with a pastel Target bedspread and generic framed art on the walls—a stuffed animal thrown on the bed for believability. Bree was nearly twenty, and her real name was Jessica Rose. Together, they'd created a fictional one-bedroom world that fans believed was real for months. A little over a year into YouTube's existence, Flinders and Beckett saw the future of entertainment being uploaded by teens online, in the form of video blogs where they recited the tedious details of their lives in short, episodic updates. Until that summer, it was mostly cat videos, comedy clips, and the occasional badly lit vlog. With the rise in attention came more scrutiny of the people making vlog life their brand. Every time Rose let her New Zealand accent slip or the audience decided she looked a little too old for her age, more people tried to analyze who the person behind the awkward teen really was. Some went as far as dissecting background sounds and local flora from her hiking videos.

Twenty-year-old actress Jessica Rose played "Bree," also known as Lonelygirl15, a lifecasting sensation.

The ruse continued until September, when the son of a Silicon Valley tech journalist uncovered Rose's old MySpace page and posted it to his dad's blog. The farce was up, and everyone knew Lonelygirl15 was a camera trick.

Instead of bringing everything crashing down, however, the sudden publicity was jet fuel to Bree's fame: Her video diaries were suddenly getting 300,000 views per clip and making $10,000 a month in ad revenue on Lonelygirl15.com. The producers pivoted to full transparency about the series being a scripted show and kept it running for years, until it fizzled out with a failed reboot in 2016.

& Tech, Animals, Entertainment, Divas & Dudes. In 2011, the gaming section split off into its own site, Twitch.tv, and in 2014, the entire Justin.tv brand became Twitch and shifted its focus to gamers. Amazon bought it later that year for $970 million.

Today, Twitch is a global social media giant, worth $4 billion with 3.8 million streamers. They turn on their webcams and invite loyal audiences into their homes while they play video games or just talk about everything—and nothing at all.

Justin Kan, star of Justin.tv, would go on to become a Silicon Valley venture capital investor.

Rise of the Camgirl

For all their experimenting and success, Ringley and Voog were missing one element that would transform lifecasting into the catalyst that turned the internet upside down: real-time interactivity with an audience. AmandaCam, launched in 1998, was one of the first to incorporate a chat system alongside lifecasting, almost a decade before Justin Kan started egging on fans from his baseball cap. Her website also had more intentionally sexual overtones than the other lifecasters to that point—users had to affirm that they were eighteen and willing to see sexual content to enter, and her still image gallery included snapshots of her shaving in a bathtub and dancing nude in her living room. Other adult webmasters were starting to incorporate webcams that uploaded images every few minutes into their full offerings. But AmandaCam tended to her fandom more than most, and live chat rooms were a large part of that.

By the late nineties, adult webmasters were also incorporating webcams as a part of their other offerings—pornographer couple Jen and Dave (see page 67) had one that posted a still photo of their office every thirty seconds, which Dave described as "the SHIT back then."

Webcam models working during the 2019
AVN Adult Entertainment Expo

As interest in home cams grew, websites sprung up that were dedicated solely to camming. Sites such as VoyeurDorm.com, which advertised "30 Cameras, 8 Women, 1 House, 24 Hours, 7 days a Week, ALL Year Round!!" rode the lifestreamer wave. By the late nineties, people were running thousands of these static-shot "homecams" from their bedrooms, hundreds of which were devoted specifically to sex on camera. TopCams.com, a link site for cams, listed 290 adult webcams in 1998; The Nose's HomeCam Page, another link directory, listed 1,200.

One of the first websites to bring several different adult home cams to one page was the AmateurCam Network. Started in 1997, the site featured around twenty women's webcams and charged a separate subscription fee for each model, ranging from $9.95 to $12.95 a month. The cameras refreshed every sixty seconds, where audiences could watch them at home in their bedrooms, bathrooms, wherever they placed a camera. "It's a network of amateur models who decided, for one reason or another, to display their private lives on the Internet. Why? Well, you'll have to ask them," the site said in 1998. "They are real people, not professionals. And, they all have their own personalities ranging from exhibitionist to shy."

Despite the emphasis on authenticity and amateurism, the models of AmateurCam Network weren't like JenniCam—they were almost always aware of the camera and were there to put on a show. The platform was a predecessor of today's subscription cam sites: Users could join models in chat rooms, call them for a private phone sex session, or browse galleries of images taken from the cams. Sites like LiveJasmin (2001) and MyFreeCams (2002) arrived soon after, with thousands of women signing up. The cam-site era changed so much about how sex work is perceived, how people interact with adult performers, how clients and fans fulfill their needs for emotional connection, and how sex workers make a living.

Bounded Authenticity, Tied Up in Capitalism

Dozens of women sat side by side at a cluttered conference table against a long wall at the thirty-sixth annual AVN Adult Entertainment Expo in 2019. Each smiled and wiggled and waved into just as many laptops and cell phones on tripods. Their booth created something of a gauntlet for the rest of the show—to get to the aisles of displays beyond them, you had to weave through a tunnel of men in ill-fitting jeans and novelty T-shirts and avoid colliding with even more women in bunny ears and bodysuits backing up to take selfies with fans and one another. One woman at the table, wearing devil ears and a kimono, spanked herself at the webcam with a paper fan. Another took a shot of dark liquor, flailing her hands and scrunching up her nose for her virtual fans. Each model at the table had two audiences and straddled two worlds: the one milling past this endless table, and the one present in their chat rooms on the streaming site MyFreeCams.

The MyFreeCams homepage is a wall of tiny thumbnail icons, each holding a window into someone's world. There are thousands of them, sitting on bedspreads or gamer chairs, illuminated by ring lights and laptop screens. All are women by decree of the site's rules, and are overwhelmingly white. Fans watching them in their chat rooms pay models in "tokens," which MFC takes a percentage of, after which models get paid out in dollars. The models set prices for certain sex acts fans might want to see them do on camera, or for vibration speeds and intensities on their connected sex toys. "Taking her private," or moving to a one-on-one video chat session, costs extra. Or viewers can tip just for watching the public show, as one might at a strip club.

On a typical Friday afternoon within those little windows, one woman sits in a turtleneck and stares at the screen, waiting for an audience to arrive. Another lounges sideways on her bed, texting absently while a chihuahua wanders around her. Click to another, who's purring into the tip of a pale dildo: "Don't you want to please me?" Six hundred and sixty-eight people watch two women have sex with a strap-on dildo. Something close to one in every five women has the hot pink silicone end of a Lovense Lush Bluetooth vibrator hanging out of her vulva, waiting for a fan to tip enough tokens to make it buzz. Another fondles her breast for a crowd of twenty-five, while someone in the chat room talks about how NASA is going to land the Perseverance rover on Mars later that afternoon.

The chat rooms that sit alongside shows are integral to the camming experience and make up their own little galaxies within the wider platform universe. Die-hard fans show up to a model's room, recognize other regulars by their screen names, and make small talk about their lives, like you would at a real-life happy hour. Together, they're performing something close to immersive theater: The fan is suspending his belief for the sake of the show while she's working—not just pretending to have fun or faking orgasms, but sometimes tamping down annoyance, anger, and disgust—to keep the theatrics of the experience going.

This is similar to the emotional labor full-service sex workers and escorts perform when they're on the job with a client. But by moving the performance to the internet, where a screen separates workers from clients, the job of regulating someone else's emotions becomes a lot less dangerous.

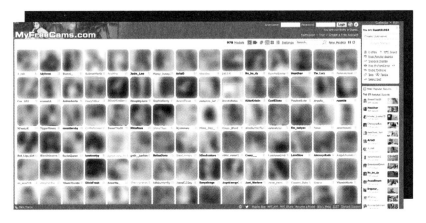

MyFreeCams homepage

Sociologist Elizabeth Bernstein coined the phrase "bounded authenticity" to describe the erotic exchange that takes place between in-person sex workers and clients: The "authentic" experience a sex worker delivers is bound within the confines of time and an agreement. Clients don't just want to get off; they could do that at home with one hand. They want to feel a connection to another person, and they want to imagine that the other person feels satisfied, too—even though this is the model's literal job, and they're performing a service.

Dr. Angela Jones, author of *Camming: Money, Power, and Pleasure in the Sex Work Industry.*

That desire for connection doesn't go away when it's moved online. It's easy enough to masturbate to porn or magazines or the thoughts in one's head without involving a livestreaming cam model or paying them in tokens. If you want a connection, you have to pay for it. Sociologist and educator Dr. Angela Jones takes the "bounded authenticity" definition to the online world, in what she terms "embodied authenticity," which she writes is the work cam models do to bring an authentic experience to online shows.

Jones argues that cam models are able to uniquely derive pleasure from their work *because* of the distance the internet provides, not in spite of it; online sex workers "are able to experience these pleasures because the computer-mediated sexual exchange acts as a psychological barrier and becomes the primary tool that models use as part of emotional management." In a world where some clients respond to boundaries with violence, and where sex workers are still seen by society, sex-work abolitionists, and the police as expendable, managing clients' emotions as a sex worker means survival. If it's safer to have sex in front of people when there's a screen between you, it's reasonably easier to relax and enjoy your work.

The cam industry broke open molds that the old studio system seemed to regard as immutable, universal truths of (primarily straight male) desire. In choosing to cam instead of joining the studio system, performers took the power back in myriad ways.

The internet empowered anyone to become an independent porn performer, not just who a casting director or producer thought was hot—which typically meant the stereotypically attractive, white, blonde, hourglass bombshell with implants and a flawless manicure (although there's still plenty of demand for that). You could come as you are, from the comfort of your home. Breaking away from the norm allowed performers to carve out new niches for themselves. You could be all the things that mainstream society tells us sexy people are not— fat, queer, nonbinary, disabled, non-white—and there would be fans waiting for you. And for many of these models, camming is the most realistic option available to them to work a healthy, flexible, safe job.

While the webcam put more control into the hands of the workers, it didn't solve systemic problems. They're still operating under capitalism, after all; the opportunity to exploit labor is always there. It's important not to fall into the trap that so many early internet pioneers evangelized at the turn of the millennium, that the creator-led internet democratizes everything.

Even though her pleasure-based argument is optimistic, Jones doesn't believe that internet-based sex work is some grand techno-utopian force. "As I'd come to learn, the camming industry is not a utopian paradise. It is an exploitative capitalist marketplace that also reproduces White supremacy, patriarchy, heterosexism, cissexism, and ableism," she writes. LGBTQIA+ sex workers have fought for platforms to meaningfully include them for years, and only recently have cam sites launched sections specifically for gay and trans models. They may be able to develop a fan base, but there are just as many trolls and harassers waiting, too—and marginalized workers within an already marginalized industry face similar stigma from their bosses at "vanilla" jobs, cops (even though camming is legal in the US and many other countries), child custody judges, and landlords as performers in more traditional porn studio work. If they're not out as sex workers in real life, cam models also face the risk of being outed as sex workers by

SPIN THE CHATROULETTE CHAMBER

The aesthetics of Chatroulette are distinct. If you were there in the early 2010s, you'd recognize the scene immediately: Two live video windows holding teenagers' eager faces crowded into a webcam frame, illuminated by their computer screen, with a sepia-toned bedroom in the shadows behind them. The site had sparse options—"Next" or "Stop"—and a chat box alongside the video feeds. Hit "Next," and you're face-to-face (or, as often happened, face to genitals) with a new, random stranger. When the conversation gets boring or you don't like what you see, the "Next" button takes you to a new stranger. It's like speed dating for meeting internet randos.

Andrey Ternovskiy, then a seventeen-year-old high school programmer in Moscow, developed Chatroulette in 2009, and within a month of launch, more than 50,000 people visited the site daily. If personal connections drive the internet, this was the most intimate, brute-force way to do it: speed dating with strangers, where the next cam could contain a friendly face, a ski mask, or a penis.

A lot of the time it was a penis. A 2010 study of the site's demographics found that as many as one in eight matches showed something R-rated. Over the years, Ternovskiy has experimented with

ways to control how much sex happens on Chatroulette—not because he's a prude, but because he's found that when users see shocking or disturbing things without warning, they leave his site and never return. In 2021, the latest iteration includes facial recognition and previews of your next match. But these are only experiments; the greater project, to him, is a reflection of society itself.

"It's not about penises, it's about giving and taking," he said in 2021. "It's about how much you contribute and how much you take . . . You can have a machine to recognize penises. But in reality, it's stupid, because you have one million ways you could be offensive."

viewers who steal their content and repost it to social media or other porn sites.

Despite all of this, the benefits outweigh the risks for most models. Informal surveys within the industry report that in 2020, on average, cam models working eighteen hours make $1,043 per week—the equivalent of a $54,000 salary per year. But that number varies quite a bit; the most successful earners make up to $6,000 per week, and low-earning beginners may only make $100 per week from the same number of hours. Top earners who work at their craft full-time make $136,500 per year on average.

Nothing accelerated the need for alternative, creator-owned online work faster than the coronavirus pandemic, when more people lost their jobs in a single year (2020) than during the Great Depression. People flocked to online sex work as a way to pay the bills. Almost half a million content creators are on OnlyFans, an adult-friendly (as of this writing) site that saw a huge boost in profit during the pandemic. The site grew from 7.5 million users in November 2019 to 85 million by December 2020. The platform paid out two billion dollars to creators globally that year alone.

The ability to work for themselves online gave sex workers unprecedented levels of control and safety in their field of work. But it's also had a splintering effect on groups that formerly relied on close, trusting relationships with other workers. Valerie Webber, a public health and porn scholar, wrote in 2021 that in her previous work as a cam model, she operated out of a brick-and-mortar building with other models who each worked out of a studio within for their livestreams. If a problem arose with the site or payment processors' strict rules, for example, a manager would knock on her studio door and explain what was going on. When she returned to camming twelve years after taking a hiatus to earn her PhD, she found that things had changed. "I'm working for a giant site with thousands of performers. I have no relationship with management," she wrote. "When I was suspended, I got no explanation, no opportunity for correction, no word about what would happen to my outstanding pay. There is a code of conduct for us to adhere to, but the rules are vague."

CHAPTER 7

The Digital Fig Leaf

SEXUAL CENSORSHIP ONLINE

"Speak plainly, and say fuck, cunt and cock;
otherwise thou wilt be understood by nobody."

–Antonia, in Pietro Aretino's
sixteenth-century work, *Ragionamenti
della Nanna e della Antonia*

HTTP Error 404

Web server cannot find the file or script you asked for

I n fall 2020, Facebook's algorithm banned a photo of a pile of yellow onions for being "overtly sexual."

The Canada-based (and ironically named) Gaze Seed Company was trying to advertise its vegetables on the largest social network in the world. But Facebook rejected the ad, on the basis of the onion's sex appeal. "I guess something about the two round shapes there could be misconstrued as boobs or something, nude in some way," said Jackson McLean, a manager at the seed company.

Facebook remedied the ban, but it's emblematic of how ridiculously overbearing much of the modern internet is about sexual censorship. Platforms, once small communities, are now overwhelmed by the endless tidal wave of user-generated content. So they employ algorithms to chase after content that's verboten—while constantly tweaking and expanding what's not allowed, so that no one really understands what's permitted and what's subject to banning. Sexual speech online exists on a crumbling cliff, and everyone is blindfolded.

None of this is particularly new. The story of sexual censorship in the US is as old as the country itself. To understand how it's spread and squashed on the internet, we can look back—way back, to this country's colonization—for context.

A Brief History of Sexual Censorship in the United States

Contrary to many retellings of the colonizers' story, the Puritans didn't cross the Atlantic in pursuit of freedom for *everyone* to worship as they pleased. After being persecuted for treason in England for pushing the king's Anglican Church to leave behind old Roman Catholic traditions like kneeling and the *Book of Common Prayer*, they set out to establish a colony that would have total control over its own brand of Christianity, and everyone under it.

When it came to sex, anything outside of biblical marriage was considered obscene and immoral; they coded obscenity laws into their "new world" as early as 1711, when the Massachusetts Bay Colony made it an offense to write, print, or publish "any Filthy Obscene or Prophane Song, Pamphlet, Libel or Mock-Sermon."

Meanwhile in their mother country, John Cleland sat in a London debtors' prison, penning the first English erotic novel: *Fanny Hill, or Memoirs of a Woman of Pleasure*, the fictional story of a woman who earns a fortune as a sex worker, falls in love, and eventually marries and lives out her days in comfort. Sexual content aside, a tale of women living happily ever after, not just in spite of but because of, a life of so-called sin was incredibly scandalous. Cleland paid his way out of jail by selling the rights to the novel for twenty guineas in 1748—while the publisher made more than £10,000 off its distribution.

Fanny fever quickly took hold in the newly founded United States. In 1786, an American bookseller tried to get his hands on a copy to reproduce himself by writing to a bookshop in London and then persuading a ship captain to ferry a copy over. By 1810, he was printing copies Stateside, and soon so were several other booksellers with printing presses. Just a decade later, three of them were prosecuted in Massachusetts for selling the bawdy book and were given jail time or fines, or both. Even showing someone illustrated copies of *Fanny Hill* could bring down an obscenity charge. These marked some of the first prosecutions for obscene literature in the US.

Undeterred and inspired by *Fanny*, more and more new American erotica writers found success selling smut— and their work mostly went unnoticed by anti-obscenity laws, as population size and new businesses outpaced legal enforcement. For bookstore proprietors, this was business. Seeing others go to jail or go bankrupt didn't stop many booksellers from peddling erotica. One of them was William

An illustration from *Fanny Hill*, an eighteenth-century erotic novel

Haynes, who established his own publishing house specializing in prurient titles in New York City.

While Haynes was making bank on dirty books, Puritan-raised zealot Anthony Comstock was building a reputation as an anti-obscenity vigilante, breaking into bars to dump out liquor and taking it on himself to tattle on erotic booksellers. He used the existing obscenity laws to stage stings against booksellers—buying erotic books, then bringing the police into the shop to show them who to arrest. He's said to have called himself a "weeder in God's garden."

Haynes learned that Comstock had set his sights on his publishing house in 1871; by then the publisher had sold as many as 100,000 erotic books in his career. Haynes received a warning letter ahead of Comstock's arrival—"Get out of the way. Comstock is after you"—and the bookseller was found dead the next day, suspected of taking his own life rather than facing whatever legal and personal hell the vigilante Puritan would bring upon him. When he did arrive, Comstock burned all of Haynes's books and destroyed the printing plates, too.

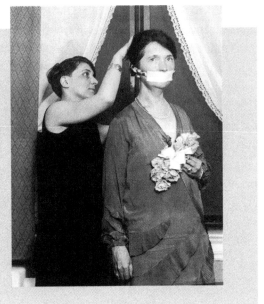

Anthony Comstock, anti-pornography crusader, and Margaret Sanger, a "family planning" activist, locked horns in the late nineteenth century.

Over the next two years, Comstock destroyed 134,000 pounds of "books of improper character," with funding from the Young Men's Christian Association, which was lobbying for anti-obscenity laws at the time. President Ulysses S. Grant appointed Comstock a "special agent" and Post Office Inspector, to enforce his "Act for the Suppression of Trade in, and Circulation of, Obscene Literature and Articles of Immoral Use," colloquially known as "Comstock Laws." With official sanctioning from the country's highest office, Comstock continued to wage a paranoid and petty war against anything he personally felt was immoral or obscene.

Comstock met his match in family-planning activist Margaret Sanger. Comstock Laws prevented her from mailing a pro-contraception magazine for working-class women called *The Woman Rebel*, and she was indicted on nine counts of violating federal statutes. She fled to Canada before trial. While she was away, Comstock arrested her husband William for selling a copy of a pamphlet she wrote about birth control methods, called "Family Limitation." Comstock died soon after, of exhaustion-induced pneumonia, and Sanger's trial was dropped.

While he was alive, the zealot's work was made simpler by the relatively condensed population of the East Coast. But the modernization of transportation, and its ability to spread illicit materials far and in secret, changed that. Transporting printed porn across state lines made US anti-obscenity zealots' missions nearly impossible: Instead of selling printed erotica and photographs in brick-and-mortar stores, peddlers carted it around the country right under their noses, in trains and car trunks. Networks of transportation decentralized the porn industry for the first time.

In the century since Comstockery began, the pace of technological advances brought us more smut in print than ever. As porn magazines started flourishing in the sixties and seventies, followed by online porn in the eighties and nineties, radical feminists—like Robin Morgan, who said in 1978 that "pornography is the theory, and rape is the practice," and Catharine MacKinnon, who wrote in 1993 that sex workers are "the property of men who buy and sell and rent them"—stepped up to take the puritanical yoke and try to impose it on everyone. Only this time, the internet's networks would be the super-highway that moved adult materials around.

The "Communications" "Decency" "Act"

"Almighty God, Lord of all life, we praise You for the advancements in computerized communications that we enjoy in our time," Nebraska senator Jim Exon, hunched over a stack of papers, said on the Senate floor. "Sadly, however, there are those who are littering this information superhighway with obscene, indecent, and destructive pornography."

It was June 1995, America Online and Prodigy were just beginning to offer access to the World Wide Web, and Exon was making a point about children's use of the internet, the spiciest topic surrounding the internet at the time. This prayer was written by the Senate chaplain, and Exon read it that day to help persuade those listening to support his new bill: the Communications Decency Act, or CDA. It would make it illegal to use a telecommunications device to make indecent material available to children, punishable with a fine of $250,000 or up to two years in prison, and make it a crime for webmasters and internet users to knowingly display anything that might be deemed "patently offensive as measured by contemporary community standards," especially sexual activity, to minors.

In other words, if you wanted to talk about sex online where a kid could see it—and the whole internet was something kids could see, in theory—you'd be in big legal trouble.

Since introducing the CDA in February, Exon had been carrying a big blue binder of printed-out porn from the internet around the Senate, pulling his colleagues into the cloakroom to look through it. While in the literal closet, Exon would urge them to support the bill, for the sake of the children.

His zany proselytizing worked, and the CDA passed as part of the Telecommunications Act of 1996 in an 81–18 vote, the day after the

Senate floor prayer. But free speech activists and federal courts immediately went to work on proving its unconstitutionality. Considering the vast openness of the web, the CDA reduced all speech online to only that which was acceptable to children—effectively babying the whole internet.

The American Civil Liberties Union argued that the vague definitions of "indecency" and "offensiveness" in the original CDA were unconstitutionally overbroad. So, they took it to court. In the 1997 ruling of *Reno v. ACLU*, Justice John Paul Stevens and the court wrote that the CDA as it was written placed an "unacceptably heavy burden on protected speech" that could potentially "torch a large segment of the Internet community." The Supreme Court declared it a violation of internet users' First Amendment rights.

Senators Chris Cox and Ron Wyden proposed adding a section to the CDA that would make it more specific: Section 230. The most famously quoted and hotly contested part of Section 230 is twenty-six words that some scholars say created the internet as we know it today: "No provider or user of an interactive computer service shall be treated as the publisher or speaker of an information provided by another information content provider." This is pretty dry language, but the implications were dramatic. It means that internet service providers, as well as platforms, are protected from what users did on their services, and won't be held responsible for the things people say or do on their sites. A restaurant can't sue Yelp for defamation if an unhappy visitor posts a negative review of their food. Or if someone goes on a small message board and starts making death threats against their neighbor, that website won't be sued out of existence. It makes the billions of conversations happening on Facebook

> **"No provider or user of an interactive computer service shall be treated as the publisher or speaker of an information provided by another information content provider."**
>
> **—From Section 230 of Communications Decency Act,** which shields internet service providers from being responsible for what people say and do on their sites

and Twitter possible; without Section 230, these companies probably wouldn't exist, let alone at the scale they do now. The same laws that shield platforms from repercussions from misinformation, hate speech, and sexual abuse material also protect what makes the internet thrive: free expression, without legal consequences for the platforms that host it. A law that set out to banish sex ended up making the whole internet flourish, instead.

That is, unless it's sexual content. Section 230 came under attack in 2016, when the Fight Online Sex Trafficking Act (FOSTA) and the Stop Enabling Sex Traffickers Act (SESTA) passed—amending the section to make websites liable for what users do on their platforms, if what they're doing is sexual. After FOSTA/SESTA's passage, it became a felony to operate an online service with the intent to "promote or facilitate the prostitution of another person." Definitions of what facilitation, prostitution, or promoting it meant are overbroad, and the ramifications of this change to one of the pillars of internet communication have been devastating for many marginalized communities.

Meanwhile, censorship of sexual speech was just getting started in the private sector.

How Sex Is Repressed Online

Human and algorithmic censorship has completely changed the power structure of who gets to post what types of adult content online. This has played out as independent sex workers struggling to avoid getting kicked off of sites like Instagram or Twitter just for existing as people—while big companies like Brazzers, displaying full nudity, have no problem keeping their accounts up.

Despite Facebook's origins as Mark Zuckerberg's Hot-or-Not rating system for women on his Harvard campus (see page 76), the social network's policies on sexuality and nudity are incredibly strict. Over the years, it's gone through several evolutions and overhauls, but in 2022 forbidden content includes (but isn't limited to) "real nude adults," "sexual intercourse" and a wide range of things that could

FACEBOOK'S "BREAST SQUEEZING" POLICY

One of Facebook's policies related to adult nudity and sexual activity on their site received a 2020 update called "Clarify Grabbing Covering in Breast Squeezing Policy," which included the question: "What are the indicators of female breast squeezing?"

The document circulates internally within the company for moderators to use when deciding which boobs can stay on the site and which need to come down. An employee leaked it to the press so that everyone could see what we already suspected: Facebook's rules banning sexual expression are arbitrary and prudish—and really confusing.

"Squeezing occurs when: there is clear indentation (e.g., dents, imprints, depressions, marks, etc.) on the female breast or clothing caused by curved fingers in a grabbing motion AND there is a clear shape change of the breast by curved fingers in a grabbing motion. Covering, cupping, or pressing the breast with palms or straight fingers [is ok, but] . . . no grabbing motion on the female breast or clothing [though some curving of the fingers is allowed], depending on the size or shape of the breast [but only if the fingers are] not in a curved grabbing motion."

A Facebook spokesperson said the company believes this is pretty straightforward.

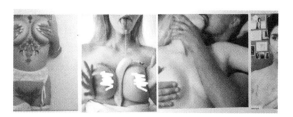

These photos, leaked by sources at Facebook, are examples of what's allowed and what's not, per the social network's internal policies. Note the lack of differences in what appears above versus below.

imply intercourse "even when the contact is not directly visible," or "presence of by-products of sexual activity." Nudity in art is supposedly allowed, but artists and illustrators still fight against bans and rejected posts all the time.

That's not to mention "sexual solicitation," which Facebook will not tolerate. That includes any and all porn, discussions of states of sexual arousal, and anything that both asks or offers sex "directly or indirectly" and also includes sexual emojis like peaches and eggplants, sexual slang, and depictions or poses of sexual activity.

An image of a cat from sexologist Dr. Timaree Schmidt's Twitter feed that got removed by Instagram.

These rules also apply on Instagram, the photo-sharing app owned by Facebook. As the number one and two biggest social networks in the US, these dictate how much of the internet sees and interacts with sexual content.

In the earliest archived versions of Facebook's terms of use, sex was never mentioned—but its member conduct guidelines did ban "any content that we deem to be harmful, threatening, abusive, harassing, vulgar, obscene, hateful, or racially, ethnically or otherwise objectionable." This vagueness gives Facebook legal wiggle room to ban whatever it wants.

The platform took a more welcoming approach to sexual speech as recently as 2007, with Sexuality listed as one of the areas of interest users could choose from, and more than five hundred user-created groups for various discussions around the topic. But the platform's early liberality with sex drew scrutiny. In 2007, then–New York attorney general Andrew Cuomo led a sting operation on Facebook where an investigator posed as teens and caught child predators.

As early as 2008, it started banning female breasts—specifically, nipples. The areola violated its policy on "obscene, pornographic or sexually explicit" material. In December 2008, a handful of women gathered outside the company's Palo Alto office to breastfeed in front of the building in protest (it was a Saturday; no executives were working).

As of 2018, Facebook lumped sex work under banned content that depicts "sexual exploitation," stating that all references and depictions of "sexual services" were forbidden, "includ[ing] prostitution, escort services, sexual massages, and filmed sexual activity."

A lot of this banned content is health and wellness education.

In 2018, sexuality educator Dr. Timaree Schmit logged in to Facebook and checked her page for SEXx Interactive, which runs an annual sex ed conference she'd held the day before. A notification from Facebook appeared: She and several other admins for the page were banned from the entire platform for thirty days, and the page was taken down, because an "offending image" had violated the platform's community standards. The image in question was the word SEXx in block letters on a red background.

The examples of this sort of thing are endless and not limited to Facebook. Google AdWords banned "graphic sexual acts with intent to arouse including sex acts such as masturbation" in 2014. Android keyboards' predictive text banned anything remotely sexual, including the words "panty," "braless," "Tampax," "lactation," "preggers, "uterus," and "STI" from its autocomplete dictionary. Chromecast and Google Play forbid porn. You can't navigate to adult sites using Starbucks Wi-Fi. For a while in 2018, Google Drive seemed to be blocking users from downloading documents and files that contained adult content. The crowdfunding site Patreon forbids porn depicting real people, and in 2018 blamed its payment processor, Stripe, for not being sex-friendly. Much of this followed FOSTA/SESTA.

Predictive text
Text message and email technology that guesses what you'll type next, before you type it. It's based on the rest of the sentence, the first letter you've typed in the next word, or an accumulation of all of your communication habits across that platform.

This is far from a complete list. There are countless stories like this, where sex educators, sex workers, artists, and journalists are censored or pushed off platforms completely for crossing these imaginary lines that are constantly moving.

Over the years, as these policies have evolved, they've been applied inconsistently and often with vague reasoning for the users themselves. There is one way platforms have been consistent, however: Images and content of Black and Indigenous women, as well as queer and trans people, sex workers, and fat women, experience the brunt of platform discrimination. This can lead to serious self-esteem issues, isolation, and in some cases, suicidal thoughts for people who are pushed off platforms or labeled "sexually explicit" because of their body shape or skin color.

TUMBLR'S NSFW APOCALYPSE

Tumblr used to be very horny.

The microblogging platform's sexual censorship horror story stands out among the rest because it threatened to destroy the site altogether. As of 2016, 22 percent of Tumblr users were consuming porn on the platform. In 2017, researchers found that more than a quarter of users were there mainly to see porn.

That all changed in 2018, when Tumblr fully banned NSFW (not safe for work) content, effectively eradicating thriving communities of LGBTQIA+ people, kink enthusiasts, artists, and illustrators. The decision was partially due to alleged child sexual abuse material on the site and the platform's inability to moderate or prevent it, but it could also be a result of Apple's incredibly stringent stance against apps that feature sexual content. Apple does not allow apps "that contain user generated content that is frequently pornographic," and Steve Jobs once said that "folks who want porn can buy an Android phone."

In a blog post about the NSFW ban, Tumblr CEO Jeff D'Onofrio wrote that "there are no shortage of sites on the internet that feature adult content." He completely missed the point of Tumblr, and of any internet community: Anyone can see boobs on the internet, but the people who build the places where conversations and kinship thrive make it what it is.

"For many, that's the one place we could find porn that represents us, made by indie performers who created their own content outside of an often racist, transmisogynist, fatphobic industry," said Kitty Stryker, a queer porn performer and consent activist. "Tumblr was where our content could exist without pushing us into the restrictions of a misogynist, male dominated workplace."

"I'm just sick of feeling like something is wrong with my body. That it's not OK to look how I do," Anna Konstantopoulos, a fat Instagram influencer, said after her account was shut down and posts were deleted multiple times. Her photos in bikinis or lingerie were deleted by Instagram moderators, while other influencers' posts stayed up and raked in the likes. "It starts to make you feel like crap about yourself."

In spite of all of this, people project their full selves, or at least a version of themselves, onto Facebook accounts. Censorship of our sexual sides doesn't stop people from living and working on the internet—unless that is your life and work.

The Specific Censorship of Sex Work

Twitter is one of the last bastions of sexual freedom on the mainstream internet. Users in the US are, as of this writing in 2022, allowed to post full nudity, close-up genitalia, and all the hard-core pornography they want. As long as no one dies in front of the camera and no minors are involved,[1] you can tweet pretty much whatever you want, sex-wise.

However, the platform does have the same issues of overbearing, inexplicable suspensions and bans. So when Twitter shuts down more than a handful of adult-themed accounts at a time, those ground tremors get noticed—and sex workers are the first to feel it.

People are often seemingly "shadowbanned," or down-ranked in the algorithm so that their content doesn't organically appear to users who don't directly follow them. Twitter has denied shadowbanning anyone, but sex work scholars and anecdotal reports from users themselves assert that it's a real phenomenon, and incredibly frustrating. Unlike a ban, where a user is notified that their account is disabled, shadowbanning doesn't usually get noticed until content creators realize their posts are suddenly getting fewer clicks and likes.

Many independent models depend on Twitter for as much as 100 percent of the traffic that comes to their paid clip or cam sites, like

---

1 This is an extreme simplification of Twitter's rules, as of this writing, but it's pretty close.

OnlyFans or ManyVids. If fewer people can see them on those sites, it directly impacts their livelihood.

"It's proof to clients that I'm a real person—a digital footprint of my existence," sex worker Lita Lecherous wrote of her Twitter profile. "Without my account, how would people get ahold of me? How would anyone see me?"

Most people who make social media a large part of their lives would feel the same, even if posting wasn't a part of their work. (If you didn't upload a vacation photo slideshow to Instagram, did that trip even happen?) And for a long time, a relationship wasn't "official" until it was "Facebook official." In certain industries (journalism and book publishing are two other examples), having an active Twitter presence and an already captive audience makes you a more appealing hire. For a lot of people, visibility online is visibility as a person in the world. If every trace of you were wiped off the internet tomorrow without explanation, how would you feel?

But for people who make their livings in the sex trade, the hostility of mainstream platforms with their hall-of-mirrors terms of use is a constant source of anxiety. Sex work communities also spend a lot of their time sounding the alarms about shifting terms of service or harmful legislation that's coming down the pipeline, on top of their already demanding jobs.

Shadowbanning

Informal term for platforms making a social media user's posts invisible to others, without them knowing. Individual community moderators have had this ability since bulletin board systems in the eighties, but social media giants like Twitter and Instagram have been criticized for limiting some people's accounts from appearing in search functions and users' timelines without notifying them; often, these end up being sex workers and sex educators.

The inability to reliably access online payment processors is yet another way sex workers are discriminated against and censored online.

Venmo is a social media platform for sending emojis along with bar tabs from your phone, and the name has become a verb—"I'll Venmo you!" Alluding to sexual services can get your account banned.

NO STRIPPERGRAMS ALLOWED

In 2018, Instagram stopped showing search results for all stripper-related hashtags—not just #stripper, but also #yesastripper, #stripperlife, #stripperstyle, #ilovetoseestripperswin, and briefly, #woman. The tags came back to search after public outcry, especially from the erotic dancer community. But platforms continue to hide dancers' content from the rest of the app—in 2020, the community called out Instagram for its "Objectionable Content" rules, which were updated to explicitly ban sexual solicitation that includes "pornographic activities, strip club shows, live sex performances and erotic dances."

Many strippers suspect that these changes are due to FOSTA/SESTA legislation (see page 116) that passed in 2018 and suppressed all sexual speech on the internet, but made it especially hard for sex workers to survive online (and, quite literally, offline as well).

Square's CashApp prohibits using its services for "obscene, indecent, lewd, [or] pornographic" purposes. In 2018, misogynists who hate sex workers started a harassment campaign to find models who used CashApp, Venmo, or Square and report their accounts to those platforms, effectively cutting them off from their income.

Snapchat, an ephemeral image messaging app mostly used by teens, has its own payment sharing system, Snapcash—but Snapcash is processed by Square. Google Wallet's terms of use call adult goods and services an "unacceptable product," banning users from paying or receiving funds for "pornography and other sexually explicit material," including but not limited to "prostitution, escort or companionship services."

And those are just the newer e-commerce native payment processors. JPMorgan Chase, Visa, and MasterCard all have a long history of discrimination against sex workers. As we saw in the earliest days of porn webmasters, these institutions consider porn "high risk," in part because of the high rate of chargebacks from customers claiming fraudulent purchases, but also because of the ongoing pressure from conservative lobbyists and anti-porn legislation that keeps the pressure on to shun porn.

In 2014, Chase Bank shut down the accounts of hundreds of porn performers. The adult industry suspected this was the doing of the Department of Justice's "Operation Choke Point," a 2013 initiative that, according to American Bankers Association CEO Frank Keating, demanded that "bankers behave like policemen and judges."

"Operation Choke Point is asking banks to identify customers who may be breaking the law or simply doing something government officials don't like," Keating wrote in the Wall Street Journal. "Banks must then 'choke off' those customers' access to financial services, shutting down their accounts."

"A lot of people have seen these bank-account closures as something remarkable or surprising," wrote Lorelei Lee, a sex worker and writer, following the mass closures. "The truth is, sex workers are discriminated against every day—fired from their jobs, passed over for jobs that they're qualified for, turned down for apartments."

PAYMENT DENIED

An incomplete list of the payment platforms that either explicitly ban, or have a history of hostility toward, users who work in the sex trade or post sexual content:

Venmo	Snapchat's Snapcash
Square	PayPal
Stripe	Intuit
CashApp	Circle
Google Wallet	Amazon payments

CHAPTER 8

Sex Sells

CLASSIFIED ADS

"Chief among the civic notabilia is the Mayor's foray or razzia among the unhappy fallen women who perambulate Broadway, the noctivagous strumpetocracy ..."

—Civil War–era diarist
George T. Strong,
March 31, 1855

It was a clammy April week in Boston when Savannah Sly saw the news: A man had murdered a sex worker at the Copley Marriott.

He bound, gagged, and robbed one escort at gunpoint on April 12, 2009, and killed another on April 14. On the sixteenth, he violently robbed a third woman. All three had arranged their meetings with him through ads on Craigslist. *Vanity Fair* called it a "new kind of murder," one in which the internet played a central role in how the killer found his victims—and how the police found him. Investigators used a trail of IP addresses and emails to track down a twenty-three-year-old medical student name Phillip Markoff, who became known as the "Craigslist Killer."

Sly first reacted to the news with shock, then they wondered if they knew the victims; Sly also used Craigslist's Adult Services section to book erotic massages and escort dates in Boston, and their network of fellow sex workers was small. Sly's next notion was more prescient: "My second thought was, this is gonna fuck shit up," they said. How would this highly publicized killing spree intensify the social stigma against online sex work?

Savannah Sly, a sex worker, musician, and activist.

"A murder in our community not only is it a gut-wrenching tragedy, and scary for everybody when a life is lost, but it fucks shit up for us," Sly told me.

National news coverage of the online sex trade was already overwhelmingly negative. Undercover cops were watching Craigslist before the murders, trying to ferret out people engaging in brothel-keeping or pimping. Sly set up their own website as a backup, just in case anything happened to the site.

In August 2010, Markoff killed himself in jail awaiting trial. By September, Craigslist folded under longtime pressure from anti–sex trafficking groups and lawmakers, shutting down its Adult Services section forever. Untold numbers of sex workers were displaced from their main source of income when it happened, and their jobs instantly became more dangerous than they had been even in pre-internet days.

If stories like the Craigslist Killer or "dead hooker" tropes in shows like *CSI: Crime Scene Investigation* are your only impressions of violence against sex workers, it might be surprising to learn that the internet has been a huge boon for their safety.

Kristen DiAngelo, cofounder of Sex Workers Outreach Project's Sacramento chapter, has worked many roles in the adult industry—in brothels, strip clubs, massage parlors, and the street. She remembers a time when violence was simply a part of the life. Now, she says, younger generations of workers have an unprecedented expectation of safety.

The internet enabled sites for warning others about bad clients, community forums where providers could share safety information, and online infrastructure that allowed them to screen new clients before meeting them in person.

Craigslist's Adult Services section was one of the first and biggest dominoes to fall for escorts doing business online. Hugely popular sites for finding and reviewing providers such as The Review Board, Redbook, Rentboy,

> "Things have gotten better—and they got better with the rise of the internet. We're able to speak across state and county lines, and nationally across countries. We're able to track predators. We never had that before."
>
> **—Kristen DiAngelo,** cofounder of Sex Workers Outreach Project's Sacramento chapter

and Backpage went down in the years to follow, each seized by the FBI after lengthy surveillance operations and undercover police stings.

The story of sex work in the United States is partly one of a constantly migrating community. Newspapers banned their ads, so they moved online. Craigslist abandoned them, so they moved to Redbook or Rentboy. Those went under, and they moved to Backpage. Backpage was seized, so they migrated to Tumblr. Tumblr banned NSFW content, so they moved to Twitter, OnlyFans, and anywhere left that will allow them to be seen, heard, and survive.

Like the history of censorship, this history of sex classifieds is another that's longer than it seems, however. In the early 1900s, under the Red Light Abatement Act, brothels around the country—in both big cities and small towns—were forced to close. Public perception about sex work shifted noticeably to saviorism. Red-light districts weren't necessarily *legal*, but they were parts of town that the police generally left undisturbed. Industrialization had pushed more families into urban life, and more white women into the workforce—while immigrants and women of color were left to seek alternative work. Now off the farm and existing outside of the nuclear family, a movement of independent, single, self-earning women started brewing.

The Chamberlain–Kahn Act of 1918, also known as the "American Plan," was made law just seven months before the end of World War I, in response to fears that sex workers visiting US military bases would corrupt and incapacitate soldiers with diseases.[1] Any woman deemed morally dubious in appearance—rose-colored cheeks, short skirts, walking alone, or being an immigrant—could raise suspicions of prostitution, leading to their arrest and forced testing for STIs. If the tests came back positive (or, more likely, if a doctor judged them harshly), they were thrown into a farm colony or forced into a hospital until they could be "cured." Historians estimate that more than 15,500 sex workers were essentially kidnapped and incarcerated by the end of World War I, many of them receiving horrific, painful procedures for their suspected diseases, like mercury pills, injections, and arsenic treatments.

With World War II came propaganda warning soldiers and their families about the evils of "unclean" women. Posters accused soldiers who "gambled" with venereal diseases of being saboteurs of their country, while others depicted curvaceous women in sensual poses alongside warnings to "protect yourself NOW." One showed a wholesome-looking young woman with the text, "She may look clean, but pickups, 'good time' girls, prostitutes, spread syphilis and gonorrhea."

---

1 Julius Caesar's army, too, was beset by gonorrhea, and during the Italian War of 1494, syphilis broke out among Charles VIII of France's troops—which they then carried home all across Europe.

The campaign to paint sex workers as dirty, disease-ridden burdens on upstanding citizens, and a threat to the future of the nation, was in full swing.

Women who escaped or avoided forcible hospitalization were left unable to rent apartments. "Abolitionist" groups that wanted to abolish prostitution altogether didn't have answers for what would happen to these women, whom they saw as helpless victims. To them, they were necessary casualties to further their cause.

This cycle of migration from place to place (physical or digital) and harmful beliefs about sex worker victimhood continue today. Online, they play out in bold relief.

A US government public health poster aimed at soldiers returning from World War II to discourage them from engaging with sex workers

A Human Occupation, Online

One of the first madams DiAngelo worked for in the seventies called all the young women under her care "pretty girls."

"She'd say, 'Pretty girl, I'll teach you how to be a lady,'" DiAngelo said. "And that's what she'd really do. Somebody could take us anywhere and be proud to be around us, from etiquette lessons to how to entertain, to how to be present and really listen and care—all of the things people think aren't a part of this. This is a human occupation."

In the eyes of California law today, that would be considered "supervising or aiding" a sex worker, which carries a jail sentence of up to six months for a first offense. At the time, before the internet enabled instant, global communication, this type of community care from veterans in the trade was lifesaving.

"It's changed dramatically, and if I hadn't had the training I had in those brothels, I probably wouldn't be standing here today," she said. "I learned how to stay safe, I learned how to take care of myself, I learned how to make sure that I wasn't exposed to anything I didn't want to be exposed to. I learned how to handle men, I learned how to defuse situations."

Back then, advertisements for escort services used to stain your fingertips black. The newsprint of each ad, rubbing off of slips of paper slipped into swingers' guides and porn magazines on adult bookstore shelves, was typically not more than two lines: a phone number and the name of a service. Maybe a black-and-white image of a leg in fishnets, or some sideboob.

Screening

Sex workers who see clients in person and set up dates online will usually ask for references from reputable past escorts, and will Google the person, check their social media accounts, verify their ID and employment information— anything that confirms they are who they say they are. This is on top of talking to the client for a bit through emails or direct messages, to get an idea of the kind of person they are.

Soon, everyone moved their ads to alternative magazines and weeklies like the *Village Voice* and *New York* magazine, where readers outside of sex toy shops could browse local options for bodywork or escort services. Newspapers as ad venues didn't last, however; the rules changed, and if you put "massage" in an ad, you'd need to show the advertising department your masseuse license. If you wrote "escort," you'd have to procure that license, too—which meant handing over legal names and identification. More visibility meant more vulnerability to police. Before, a madam or independent group of workers could use pseudonyms and designated phone lines that would be hard to trace back to one person; not so with these new requirements.

Former sex worker Kristen DiAngelo, in a Sacremento, CA, massage parlor.

Usenet groups like alt.sex .prostitution brought the old newspaper and magazine ads online, but there was limited ability to filter preferences (Blonde, brunette, or salt and pepper? Erotic massage or girlfriend experience?). Subgroups like alt.sex.femdom or alt.sex

.telephone might narrow your search a bit, but your chances were only as good as your deftness at navigating Usenet.

On the World Wide Web, one of the first advertising platforms to come online was Rentboy.com, a site with a self-explanatory name— male escorts posted ads, revealing as much or as little as they wanted in the way of real-life identification. Jeffrey Davids founded the site in 1997[2] and ran it like a combination of Jay Gatsby and a responsible nineties sitcom dad: The company hosted an award event called the HustlaBall, as well as regular parties and cruises around Budapest and Prague. Rentboy's ethos revolved around safe, fun sex that went hand in hand with the destigmatization of sex work. Davids wrote in 2008 that Rentboy stood for pleasure and fun, but also worked for political and social change on behalf of male sex workers. "In the eleven years since we began this site, we have been working to change the image of male sex workers from a dirty dead-end job to a respectable career," he wrote.

Arranging dates on Rentboy was exponentially safer for client-escort meetups than cruising in parks, bars, and backrooms. But it was more than an advertising platform and party scene. Rentboy was a community effort in harm reduction. The company sponsored classes on web design, HIV prevention, individual rights when confronted with law enforcement, and more, and gave website perks to those who attended, like free weeks of ad space. By 2009, there were 40,000 escorts using the site, and Davids claimed to call every one of them personally when they signed up to verify their identities (although they could stay completely anonymous online).

Rentboy was a popular site where gay sex workers and clients could meet and make arrangements in a safer environment than on the street.

---

2 A year before Google.

Sex worker rights activist Kaytlin Bailey calls the time after escort ad sites became popular, but before widespread surveillance technology, a "golden age" of advertising for sex workers. When she posted her first ad online, she got a hundred emails in the first twenty-four hours; this enabled her to look for reasons not to see someone, instead of chasing clients. Responses from rude and overly terse potential clients were filed to trash, along with anyone who couldn't follow her screening directions. This put her in a position of control over her own work.

Reviews and "Rip-Offs"

The nineties and early aughts saw a boom in platforms built for interactions between sex workers and clients. The founder of one of the biggest sites for advertising and reviewing providers was a client. But by most accounts, he was a vindictive one.

David Elms launched The Erotic Review in 1999 as a message board, ad site, and review platform for clients like himself to rate the escorts they visited on a scale of one to ten (ten being a once-in-a-lifetime experience). On TER, clients are "hobbyists," the hobby being hiring providers for sex. Hobbyists could write detailed reviews of escorts—and escorts could do the same about their clients.

"I'm a hobbyist, and I was getting ripped off," Elms told NBC in 2006. "There was no way to hold people accountable for their actions. There had to be a way to get this information out. If a guy got ripped off or he received good service, then he could tell somebody."

In 2008, the site was receiving 300,000 visitors a day, with half of those logging on more than once per day. Elms told the *Riverfront Times* that he collected data on every hobbyist that registered. On average, he said, they were middle-class men between the ages of thirty-five and fifty-five.

TER's legacy is complicated. The site empowered thousands of sex workers to take control of their work and warn others about bad dates. Providers had been doing this on a local, smaller scale for years already, by sharing lists and resources online among other escorts. On

TER, the process was more consolidated and accessible. Good reviews from clients helped boost their reputations, while bad reviews could threaten to tank a career—and negative reviews could crop up over anything, including petty qualms about their real-life appearances not living up to photos, an escort's unwillingness to bend on preset boundaries, or personal vendettas. Many sex workers have a love-hate relationship with review sites.

"Men in middle management are just bad writers, and they're usually just writing their fantasy," Bailey said. She said she'd sometimes read reviews after dates and realize that she and the client were on different planets the whole time. "It'd be like, 'Wow, we really had different experiences of what happened, and it's interesting what details you're choosing to focus on here.' But a few good reviews helped establish my legitimacy. From the buyer's end, I understood that we're both taking a risk meeting another human being."

Robyn Few, a former provider and cofounder of Sex Workers Outreach Project's San Francisco chapter, once said she hated that women were being rated as if they were "subhuman." But there were two sides to this coin: "When providers have a bad client, they write about it . . . It's one way to out the bad guys." If clients wanted to write nasty reviews about being "ripped off," escorts could play that game, too.

Elms probably didn't intend to be the progenitor of safer working conditions for the hundreds of thousands of workers using his website. In 2006, the same year he was giving interviews to national news outlets accusing women he hired of ripping him off, police were called to a hotel in Manhattan Beach, California, where Elms was staying with an escort. He

> "It was this period of time that empowered individual sex workers to seize the means of production—we were able to take our own photos, and establish our own brands, and communicate directly to clients, but not in a face-to-face way, which really mitigates a lot of the danger."
>
> —Kaytlin Bailey,
> sex worker, writer, activist

had a loaded semiautomatic weapon in the room. The escort told police that he had forced her, at gunpoint, to perform oral sex on him, but the deputy district attorney said the woman didn't have enough evidence to press charges.

By then, workers on TER had been coming forward to accuse him of blackmail and extortion for years. Elms would ban their accounts, they claimed, and then try to talk them into meeting him for sex to get back in his good graces—and back on the site. Some accused him of rape. Others claimed he and his site moderators accepted bribes from big escorting agencies in exchange for fluffed-up ratings and rejected client reviews that weren't "juicy" enough, encouraging hobbyists to stretch the truth or outright lie about what services providers offered. Elms denied it all.

Many of these claims came to light through a blog called sexwork .com, run by a webmaster who called himself "Dave in Phoenix," a man on a mission to take down Elms. Dave posted dozens of emails to his site, allegedly from escorts and TER users. Their virtual feud escalated, until Elms was arrested in 2009 for trying to hire a hitman to kill an unidentified man in his sixties and a woman in her thirties. Dave claimed in the press that he was Elms's intended mark. The Cayman Islands–based parent company of TER and its staff "parted ways" with Elms that year.

■■■■■■■

Just over two weeks after Elms first registered theeroticreview.com, Mountain View techie Eric "Red" Omuro registered sfredbook.com, another site for escort ads and reviews. It started with the Bay Area, focusing on reviews for erotic services in San Francisco and the surrounding areas. It expanded beyond Northern California a few years later, and switched to myredbook.com—but mostly, people just called it Redbook. It had a review section and submission form (with sections for rating face, body, attitude, and service on a scale of one to ten), message boards for all kinds of topics, and a classified ads section. Like on Usenet, MUDs, cam chat rooms, and anywhere sex brought masses of people together, conversations ranged from the erotic to the mundane. Threads with titles like "Capitalism, an innovative and viable system?

By Chomsky" and "Marines Kick Ass in Iraq" went in the miscellaneous politics and culture section, and sports talk went on in the "Pool Hall," where people debated Shaquille O'Neal's basketball performance and traded golf club recommendations. One Redbook member said he came for the strip club recommendations, got wrapped up in the engaging forum community, and stayed for four years.

Redbook's clientele wasn't necessarily more genteel than TER's hobbyists; sample reviews on the site shortly after it launched featured such perceptive lines as "Cute face and OK body (kinda saggy in some areas)" and "She said that this was not allowed, but after asking if I was police, and some other suspicious questions, she took the towel off and started the massage." But it had a lot less drama surrounding it than TER. Both of their homepages looked like something you could browse at work without being noticed, if you were feeling bold. Craigslist, TER, and Redbook, along with a few influential local sites like The Review Board in Seattle, ran the game for years.

Then, in 2004, two antiestablishment newspapermen named Michael Lacey and Jim Larkin launched a Craigslist competitor called Backpage.

Backpage was a study in plain, corporate cornflower blue, early-2000s internet blandness. At first, its offerings were Craigslist's near-identical twin: You could find a job, a house, or a bike on its user-generated listings. Lacey and Larkin's main focus at the time was their media conglomerate of local alt-weeklies called the *New Times*. In 1989, the *New Times* launched a section of adult classifieds in its literal back pages, called the Wildside, revenue from which helped them expand and open weeklies in major cities around the country. But by the early 2000s, online classifieds, especially Craigslist, were siphoning ad revenue from print publications—including their own. Instead of trying to beat them, Larkin and Lacey joined them.

It was a decision that became a life raft for the company's future. They bought Village Voice Media in 2005 and merged it with the *New Times* group for a combined seventeen publications nationally, but the state of media advertising was already in decline. Backpage buoyed them, but it was almost too good at what it did. In 2009, its twin flame

Craigslist's legal battles started sending a surge of sex workers and clients its way.

While Backpage grew, Craigslist was busy trying to quell legal and public criticism about its adult offerings. It started requiring credit card payments to post adult listings in 2008, after the National Center for Missing and Exploited Children (NCMEC) and the attorneys general of forty states demanded that it implement better safety measures to prevent child exploitation. Craigslist was already safe, and used by tens of millions of people for legitimate purposes, Craigslist CEO Jim Buckmaster said, but the pressure from these groups forced the change. It was clearly an attempt at stopping adult prostitution, not child abuse: "Prostitutes will hopefully stop using Craigslist to break the law, knowing that their posts could lead to arrest and conviction," Connecticut attorney general Richard Blumenthal said, after the change.

Craigslist renamed Erotic Services to Adult Services a month after the Craigslist Killer's spree. Blog posts from Craigslist administrators tried to defend the site against allegations that its adult ads were courting danger. One blog post made the point that there were dozens of notable "Lonely Hearts killers" who historically used newspaper classifieds to find their targets—more than there had been instances of high-profile Craigslist-based murders.

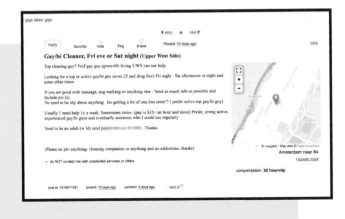

An ad from Craigslist's Adult Services section

After the semantic shift from "erotic" to "adult," sex workers moved to other parts of the site, and coded the language in their listings more heavily, offering "French lessons" instead of being explicit about what was for sale. Blumenthal swore to find anywhere sex workers migrated to on the site. "We are going to be extraordinarily watchful," he said. "We are not going away."

Attorneys general from seventeen states sent a letter to founder Craig Newmark and Buckmaster, demanding the site shut down the section entirely, with more allegations about enabling sex trafficking. Legally, Craigslist was well within its rights to keep the category up; Section 230 of the Communications Decency Act protected them from liability for what users posted. But the public and legal pressure was too much. In August 2010, the Adult Services section was censored with a black bar, then disappeared entirely.

Sex trafficking
The Department of Homeland Security defines human trafficking as using force, fraud, or coercion to exploit someone for their labor. Scholars believe that "sex trafficking" as a specific term was coined in the eighties and nineties by anti-porn feminists.

Buckmaster seemed to regret the decision a year later. "For a long time we tried to do what, in our minds, was the principled thing," he said in a 2011 interview. "We ended up doing the pragmatic thing."

As Craigslist fought and floundered to keep critics off its back, displaced workers migrated again, to Backpage. "It is an opportunity for us," Backpage CEO Carl Ferrer wrote in an email to staff. "Also a time when we need to make sure our content is not illegal." With this wave of new users migrating to Backpage, the state turned its lidless eye toward Lacey and Larkin.

Sex-trafficking lawsuits and allegations started rolling in shortly thereafter. In 2009, a girl claiming to have run away from home and into the clutches of a pimp who put her on Backpage sued Village Voice Media for facilitating prostitution and not trying to stop it. The case was dismissed on the grounds of Section 230 protecting the site from liability, and Backpage hired a former federal prosecutor to help make the site watertight against such abuses. They also started reporting suspected minors to the authorities. By their own accounts, the owners didn't want child abuse living on their site. No reasonable website operator would.

Elsewhere, the walls were closing in. The Department of Justice, FBI, and IRS seized Redbook in 2014, alleging that the site was engaged in "money laundering derived from racketeering based on prostitution." The FBI took Omuro into custody, charging him with facilitating prostitution over the internet, along with twenty-four counts of money laundering. He became the first operator of an adult classifieds website to face federal charges for facilitating prostitution, and was ultimately sentenced to fifteen months in prison.

"Ten thousand sex workers up and down the state of California posted on that site," DiAngelo said. "So in taking it down, what the feds really did was put ten thousand people out of a job overnight, with no help or ability to provide for themselves." Sly described these types of seizures as "like punching in to work and seeing FBI tape all around your building."

The following summer, feds raided the Rentboy offices under suspicion that the operators were conspiring to violate prostitution offenses covered by the Travel Act, a law that enabled federal agents to get involved, including Homeland Security. They took Davids into custody, along with several staffers.

"Those who advertised on Rentboy.com are now left potentially exposed, their listings in government custody, and for now are largely out of work," wrote journalist Melissa Gira Grant, who attended their trial in Brooklyn. "Rentboy was their hiring hall, a community center, one place where advertisers could manage their work and find one another [. . .] They are charged with providing a website where escorts can advertise, but more so: for doing this without hiding."

Davids, who pleaded guilty to promoting prostitution, stood in front of a judge at his sentencing two years later. From the bench, Judge Margo Brodie admitted to him that she'd lost sleep over deciding his punishment. She asked him why she shouldn't send him to jail.

"I did my best to run a company that was doing good for people, not as a criminal racket," he said.

"The very thing that was illegal, it also did a lot of good," the judge replied. She gave him six months in prison, less than half the minimum sentence.

Meanwhile, Lacey and Larkin tussled in their own grudge matches. Protesters picketed around the *Village Voice* offices,[3] while the publication ran editorials and features defending itself against the myths and rumors circulating about Backpage facilitating sex trafficking.

The pair sold their newspaper business to focus on Backpage in 2012. In July 2013, forty-nine attorneys general petitioned Congress to amend the Communications Decency Act so that they could go after Backpage. "It is ironic that the CDA, which was intended to protect children from indecent material on the internet, is now used as a shield by those who intentionally profit from prostitution and crimes against children," the letter said.

As the site grew, its owners deflected more and more civil lawsuits. In 2014, three women sued the site for enabling their traffickers to post their ads while they were fifteen years old. The women claimed that Backpage not only provided a space for them to be trafficked, but also tailored the site to better serve their abusers. This and many of the lawsuits levied against them were dismissed under CDA Section 230

> "Information provided to us by [FBI Agent Steve] Vienneau and other members of the Innocence Lost Task Force confirm that, unlike virtually every other website that is used for prostitution and sex trafficking, Backpage is remarkably responsive to law enforcement requests and often takes proactive steps to assist in investigations."
>
> —From internal emails written by US attorneys in 2012 regarding their case against Backpage.com

---

3 One protest of about fifty people from the Coalition Against Trafficking in Women and elsewhere stood in the rain. One speaker took a megaphone and announced that "this is the Holocaust of another generation. It's raining now. These are tears from God."

protections, but press coverage, along with growing outrage from anti-trafficking groups and government pressure, stayed on them.

In private emails, the feds praised Backpage for years of helping them find trafficking victims. After an expansive investigation into Backpage in 2013, they traded emails saying that following interviews with more than a dozen witnesses and review of more than 100,000 documents, none of the "smoking gun admissions" to trafficking they hoped to find ever manifested.

But the FBI didn't come forward with this information.[4] Doing so would disrupt years of the public's sex-trafficking paranoia, and the feds wanted Backpage gone—they just hadn't figured out how to finish it off yet.

The gap in Backpage's armor, ultimately, would be the ways they tried to comply with demands to stop traffickers from finding girls on the site. Trafficking prevention organizations suggested they prevent users from searching for specific terms like "incest" or "Lolita." Ferrer tried a sequence of moderation practices over the years, including auto-banning words like "fresh" or "little girl." This was frustrating for a lot of clients and advertisers—"little girl" is a phrase grown adults are allowed to say to one another in the bedroom, after all—so he set up a system that would automatically flag to ad writers what words got their ad banned. This editorializing opened them up to accusations that they were a publisher, not just a host, and therefore outside of CDA's protections.

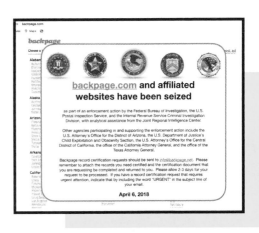

The FBI seized Backpage on April 6, 2018.

---

4 The emails from that investigation, essentially proving that the FBI found the many trafficking accusations levied against Backpage were a lie, weren't exposed until 2019—a year after the bureau seized the website.

As journalist Elizabeth Nolan Brown wrote after the emails were made public:

> Years of much-hyped horror stories about the site and heinous claims about its leaders had been coming from all angles— Democrats, Republicans, women's groups, religious groups, attorneys general, actor-activist Ashton Kutcher, state and national lawmakers, the *New York Times*, the McCain Institute, the FBI, movies, newspaper ads, billboards, and much more. The preferred narrative about the site was clear, and nearly impenetrable.

In 2017, Congress called Lacey and Larkin in for a hearing to testify against the allegations that they were facilitating sex trafficking. Senator Rob Portman introduced the Stop Enabling Sex Traffickers Act later that year, which would amend Section 230 to carve out suspected sex-trafficking activity posted by users as an exception to what website operators would be liable for. Senator Ann Wagner introduced the Fight Online Sex Trafficking Act, and the two were combined into one piece of legislation that President Donald Trump signed in April 2018.

Free speech advocates and sex workers fought passionately against FOSTA/SESTA. But Kamala Harris, then senator and formerly attorney general of California, championed the bill and had been holding Backpage up as an example of the type of site that allowed the evils of trafficking to run amok. FOSTA/SESTA would put a stop to that, its supporters claimed, while deflecting all criticism and concerns from the people who actually use those sites for their consensual, adult livelihoods. But less than a week before Trump signed it into law, the FBI seized Backpage. They never needed new legislation to make it possible, but the bill needed Backpage to sail past the president's desk.

This law would prove disastrous to all sorts of marginalized communities online and off, and completely ineffective in stopping sex trafficking.

Plug and Play

INTERNET-CONNECTED SEX TOYS

"Just twist the base and away she goes.
Gives fast, penetrating comfort.
Makes strained, sore muscles feel new.
Stimulates circulation, too.
Five minutes does the job.
Give it to her."

—Sixties massager advertisement

While the boys at Stanford were getting ARPANET up and running in the seventies, a young Dell Williams was trying to buy a vibrator at a Macy's in New York City.

She'd attended one of Betty Dodson's sex education workshops, where the preeminent feminist voice for masturbation-as-radicalization recommended the Hitachi Magic Wand. This was before Hitachi became a household name in mind-blowing orgasms; the device was still being marketed as a muscle massager. But its reputation for off-label uses was getting around, and Williams wanted to find out for herself.

"What do you want it for?" the greasy guy running the register in front of her asked. Loudly.

"I left Macy's that day," Williams wrote in her memoir, "clutching my precious, anonymous brown shopping bag and thinking: Someone really ought to open up a store where a woman can buy one of these things without some kid asking her what she's going to do with it." Williams opened exactly that store, Eve's Garden—located around the corner from Carnegie Hall—in 1974. It was the first feminist sex toy shop.

Three years later, in San Francisco's Mission District, sex therapist Joani Blank opened Good Vibrations, the city's soon-to-be-storied sex toy shop. The shop was more than a place to buy dildos. It became the locus of the sex-positive movement in the West Coast, at a time when *Deep Throat* was hitting the mainstream.

The sexual revolution of a generation started in sex toy stores, by women seizing the means of orgasm.

Since then, the sex toy industry has exploded. The global market is worth more than $26.6 billion, and analysts expect it to reach $52.7 billion by 2026. A large part of that growth, they predict, will be in toys that are connected to, and controlled by, an app on your phone. Now, everything we do can be augmented by mobile apps—paying bills, ordering food, dating, and, of course, sex.

"Many [investors] are wary of missing out on what may be one of the last great untapped retail markets in the world," wrote Andrea Barrica, CEO and cofounder of pleasure education platform O.school, in her book *Sextech Revolution*. "But they're also nervous. Investors are largely older men, which means they sometimes don't understand the problems to be solved. Or they answer to more conservative institutions that won't invest in 'vice.' Stigma keeps them from sextech."

Stigma has kept marginalized people locked out of their sexual power for eons. Barrica grew up in a strict Filipino-Catholic household, immersed in a purity culture that told her there was only one model for acceptable sex: straight, Christian, and virginal until marriage. Anything else was sinful, or would end in rampant STDs, like the medical photos her school health teacher showed in class. Her first experience of someone else affirming her sexual needs was from a salesperson in Good Vibrations, and it would lead the naive, repressed Catholic

> **"My investors may not know the structure of the clitoris, but they sure understand those numbers. And nearly every investor I speak to is intrigued by the space."**
>
> —**Andrea Barrica,** in her book *Sextech Revolution.*

to become a sex-tech entrepreneur and a respected voice in helping others find their personal pleasure.

Stores like Good Vibrations and Eve's Garden, with trained and welcoming staff selling products on clean, brightly lit shelves, just didn't exist until then. You'd order a sex toy in the mail from the back of an erotic catalog or in person at a porn shop—not exactly a welcoming space for young women and nonbinary people.

"I encouraged women to try vibrators," Good Vibrations founder and sex therapist Joani Blank told the *San Francisco Chronicle* in 2003. "So I just thought there should be a non-sleazy place for people to buy vibrators. It's that simple."

The internet brought yet another leap forward in pleasure accessibility. It did for sex toys what it also did for porn: took an experience previously relegated to socially stigmatized in-person shops and brought it home. This meant that a wider variety of people could now access sex toys that were once out of their grasp—anyone with internet access and a credit card could safely approach new ways to control their own pleasure.

In 2019, Minnesota State University researchers Dennis Waskul and Michelle Anklan surveyed 218 women about their first experiences with vibrators. More than 36 percent said they bought their first vibrators at a sex shop, but many of those reported having an unsettling experience: "I felt like there were only men in the store and they were undressing us with their eyes the whole time," one respondent said. Another: "The shop I went to had male clerks that seemed 'seedy' rather than helpful, had creeper sneers and asked questions that felt prying versus offering recommendations based on what had good reviews among customers." Almost a quarter of respondents said they'd ordered their first vibrator online, mostly through Amazon.com.

Amazon launched its Sexual Wellness category in 2003 with condoms and lube and expanded to 60,000 items, including toys, by 2010. The monolithic retailer sucked up so many customers that even Good Vibrations started to struggle. In 2012, after waning sales due to online big-box stores' influence, the sex shop posted a notice on its website seeking investors—and found a buyer, adult toy seller GVA-TWN, to take on the enterprise while retaining the sex-positive spirit of the business. More potential customers moved to online shopping,

A contrast in sex toys from two eras. Right: Joani Blank, founder of Good Vibrations, San Francisco's iconic sex shop. Left: Andrea Barrica, sex-tech entrepeneur

while more independent retailers put up websites to keep pace with the e-commerce boom.

Waskul believes that the internet played a big part in driving the sex toy market forward. "I'm completely convinced that the internet has been the driving force behind the dramatic increase in sex toy use—especially among women and particularly with vibrators," he said.

But the demand was always there.

"No market needed to be created; they merely needed to innovate a means by which people could purchase and receive those products with the utmost confidentiality," Waskul said. "The internet has simply accelerated that trend."

Do Androids Dream of an Electric Penis?

"Some day your sex life could be shut off for failure to pay your electric bill," David Rothschild wrote for the *Chicago Tribune* in 1993. "In case you've been too busy trying to program your VCR to notice, cybersex—or digital erotica—has arrived. It runs on regular household current, you'll never have to touch another person to experience its pleasures, and it may eventually turn you on more quickly than you can turn it off."

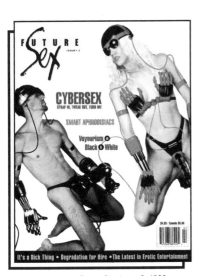

Future Sex, issue 2, 1992

Few things better embodied the cautious optimism of computing in the eighties and nineties than how we imagined fucking our computers. One of the voices grounding that giddy, nervous time was Lisa Palac, the editor of *Future Sex* magazine.

As many young people do in the process of navigating the deluge of voices and viewpoints vying for their minds, Palac tried on a series of worldviews in her adolescence and early adulthood. Raised Catholic in all-girls schools, she went from a childhood curiosity about sex, to full-on anti-pornography second-wave feminism in college, to a slow awakening to her own inner sex life. She got her sexual education in spite of not finding it in church or through pop culture, even as Cher showed her belly button on TV, rumors of Jimi Hendrix's "guitar" size flew, and David Bowie's bisexuality was hotly debated. But, it being the seventies, something, of course, was conspicuously missing.

"Despite all the sex clues hidden in pop culture, I came across absolutely nothing about female masturbation," Palac wrote in her memoir, *The Edge of the Bed: How Dirty Pictures Changed My Life*. "Led Zeppelin sure wasn't singing about the clitoris, and there was no episode of *The Brady Bunch* where Marcia finds her clit and comes. Even in the sex magazines I saw, women just spread their legs, they didn't touch, and it gave me the impression that just spreading would result in a deep state of ecstasy."

At twenty, like the Isaac Newton of masturbation, a vibrator fell out of a closet while she was moving into her new apartment and hit her on the head. It was the first time she had ever seen a sex toy in real life. She had her first real orgasm thanks to that left-behind toy (which she didn't realize at the time was actually a buttplug), and eventually made her own pilgrimage to Good Vibrations in San Francisco's Mission District in 1986. She bought a copy of *Coming to Power: Writing and Graphics on Lesbian S/M* and read it on the plane home in the middle seat, right through the descriptions of girl gangbangs and whippings. She started voraciously reading all the feminist pornography media and theory she could find, including Candida Royalle's feminist porn videos and *On Our Backs*, the first women-run erotica magazine.

Palac met feminist writer Susie Bright in 1988, and soon accepted a job at *On Our Backs*, where Bright was the editor.[1] She became the

---

1 This is a seriously simplified version of Palac's whirlwind visit to San Francisco to meet Bright for the first time, including the first night at a party where Nina Hartley did a live strip show and then Bright and Palac got their labias pierced in Oakland the next morning.

ON OUR BACKS

Entertainment for the Adventurous Lesbian

On Our Backs, an erotica magazine run by women, aimed at the lesbian community

editor of *Future Sex* in fall 1991, inheriting a pile of manuscripts and half-done photo sets from a previous editor's failed attempt to get the first issue out the door.

The *New York Times* called Palac the "queen of high-tech porn" in a 1992 story about her and the first issue of *Future Sex*. She was reluctant about the title and skeptical of the so-called future of sex. She just wanted to make a forward-thinking magazine. "What the hell was 'high-tech sex' anyway? Computerporn? Fucking robots?" Palac wrote. "Part of my disdain was, admittedly, rooted in fear . . . How could technology, which I always viewed as alienating, densely mathematical, and potentially deadly, possibly enhance the highly sensual experience of sex?"

Besides, the first issue was what the publishers—two men, one a lawyer, the other a doctor—wanted to print, plus what her predecessors left unfinished. And it wasn't very imaginative. The second issue was what she wanted: More than just a horny version of *Wired* magazine, it engaged thoughtfully and differently with the current moment. And that moment, in early nineties San Francisco, was high-tech.

She self-educated by reading future-forward thinkers like Howard Rheingold and Timothy Leary, joining The WELL (see page 8), and going to tech conferences. Something started to click. People in these spaces talked about the internet as being on par with the invention of fire, with the power to transform daily life—and especially how we communicate. "Since sex, at its core, is about communication, I was jazzed," Palac wrote. But her first exposure to online porn was uninspiring. "I still remember waiting an hour to get a porn picture, only to be so disappointed," she told me in 2021. "Like, 'Oh, that's what we waited for so long to download.' In the beginning it was just all very mysterious with this great promise of education and liberation."

That promise came true in many ways. Hundreds and hundreds of *Future Sex* readers emailed her about their sex lives, with questions, stories, and confidences. Palac still struggled with popular perceptions of cybersex, however. She believed the most exciting technology available at the time was the simplest: writing on bulletin board systems. BBS users were already crossing great virtual distances to have sexual encounters. But that didn't translate visually; people wanted to see the future of cybersex, like something out of *Star Trek*.

To help with the second issue of *Future Sex*, Palac called Mike Saenz, who'd already created the *Virtual Valerie* and *MacPlaymate* CD-ROM games. Together they made a plan to create a speculative "cyber-sex suit," which ended up on the cover of issue two in January 1992. Helmets with fully adjustable stereoscopic displays, "tactile data playback" gloves, genital harnesses with "silky-soft SIMSKIN" that simulated erectile tissue—and, of course, a cyborg hand bra for women. The models "wearing" the suits (which were just 3D renders overlaid on their naked bodies) seemed to be experiencing manic glee that fell somewhere between a Newport ad and winning at *Space Invaders*.

This wasn't the first time someone imagined how far-out cybersexual hardware might look in the real world. Information technology pioneer Ted Nelson first used the word "dildonics" in 1974, to describe an invention that turned sound into something you could feel in your bones, literally.

Howard Rheingold coined the word "teledildonics" much later, in 1990, for his *Mondo 2000* essay, which referenced How Wachspress's patent (see page 150) for the "Radio Dildo." "The first fully functional teledildonics system will probably *not* be a fucking machine," Rheingold wrote. "You will not use erotic telepresence technology in order to have sex with machines. Twenty years from now, when portable telediddlers are ubiquitous, people will use them to have sexual experiences with *other people*, at

Cybersex suit
In the nineties and early aughts, future-thinking tinkerers started imagining what it would be like if a sex toy covered one's whole body, for a physically immersive experience.

Teledildonics
The field of internet-connected sex toys.

THE RADIO DILDO

An inventor named How Wachspress filed a patent for an "audiotactile stimulation and communications system" in 1973 and described it this way:

Random or controlled electronically synthesized signals are converted to sound waves that are directly coupled to the skin of a life form, such as a human body, to stimulate the skin or internal portions of the life form and to communicate the intelligence, sense or feeling of the sound to the brain, bypassing the ear as the channel for reception of audio information. Control signals are derived from biopotentials or other sources, to modulate an electronic synthesizer.

Nowhere in the patent does Wachspress mention sex or eroticism. The closest he comes is "probe" and talk of insertion into "orifices." But based on a flyer about the "Radio Dildo" on Wachspress's website, it's clear that between the lines, that's what he was imagining.

RADIO DILDO
PATENT #3,875,932

KDIL TRANSCRIPT

Diagram from the patent application for the Radio Dildo

a distance, in combinations and configurations undreamt of by precybernetic voluptuaries."

In that essay, Rheingold also put forth the idea of the cybersexual body suit, "something like a body stocking, but with all the intimate snugness of a condom." It would be full of tiny vibrators that would convey tactile sensations like the softness of silk, human flesh—or something more firm.

Others tried out the suit concept, too. Artist Stahl Stenslie created the cyberSM suit in 1993. A black, strappy latex bondage set with wires dangling from the wearer's arms, chest, and torso, the suit was the "next logical step" from BBS and MUD sex into the future, according to the artist's statement. Users could assemble a 3D body on a computer screen using pre-scanned nude models to interact with another person in a virtual world; the people in the suits remained anonymous to one another. The cyberSM suit premiered by connecting two people from Paris to Cologne, though the details of what they actually felt were vague.

One company tried to bring Rheingold's description of a full cybersex suit to life—and failed. Porn production giant Vivid Entertainment created a cybersex suit in 1999 that looked a lot less high-tech than Palac or Stenslie's wire-spaghetti and latex outfits. It was a black neoprene leotard outfitted with thirty-six sensors and actuators located over the entire body. Someone controlling the suit could select from five settings to activate sections of the suit: tickle, pinprick, vibration, hot, and cold. It also fit with Vivid's push for CD-ROMs, as the suit could come with a DVD that interacted with it.

"To be honest, it's nothing magical," Vivid president David James told MSNBC in 1999. "I'm sure a pair of college students could have probably sat down and come up with something far more futuristic than we have here. The big advantage we've got, of course, is our marketing ability to first of all have it made and then be able to sell it worldwide."

The company spent $180,000 on development, but never got to sell the suit. There was one big problem: They couldn't guarantee the suit wouldn't kill somebody. Getting approval from the Federal Trade Commission meant demonstrating the product wouldn't short out a pacemaker, which Vivid could not prove; they abandoned the idea a year later.

We don't have real full-body cybersex suits yet, but we do have something else Rheingold predicted: a massive market for internet-connected sex toys that can be controlled from across rooms with a Bluetooth remote or across continents with an app.

"Step 1: Put the Machine on Your Penis"

"She gives good internet," a stripper named Jackie Lick said between moans to a captivated audience at the 1999 Erotica USA conference. She was on stage demonstrating one of SafeSexPlus.com's internet-connected sex toys, where another participant controlled her vibrator from across the country.

If the nineties were for dreaming and prototyping about a technosexual future, the turn of the millennium was for making it happen at scale—or at least, trying to.

The sex-tech market went through puberty with a series of clumsy, colorful iterations of toys controllable over the internet. There's some debate about which one earned the title of the first true internet-connected sex toy, but a series of inventions in 1999 tried to break the internet's fourth wall: the monitor.

Technosexuality
A word with two meanings. This is the idea that technology shapes sexuality, and also the phenomenon of being sexually aroused by technological themes or aesthetics.

"If you can control a sex toy through your monitor, you can control just about anything," SafeSexPlus.com founder Allen Hadazy once said. "Controlling devices remotely through an everyday internet connection isn't the future. It's here now." Hadazy developed software that controlled a penis-stroker device—he elegantly named it the "RoboSuck"—by reading a computer screen's brightness. Turn the brightness up, and the toy's pace intensified. (The sensor was suction-cupped to the screen, for double entendre effect.)

In 2000, a company called Digital Sexations combined the well-established appeal of cybersex chat and the futuristic allure of a dildo connected to your PC. Their "Black Box" kit could support up to four sex toys via serial ports plugged into a computer, and connected to a chat interface that controlled each from afar.

By 2001, the Virtual Sex Machine—an automatic fuck-tube that claimed to move with the motions on the screen—started getting media attention, although it had been in development since 1996. It cost $439.69 plus shipping and handling for the machine, a "digital interface" video player, lube, cleaning solution, and a carrying case that looked like a jewel heist briefcase. Its website got straight to the point:

Step 1: Put the machine on your penis
Step 2: Choose any of the Girls
Step 3: Sit back, relax, watch, and FEEL IT!

The History Channel's *Modern Marvels* show featured it in 2001, as did Glenn Beck's show on CNN. "For the expense of one good date, now you have an experience you can have anytime," the toy's designer, Eric J. White, told Beck. "And that, my friend, is a scary thought," the host replied.

For someone who talked often to the press about careful marketing, White pitched his own product as something for men who

TELEVIBE

The Lady Calston Televibe was an early 2000s distance-sex device that rode the internet sex hype, despite not exactly being internet-connected.

Users could pair it with their landline phone, cell phone, or PC; anything with a touchpad and a connection to a phone line would work.

The package came with a "Foxy Lady for Men," a tiny white headless torso with breasts and a vulva, bisected by a metal Frankenstein diode connected to a central battery-powered unit, itself wired to a PC or phone. Women's versions came with the "G-Pulse," a hot pink bullet vibrator with a slight curve at the tip, connected the same way.

The Televibe used a sixties technology known as "dual-tone multi-frequency signaling," but most know it as "Touch-Tone," the Bell Systems–trademarked word. With the Televibe—and a small handful of other proto-internet remote sex toy contemporaries—one person could control another's toy by button-smashing.

aren't willing or able to get laid otherwise. "It adds another level of marketing ability to (an adult movie) star," he told CNET. "When you're done with her, you put it back on the shelf

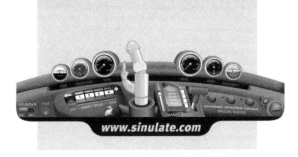

Control panel for the Sinulator

and close the door. You don't have to take her out to dinner."

White wanted to be "the guy who invented virtual sex," he said in 2007. By then, he was already too late by several years.

The Sinulator, a software and hardware setup, debuted in 2003. The full Sinulator package included a USB transmitter, vibrator, and controller. Users would install an application on their computer, then attach the vibrator to the controller. They'd register the device with a unique name on the Sinulator website and from there, anyone who knew that toy's name could operate it from the website's control panel. Wired described the panel as "a grown-up version of a driving toy for [a] baby, with buttons and levers and sliders that you manipulate with your mouse."

It cost $279 when it debuted and dropped to $119.95 a year later. Customers were required to sign up for a subscription to use the Sinulator's web-based features: $39.95 for sixty minutes of play a month, up to $299.95 for 900 minutes.

For a more private audience, the HighJoy combined online dating and teledildonics—and put the whole messiness of finding a cyber-sex partner under one virtual roof. The Doc Johnson High Joy Enabled iVibe Rabbit was a five-and-a-half-inch clear purple vibrator that connected to a computer through a chunky serial port cable. "Imagine engaging a partner in an Online Sex session at Highjoy.com, and having an orgasm with them hundreds of miles away," the product page said in 2005. Moving your mouse over a control panel moved parts of the dildo in tandem, making the shaft and head rotate or the clitoris-stimulating bunny ears pulsate.

Membership to use the HighJoy system was $7.95 a month, but according to a Salon journalist who took it for a test run in 2005, anyone could join, toy or no toy—and fewer than fifty out of ten thousand members using the system actually owned the device. Most just wanted to talk, without the toy. Like Operation Match, the thrill was less in technology and more in the excuse to talk to similarly open-minded people who were also exploring sexuality over the internet, serial port not required.

Exploits and Vulnerabilities

With the arrival of widespread wireless internet, we became physically untethered from our computers. The metaphysical connection between ourselves and our online lives, however, grew stronger. Our pockets held the world's knowledge, or close enough—as well as the potential for a world of connections. When the first iPhone launched in 2007, 47 percent of Americans were using broadband at home, and 1.4 billion people were online worldwide.

Soon enough, the Internet of Things connected everything in our homes to the web: washing machines, lamps, doorbells, air conditioners—it can all be controlled from your smartphone, if you wanted to live the Jetsonian dream.

Wi-Fi and Bluetooth enabled sex toys opened up new possibilities for cordless, remote-controlled action: Instead of sitting in your desk chair, you could lie in bed, take the train, and sit across from your lover at a restaurant, all with a remote-controllable buttplug or vibrator in your pants and a phone app or remote in their hands. But all this freedom also opened the doors for more nefarious activities: Hackers used openings in poorly secured apps and device design architecture to take control of people's sex lives, and toy makers themselves siphoned off more private data about what we do in bed than ever.

The Lovense Hush buttplug can be controlled
by smartphone from around the world.

CLUB LOVE

All of this hype around sex toys controlled over the internet resulted, predictably but not inevitably, in the corporate exploitation of sex workers.

On Clublove.com—a site run by Seth Warshavsky, who made $77 million off Pamela Anderson and Tommy Lee's stolen sex tape by posting it online—voyeurs could watch women in a peep show–style environment through webcams set up in the Seattle Club Love headquarters (although most of it was pretaped).

During a staff meeting one evening in September 1999, the director of talent told the performers that starting Monday, they'd be required to use a SlimLine vibrator with a camera inserted in the tip that would broadcast a gynecological view to their internet audience. More egregious: They'd have to take turns using the same one. The plastic dildo can hold bacteria, whereas steel, glass, and silicone can be sterilized. It was also corded, so it would never be thoroughly cleaned between uses. Rumors of workers with herpes at Club Love were already swirling in the Seattle sex industry. "It's a pussy sweatshop," one source told *The Stranger*.

The SlimLine announcement was only the latest in labor abuses alleged by women who worked there: across eight-hour shifts, they were required to masturbate eight to thirteen times per shift minimum, a demand that led several to quit on the spot. Some of those same workers then filed a complaint with the Department of Labor & Industries.

Usually, hackable sex toys don't pose an immediate or visceral risk to one's genitalia. The worst a hacker could do to most consumers if they could access the Bluetooth controls of a sex toy—as researchers did in 2017 with the Lovense Hush buttplug—is turn the thing up and down or on and off.

An out-of-control dildo or buttplug sounds unpleasant, but it would be a creepy mood-ruiner at worst. More often, the data leakage is seen as the bigger intrusion: In 2017, the makers of the Bluetooth-enabled We-Vibe vibrators line settled for millions in a lawsuit that alleged the company was collecting data about people's settings preferences and usage that were connected directly to individual accounts and email addresses. We-Vibe's parent company, Standard Innovations, admitted no wrongdoing, but the lawsuit marred the public's trust in connected sex devices.

Sex toys tend to be privacy-leaky because the companies making them are usually new to the Internet of Things and have never had to figure out how to—and how not to—store user data before. Many don't even have privacy policies.

The fears and flaws swirling around connected sex toys reflect how we still view the Internet of Sex as a bit mysterious. Yet we keep grappling with them, along with the questions we've always had about selfhood and embodiment, since the earliest days of cybersex and long before.

Are our continued attempts at connecting sex toys to the internet just another way we're trying to locate our bodies physically, across distance and cyberspace? "With internet-connected sex toys, images, and video, the body is simultaneously both 'here' and 'there,'" Waskul told me.

We split ourselves across space, but are still dislocated. Some people are into it, but many are not. For many, the allure is in the absence of the body; the thing we're burdened with AFK is the real ball and chain, not wires or cables.

But then, we can never really be in two places at once.

For a long time, a sex toy was one of two things: a hole to fuck or a shaft to be fucked with. Lateral, on a track, going in and out. In the last few years, those early dreaming days of the nineties are coming back, spiritually at least.

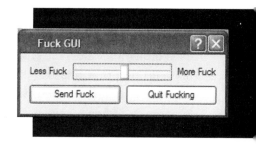

More people have their hands on more toys and more ways to take hold of their own pleasure. There's been a shift away from replacing the experience of real-life sex toward enhancing those experiences and our imaginations.

> "I think that sex toys now are moving away from realism: The idea that a person would only want to masturbate with a replica of genitals is kind of going away. People are more focused on both the utility of a device (does it give me an orgasm?) and the design: They want something that looks beautiful."
>
> **–Hallie Lieberman,** sex historian and author of *Buzz: The Stimulating History of the Sex Toy*

Now, sex toys—internet-connected or not—are shaped like beans, long elegant squiggles, and cartoon sea animals, and are cast in colors that look nothing like human flesh. They're without gender or prescribed use, moving in whatever direction feels best to the person.

On the opposite end of the sexual-wellness spectrum, away from the amorphous and pleasure-centric, there's the very literal, hyperreal, and futuristic. Instead of meeting your distant friends and lovers in text-based cyberspace, "virtual reality" now means strapping a headset to your face and feeling like you're in the room with them. Or, in the room with porn stars.

Thirty years after Rheingold's predictions about virtual reality and teledildonics, those applications have mostly arrived. "As we look back on the history of internet sex it has never been sex machines that have motivated these passions—it has always been innovations in means by which people can communicate with other people that have brought about creative sexual applications," Waskul said. "I see no indication that this will change anytime soon. Sex machines are interesting to talk about but, in any co-present or virtual context, it's a lot more exciting to fuck another person."

Algorithms, Monopolies, and MindGeek

The internet is not
something that you
just dump something on.
It's not a big truck.
It's a series
of tubes."

**—US Senator Ted Stevens
(R-Alaska)**, 2006

n the beginning, porn websites peppered the web with a constellation of twinkling backgrounds, neon hyperlinks, and twitching nude GIFs. Each site was run by a model (or a couple, or a small group of models), studios, or fans—all showcasing carefully curated photo galleries in wireframes and thumbnails that took longer to display on the screen than they did to shoot. Nude bodies loaded onto the page in packets of data, trickling down the screen in a digital peep show.

"You could cook Thanksgiving dinner and come back and the GIF would be downloaded," adult-industry veteran Angie Rowntree said. "There was no immediate gratification . . . *at all*." She founded women-focused Sssh.com in 1999, after her husband Colin started the BDSM website Wasteland in 1994, making them some of the earliest online pornographers that still operate studios today. The first website that they ran together, phoenixgrp.com, had fiery, animated flame GIFs and everything.

"It was so hot," Rowntree said, then laughed. "Oh, it was horrible."

The Rowntrees had front-row seats for some of the most important years in the adult industry. Colin, seeing the new horizon of the internet, set up a BBS as an online companion to mail-order catalogs for fetish wear and Celtic jewelry they produced, for subscribers and fans of the catalog. With the internet came an opportunity to deliver what subscribers wanted digitally, catering directly to their desires. Soon, they realized that people stopped ordering the whips and cuffs and were just looking at the pictures. Colin moved Wasteland to its own website, and they started charging $10 for three months of access to photos and short clips. From there, they became a full production studio, writing and directing the porn their members wanted to see.

Landing page for Sssh.com, as it appeared in 2002

While they were walking around an adult industry conference in Vegas in 1998, Angie noticed that nothing on display was speaking to women—or to her, more specifically. "It was all very much from a male perspective," she said. "It wasn't that I hated it, it just didn't feel right. I asked people at the trade show and they said the regular things, that women aren't visual, women won't pay for porn, women don't like porn. But I'm visual."

She and one of the staffers from their website went to Barnes and Noble and scattered all the women's magazines they could find on the floor of the aisle, studying what their headlines were saying about sexuality. A lot of them focused on finding what a male partner liked, and not what the reader herself might actually enjoy in bed. "So we decided that we would take these concepts, and just be very blunt and show everything. Where they stopped, we continued. But we still didn't really answer the question of what women wanted to see."

Tube sites
These are YouTube-like platforms where users upload porn, usually for free. Pornhub, Videos, and xHamster are the most-trafficked tube sites year after year; Pornhub claimed it had 115 million visits per day in 2019. For comparison, the websites of the most-read news outlets in the world take a month to clock that many visitors.

One of the first things Angie did after setting up Sssh.com was open a membership survey, asking viewers about their sexual fantasies and what they wanted from a porn site subscription. Respondents cared about two things: whether their sexual appetites were "normal," and that the website they were paying to watch sex on wasn't "dirty or sleazy."

The link directories of the nineties (see page 58) proliferated into the aughts, using affiliate programs and ad sales that made them profitable without producing anything new.

Then, something shifted. Porn websites started evolving from small webmasters' hobby projects to huge machines of revenue and influence. Sexual preferences, fetishes, and fantasies became concentrated down into categories, tags, and keywords. Subscribers started sending Angie and Colin links from new sites called Pornhub.com and

YouPorn.com, where porn was free, as examples of the types of films they wanted to see next.

To the webmasters at the time, these years represented a shift in business that's hard to overstate. "Before the tubes, the typical porn aficionado knew where they could go see free stuff—like Persian Kitty—where there were links of '12 Free Photos and Videos of the Day,' or whatever it may be," Colin said. These were all sponsored through affiliate programs by a paid site: If you saw something you liked and wanted to see more, you might go to the site hosting the images and sign up for a weeklong trial with your credit card, which then became a subscription.

In the mid-2000s, that model changed. "It was the most horrific nail in the coffin," Colin said. "The consolidation of free video porn into tubes. It was a perfect storm . . . Those things all happening in 2008 changed porn forever." He estimates that close to 70 percent of the porn companies that existed in 2006 no longer did by 2012. "We had to crawl back. We were lucky to have survived. Most didn't. It decimated the industry."

The Algorithmification of Porn

When you work as a developer for one of the biggest porn websites in the world, you stop seeing gangbangs and stepsisters and peer between the lines of code representing so many nipples and anuses—to something else.

"When you know the average amount of time that someone spends on the website, you know how long people are . . . *going* for," said Brandon Reti, a mobile developer for the porn company formerly known as Manwin.

"I think the average amount of time was like seven minutes," he said. "And once you factor in saying, 'Okay, let me find a video and get settled in,' it's like three minutes. It's not long."

Reti worked there during its earliest stages, from 2010 to 2013. That company would soon become one of the biggest names in porn: MindGeek.

This get-in-get-out user behavior was a shift in itself, away from spending time trawling custom-made porn clips on bespoke, flame-GIF-covered websites. Studios started making more content that would cater to keywords and search queries, to show up high in the search results on tube sites. The films they made were spliced into short clips, the plot boiled down to a blunt title. "VISITING BUSTY STEPSISTER'S COLLEGE DORM" tells you all you need to know about what's on offer in a three-minute video, even if what the video delivers is simply a small bedroom, two young adults, and no dialogue.

The whole reason Manwin (later renamed to MindGeek) was successful was because of data. Reti confirmed that they treated it like a real tech business. And that all started with the man who hired him—German tech nerd and Manwin founder Fabian Thylmann.

As a teenager in the late nineties, Thylmann was perusing CompuServe's porn forums when he had the idea that would forever change the adult industry.

Those forums were for exchanging porn site login information—at that point, mostly paywalled or subscribers-only—for free, or a fee, but definitely without the site owner's permission. Thylmann was still too young to subscribe to those sites, which usually required a credit card as proof of being legal age (and to pay for the subscription), but he was old enough to start learning the trade from the pirated side of things. In a 2019 interview, he called this practice of finding and sharing logins for paywalled sites "a sport."

In 2004, Thylmann cofounded Too Much Media, a holding company for online commerce products. One of those companies was Next-Generation Affiliate Tracking Software, or NATS, an affiliate-linking system that would win awards from adult trade organizations. That same year, entrepreneurs Stephane Manos and Ouissam Youssef founded Mansef, a Montreal-based software company with a

Fabian Thylmann, who started Manwin, which would later become MindGeek after he sold his stake in the company for a reported $82.7 million in 2013

THE RISE OF FREE VIDEO

Even though Pornhub is now the household name for free porn, YouPorn was the first-ever porn tube site, launched in 2006. It blatantly copied another free video streaming website's aesthetic and business model: YouTube.

YouTube went live just one year before YouPorn, and initially looked more like a dating site than a video-sharing platform. Its main search function was in "seeking" format ("I'm a male seeking a female between 18 and 45," for example). An earlier version of the site literally was a dating site called Tune In, Hook Up—but it didn't take off.

That a porn site would copy YouTube makes sense. The first-ever video on YouTube.com, uploaded by the platform's cofounder Jawed Karim on April 23, 2005, is a dick joke about elephant trunks. Karim said in a later interview that the version of YouTube as we know it today—designed to encourage viral video sharing—was partially inspired by tabloid website videos of Justin Timberlake exposing Janet Jackson's breast on stage at the 2004 Super Bowl. Jackson caught severe public backlash for the incident—it effectively derailed her career at its peak—and she said it was "truly embarrassing for me to know that 90 million [actually 140 million] people saw my breast" on television. Through online tabloid videos, those viewers increased exponentially, and the incident lived on repeat forever. YouTube's twentysomething male founders were inspired and decided to replicate that frenzied watching and sharing on one platform, with users uploading videos themselves.

Seeing YouTube's wildfire success with free video, the founders of YouPorn molded their site in its image, down to a copycat logo of YouTube's signature red button and the simple grid layout for videos.

Manwin bought YouPorn in 2011, following a 2010 lawsuit against YouPorn for secretly harvesting user browsing data.

tight-knit staff; the head of the HR department used to babysit the CEO. They opened a few porn sites, including Pornhub, but kept the adult side of the company secret from their families. On its public-facing web pages, Mansef never copped to what they were up to behind the scenes, billing themselves as "an internet based company specializing in web programming, more specifically web-based Content Management Systems (CMS)," that was "constantly pushing the boundaries of cutting edge web technology, with a strong emphasis on object-oriented software design practices and principles." It was just a tech company, to anyone not looking closely. Thylmann saw the potential in the online adult industry and Manos and Youssef's serious, data-driven treatment of porn; he bought Mansef from them in 2010, changed the name to Manwin, and got to work building an empire.

Thylmann knew the money was in free porn for the masses, and the fastest way to get there was not to pay for it—or let other people steal it—and monetize whatever people were willing to pay for. It was all profit. And he'd grab it with data.

Manwin started hiring tech talent in Montreal. When Reti applied for the role of mobile product manager, he'd been working at a company that specialized in mobile phone ringtones and wallpapers. His former boss was skeptical that this new iPhone thing would take off. The iPhone had just launched in 2007, and Reti wanted to work at a new company that understood the gravity of Steve Jobs's new invention and the new, unharnessed market it unlocked. The mysterious Manwin, with its massive traffic numbers, seemed to be on to something. It wasn't until late in the interview process that he learned the gig was in the adult industry. But Reti was sure that if taking the job sullied his career in tech, any future employer that couldn't see the progressive future that porn entrepreneurs were building online wasn't worth his time, anyway.

By the time Reti came aboard, Thylmann was in the process of acquiring every porn website and studio that would sell to him. He landed a nine-figure loan from a secretive Wall Street funder in mid-2011. Between 2010 and 2013, he used this massive infusion of private equity to turn the porn world into an oligopoly.

Because he poured so much capital into acquiring and launching all these websites and studios, Thylmann needed to make it back, fast. Some of the sites featured subscribers-only content, while others were free and filled with user-generated content. Still others, like Pornhub, were a mix of premium subscription access and scads of free videos. "Monetization, and then blending that with customer experience, are the two things we were looking at," Reti said. "What if people don't look at more content? You have to make something enticing to click. You've got a category—let's say, amateur—and you've tried three, four, or five different titles, and you see which one gets the most click-throughs. You leave it there for a couple of days, swap it out, redo it, redo it, and redo it . . . and you're running all these tests all the time." They'd repeat this not just with category titles but also thumbnails, featured channels, anything on the site within their power to tweak, which was everything except the content of user-uploaded videos themselves.

A/B testing
Experimenting to find what makes visitors click links, buy products, or stay on the site longer. There are usually "A" and "B" versions being tried at random on visitors, with the winner being the one that performs better. News article headlines, promoted tweets or Facebook ads, and images are some of the things site developers often A/B test.

At Manwin, site developers and programmers were doing this sort of exhaustive A/B testing constantly, where a user in one zip code (or other demographics) would see one version of a category's lead image or video titles, and their neighbor in the town over would see another. They'd take the one with the most click-throughs or conversions to a paid website, and roll that out to everyone. The goal was to get visitors to buy subscriptions or, short of that, view as many advertisements as possible.

Brandon calls this a "washing machine" effect between free and paid sites. "When you have forty million people visiting your website every day, if one in five thousand, or even one in ten thousand buys something, the numbers are astronomical," he said. "So even though the click-through rates are lower, the amount of money that you're generating is batshit crazy."

The work they did at Manwin paved the way for how the rest of the adult internet—the rest of the internet, period—operated. They patented pop-up technologies and standardized banner ad sizes that became the staple of websites and are still in use ten years later. The shark-eyed tech start-up capitalism in which Thylmann specialized was its own innovation: tube sites like XVideos and xHamster, both founded in 2007, followed a similar recipe of free content, advertising, data collection, and site testing based on user data. With YouTube's launch just two years prior, 2007 was a golden age for the video platform. Anyone could become a breakout star with a digital camera and something to point it at.

Tech entrepreneurs saw how YouTube's user-generated business model translated neatly to porn, and ran with it. With the dry winds of the 2008 recession at their backs, plus a burgeoning culture of internet users who prided themselves on never paying for anything—Napster, LimeWire, and BitTorrent were the preferred media-gathering methods—the timing was perfect.

The economy was crashing, and people had maxed out their credit cards and were hunkering down for the recession. Porn was both a luxury item *and* the product of deeply stigmatized labor that even its consumers considered devoid of value. The tubes were ready with free porn aplenty. The only cost to users was all the data the sites could vacuum up from their habits—IP addresses, locations, age, gender, and whatever else they'd disclose through their computer's stored data cache or their free sign-up profiles that made commenting possible. They no longer needed anyone to actually click on those advertisements for little blue penis pills or semen volume–boosting elixirs. Time on page replaced click-through rates as a meaningful

RATES
Click-through rate: A metric seen by website administrators to know how many people click through the links on their site.
Bounce rate: The percentage of people who visit one page on a site and immediately leave.
Conversion rate: The number of visitors who do something that the site owner wants them to do—actions like signing up for a newsletter, buying a subscription, or downloading software.

advertising metric. And the tubes trained viewers to never expect to pull out their credit cards for porn again.

Thylmann sold his stake in Manwin in 2013 (following tax evasion charges, for which he was sentenced to 16 months in

Feras Antoon, former president, and David Tassillo, former COO, of MindGeek. Both resigned from their positions in 2022.

prison in 2016) to the company's senior management, Feras Antoon and David Tassillo. They changed the name again, to MindGeek, but kept the company's ferocious appetite for its competition: The new leading duo acquired whole networks of sites, bought up dozens of platforms, and opened new studios, all now under the MindGeek umbrella.

"A kid in a candy shop"

Philosopher Roland Barthes suggested in an essay analyzing strip-tease that the woman is desexualized the moment the last scrap of clothing comes off. The show is "a spectacle based on fear, or rather on the pretense of fear, as if eroticism here went no further than a sort of delicious terror." Anyone who remembers opening a tube site for the first time and being assaulted with advertisements for vinegar-based penis enhancement and animated GIFs of reverse-cowgirl-anal at 3x speed is familiar with this "delicious terror." These, combined with blocky, brutalist grids of thumbnails and screaming capital-letter titles, are a jarring user experience. Not a pixel of browser real estate is wasted on a site like Pornhub or XVideos.

We've never had more processing speed, design knowledge, personal data, and sheer volume of content floating around online than we do today. Unlike the lovingly crafted porn websites of yore, working with so much less technological power, tube sites today kind of look like shit, while the rest of the internet evolved into user-friendly, pleasantly sleek, veering-toward-prosaic design theory. So why do so many porn sites, once on the cutting edge, still look like that?

Some porn scholars believe that it is on purpose—that tube sites are motivated to throw just enough grit into the gears of porn viewers' browsing experience to make them keep hunting for the perfect video for as long as possible. Following the free thumbnail galleries of the nineties and YouTube's influence in video streaming, the sites are mainly grids with sidebars full of categories and those long, erratically animated advertisements.

Part of tube sites' design is in how they dangle their smorgasbord of content in front of visitors as the first number they confront. Before Pornhub banned unverified uploaders in December 2020, it hosted 13.5 million videos; XVideos hosted more than 9.7 million in June 2021; YouPorn breaks their numbers down by category, with 180,000 in Amateur, 60,000 in Anal, 82,000 in Big Butt, and so on. These numbers are visible in the search bar, so viewers are able to confront them before anything else, as they're about to wade in.

Patrick Keilty, professor of media and technology at the University of Toronto, calls this the "search for an imagined perfect image," an unfinishable quest tube-surfers embark on when they're clicking through hundreds of categories and tags. "The porn industry wants you to feel like a kid in a candy shop," he said.

> "It's a buffet. You go to a buffet, and you're a non-gluten vegan. You're going to walk the buffet until you finally find something you like. If you give people a plethora of choices, they'll eventually choose something."
>
> —**Brandon Reti,** former mobile developer at Manwin

Since their beginnings, porn sites have always pushed the technological envelope—faster, faster, load it faster, stream it *almost* live, close to live, and finally in real time, trying always to close that impassable gap between viewer and performer. Many sites, even the most well-funded ones, look brutish and amateurish because they're holding on to that dual allure of homemade "authenticity" and presenting themselves as massive, bottomless repositories of lust.

All the big sites—Pornhub, XVideos, RedTube, xHamster, etc.—are this way. The eye is drawn clockwise from the top left logo and search bar (usually with its total number of videos), down across a bunch of animated GIFs that might spring to life if you move a cursor over them, to a big, long ad on the right side that's usually animated on a loop, back around through a grid of thumbnails and categories before returning to the start, at the logo and search bar.

"Those are all old strategies. The mall was always that way, IKEA is designed that way, the Parisian arcade from the nineteenth century, an open-air market—you could argue that the design of these kinds of consumer spaces is ancient, and then [tube sites] are just participating in something that's always been there," Keilty said. These systems are ostensibly meant to help consumers find what they're looking for, but they're made with the company's best interests in mind: It's best if the shopper keeps looking, stumbling through more goods as they seek.

A lot of this consumer-behavior calculus is done with user data. Pornhub was one of the first to make their site's traffic patterns and user data collection into content; perhaps taking cues from the website hit counters of old, its "insights" blog posts usually touted the numbers of visitors with year in review reports. But they also exposed how much information the site was gathering about visitors: A 2013 report done by the company, "What Are Americans Searching for on

Some say the brutalist, no-frills design of "tube" sites is highly intentional.

Pornhub?" broke down search terms by state, and a 2015 report focused on millennial interests. By making mass data collection fun and cute—*Can you spot your fetish on this infographic about what porn people in* your state watched during the Superbowl halftime show?—they've made it less scary.[1]

Porn sites are constantly collecting reams of data about their users. So is almost every other website on the internet, including the ones we use most, like Google, Facebook, and Amazon. The longer visitors wander around the site, the more data a site is able to gather, and the better "time on site" and "attention retention" statistics look for advertisers.

It makes sense, then, that modern tube sites are designed to keep visitors meandering from MILF to Hentai to Babysitter for as long as possible.

> "But porn search engines . . . suck. They're really bad. I see it as a conscious decision to create a suboptimal way of navigating through the website in order to generate more page views..."
>
> **–Sophia Chen,** doctoral candidate at the University of Michigan

Categorization of Sexuality

The flattening effect of mainstream porn's tags, categories, and titles forces people into neat boxes bound by age, gender, sexual orientation, and race. This doesn't just happen to viewers, who are regarded as products themselves by companies, but the performers, too. They shove humans—soft, messy, fluid things—into literal boxes on a page. But the full range of human sexuality can't be boiled down to a hundred neat categories, or even two thousand keywords.

Across the internet (and beyond, in surveillance technologies, carceral systems, financial systems, and anywhere humans program computers to make decisions) the people who built websites and algorithms coded their own biases into the products. It's no different in the adult industry.

---

1 Other social media sites do this, too: Spotify's custom-made, algorithmically generated weekly playlists, or Facebook's "On This Day" memories feature, and Google's Year in Review, to name just a few.

In her research study "For Black Models Scroll Down: Webcam Modeling and the Racialization of Erotic Labor," sex work scholar Angela Jones examined how camming website MyFreeCams (MFC) incentivizes models and visitors to play by an algorithm's rules. "If a behavior or action is legal, and there is a market for it, capitalists love it—even if it's racist. White Supremacy and capitalism are bedfellows," she wrote.

On many social media platforms today, users are incentivized to uphold a status quo by rewarding what's already popular. On MFC, this manifests as the CamScore, an algorithm that ranks models based on their earnings. Models who earn more tokens from fans are ranked higher, in the first two rows of the MFC homepage. There's no other real discovery process for using MFC other than browsing the homepage and adjusting a few demographic filters to one's own preferences. Models who conform to Western and European beauty standards of whiteness and thinness are consistently at the top of the page.

Jones theorizes that the website's founders and moderators created the CamScore and made it publicly visible to stoke competition among models trying to outperform one another. And that means more money for models means more revenue for MFC, which takes on average about 40 percent of earnings.

As a company, MFC talks about the CamScore sheepishly. "Unfortunately, finding an order that is satisfactory for everyone is a more difficult task than it may seem," says MFC's informational Wiki.

"The structure of the website and the creation of the CamScore embed sexual racism into the cam site."

—**Angela Jones,** sex work scholar, speaking about MyFreeCams.com

"Although CamScore is not perfect, we have found it to be better than our alternative options."

—**MyFreeCam's informational WiKi**

The company is also careful to note that one's CamScore can be hidden from visitors—but this doesn't change the fact that the site sorts everyone according to CamScore by default, and the top thousand models are rewarded with bonuses for their CamScores. It's not just a number—it translates to a tangible, financial reality of those working on the site.

The popularity of white, thin, Western models becomes a self-perpetuating cycle: They rise to the top because they're who get the most interaction, and they get the most interaction because they're at the top.

"Those who run the site have created an environment that nurtures sexual racism, even if they did not themselves create racist cultural scripts," Jones writes.

Tube sites follow those racist scripts, too. "Interracial" porn, generally accepted as code for "white woman and Black man," has been around for decades and predates the internet, but it's still a massively popular porn category today. Porn workers of color frequently voice their opposition to these roles as racist, perpetuating damaging stereotypes about hypersexualized Black men and women versus innocent, pure white women. This is compounded by the fact that Black women experience discrimination from directors and studios, as well as pay disparities compared to others in the industry—while white women are often able to charge more for these interracial scenes as a marketing ploy, or refuse to work with Black men altogether.

Under the blunt thumb of an algorithm that's looking for patterns and trends instead of interesting nuance, these are categories (and stereotypes) a lot of big sites lean into fully. And they get clicks.

The "Big Beautiful Woman," or BBW, category is another example of this dynamic. BBW is a popular search term on many mainstream tube sites, as well as camming platforms and custom content subscription sites. It's also highly stigmatized, doubly so for a fat sex worker, and in multiplicity for one who is fat and also Black or brown, nonbinary or trans.

When Jessie Sage, an academic and BBW sex worker herself, investigated what it means to be a BBW, she encountered nuanced challenges faced by women in the industry. "I resisted BBW but when I finally embraced it, my sales went through the roof," performer Dahlia Dee told Sage. Being a "big beautiful woman" set her apart from thousands of straight-sized models. "If I was a skinny chick, I wouldn't stand out." Shy Spells, a Black BBW performer, told Sage that racism and fatphobia often go hand in hand, and she has to work harder to be seen online. "I have had some viewers tell me that they would never book a show with a fat girl. . . . There is a lot of the N-word, and to be honest, I think the Black comes up first, before the fat."

Breaking these longstanding molds of what a "porn star" looks like (thin, white, blonde) is not simple. For example, who is allowed to call themselves a BBW—or a "Super-Sized BBW"—and who isn't is up for debate. Male performers have a parallel to BBW, called "Big Handsome Man," or BHM, who've been shunned by the mainstream studio system for not having an eight-pack or an eight-inch penis.

Performers like these, as well as queer, non-white, non-gender-conforming actors, frequently work independently. They may never have the backing of a big-name studio, but they can leverage tube sites like Pornhub to get their work in front of wider audiences. And subscription services within the platform allow performers to be paid by fans within the tube-site ecosystem.

Most people working in the industry don't view tube sites as pure evil, or even wish that they'd disappear. At this point, they're a part of the landscape, and often easier to work with than fight against.

Left: Jessie Sage, academic and BBW sex worker. Right: Shy Spells, BBBW sex worker.

Around 2011, something curious started happening with Angie's Sssh .com member survey. Instead of slow titillation and fantasies that typically dominated the requests, women started demanding porn that went straight to the point.

"I remember to this day, the very first submission that we got that was the complete opposite of what we normally heard," she said. "Somebody wrote, 'You know what I want to see? I want to be bent over my boss's desk and *fucked*. I don't want anybody to talk. I don't want any music. I want him to hold me there, pull my hair, and just fuck me silly!'"

She attributes this shift in tastes in part to the first *Fifty Shades of Grey* novel published that year. "Our submissions became way edgier, way more hard-core, and way more explicit," she said. People were emboldened to fantasize about rough sex for sex's sake, far outside of the soft pink, beach-read style of "porn for women." But at the same time, the free porn proliferating online was introducing more people than ever to kink and BDSM.

While *Fifty Shades* thrust bondage and rough play into the mainstream, tube sites were laying the groundwork for low-commitment porn viewing. Sssh.com members talked about seeing clips they liked on a tube site and wanting to see more of it, with a higher production quality that Angie could help deliver.

For all the damage they did to the adult industry, the tubes did open up a new realm of experimentation and exploration for viewers. Sometimes, you don't know you're into something until you see it; when it's not behind a paywall, but floating freely among nine million other tagged, categorized, and algorithmically sorted fetishes, it's easier to stumble into something new.

The Rowntrees haven't changed their business model much in the last two decades, even as everything around them has. The Wasteland and Sssh websites have gotten their own upgrades and redesigns over the years, of course, but they're fundamentally operating in the same way they have since the nineties: listening to their audiences and making the films people want to see.

In 2014, someone called in a bomb threat to the Manwin headquarters. Reti got up from his desk, where he and his team had just pushed out a new feature for live testing, and evacuated the building to wait in Manwin's parking lot for security to declare it safe to return. While he paced and squinted at his phone in a Montreal spring drizzle, a friend texted him with a new start-up opportunity: "I wanna know if you can do for me, what you can do for Manwin."

"I'm in mid-deployment for site tests during a bomb threat," he replied. "I can do it."

Security sent the Manwin employees home for the afternoon, and Reti decided to submit his resignation. "Enough is enough," he recalled thinking to himself that day.

"Porn's not going anywhere," he said. "It's never gone anywhere, and now is not the time that it will go anywhere. It's a part of human existence. Death, taxes, and pornography. They will always exist."

The End of the of the Beginning

Consider the "Cybersex Addict"

A VIRTUAL SEXUAL EDUCATION

"I don't want to be horny anymore, I want to be happy. I don't wanna fuck, I want to love."

—Anonymous Pornhub comment

Porn as addiction is a pathology of the internet age. In the pre-internet days, psychologists who believed in sex addiction as a clinical condition considered pornography use was a "victimless behavior," a symptom but not an affliction unto itself. It wasn't until internet-connected computers started appearing in family rec rooms in the late nineties did the idea of someone getting so hooked on internet porn that it could ruin their lives enter the mainstream.

Part of that notion began with the work of Dr. Kimberly Young. She'd written the first survey to assess and diagnose internet addiction a few years prior and founded the Center for Internet Addiction in Pennsylvania. "We're a nation of puritans," Young said in 2000. "This is the first time in our history we've had something so uncensored in our homes. You can get to very objectionable material in a few keystrokes—even by accident—and then it's hard to get out of the site."

The web was only a few years old when Young first noticed a disturbing trend: People who logged on sometimes couldn't bring themselves to log back off. She hadn't set out to study cybersex or online porn in particular when she pioneered the field of "internet addiction" as early as 1995, but she clearly felt that the lure of cybersex was a big part of this growing problem.

To get to the bottom of why and how the intrusion of a tan box of wires and chips could severely upend lives, Young created a short Internet Addiction questionnaire and posted it around Usenet in November 1994.

Young found that 80 percent of the nearly five hundred respondents qualified as internet addicts by her self-styled definition. She conducted longer interviews with several of the respondents, cataloging stories of destroyed families, lost jobs, and crumbling marriages—all linked to the arrival of the internet in homes or workplaces. One thing many of them had in common: sexual relationships that happened online.

Young herself was ghosted by a man she met on the BBS group alt.personals while researching her 1998 book, *Caught in the Net*. The experience gave her a firsthand look at how online relationships form with speed and intensity. She projected her own desires onto her connection from the moment she responded to his generic personals ad about enjoying walks and candlelit dinners, with the assumption that he was romantic and cared little about physical appearance. Their email dalliance escalated to real emotion, at least on her side: "In many ways it was like having a conversation with a part of myself."

Perhaps this experience jaded her, coloring her view of the people she diagnosed with internet addiction. Regardless, the common thread through many of her so-called addicts' stories was sexual connection: They got a taste of affection from internet strangers on services like Usenet, MUDs, or AOL's People Connection chat rooms, and were willing to risk it all to chase that thrill.

When the internet was still new and people were still unaccustomed to the strange world of connectivity, worries about cybersex addiction loomed large. Kids stumbling into online porn was one thing, but what if adults fell down the rabbit hole of role-playing, flirting, and one-handed typing—and couldn't crawl back out?

Psychologist Mark Schwartz said cybersex was "like heroin" in 2000 and an epidemic in 2008. "There isn't a week that goes by where I don't get two calls [about sex addiction]," he said. But neither internet addiction nor porn addiction are in the psychologist's diagnostic manual, the DSM-5, and among mental health professionals these diagnoses have always been controversial. Some psychologists now believe drawing such strong parallels between internet compulsivity and addictions like gambling or alcoholism is flawed. And not being unable to log off at the expense of relationships and personal health is usually a sign of other issues, like depression or bipolar disorder. But the idea of internet addiction has stuck around anyway. Today,

Ghosting

When someone you're pursuing suddenly stops answering your messages and disappears without explanation. It was coined around 2014 to describe one of the worst sins of online dating—but as many as a quarter of online daters admit to doing it.

Porn addiction

Some researchers believe that people can develop a compulsive habit with viewing porn. Porn as something one can become physically addicted to, however, is a matter of debate among clinicians.

Internet and Technology Addicts Anonymous guides members through a 12-step program like Alcoholics Anonymous (complete with a spiritual awakening at the end). "Digital detox" retreats fill up with people who can't put their cellphones down, and worries about porn and sex addiction go hand in hand with this new-age anxiety.

As the internet grows up, sexologists are taking new approaches to this issue. Some researchers have theorized that hypersexuality, or what some clinicians might call sex addiction, isn't different from having a high libido. Others have found that self-proclaimed porn addicts often feel high levels of shame around their own behavior, even though they're relatively normal. One study led by neuroscientist Nicole Prause showed that LGBTQIA+ people, especially gay men, are more often labeled sex addicts than straight men—a harmful stereotype that perpetuates the idea that queer sexuality is somehow wrong. It's also a sign, according to Prause, that porn and sex addiction is a moral diagnosis, not a medical one. "I think the overrepresentation of homosexual men in sex addiction centers is strong evidence that the diagnosis is primarily used for social control of sexuality, rather than treating any actual disease that should affect all men equally," she said.

For a disorder many psychologists question, a lot of people turn to internet strangers to beg for help. Reddit, a message board with millions of users bonding with one another about everything from gardening to running to their favorite OnlyFans models, is home to multiple communities devoted to breaking what they feel is the death grip of a serious mental illness that keeps them clicking back to pornography.

Young- Internet Addiction Diagnostic Questionnaire
1. Do you feel preoccupied with the Internet (think about previous online activity or anticipate next online session)?
2. Do you feel the need to use the Internet with increasing amounts of time in order to achieve satisfaction?
3. Have you repeatedly made unsuccessful efforts to control, cut back, or stop Internet use?
4. Do you feel restless, moody, depressed, or irritable when attempting to cut down or stop Internet use?
5. Do you stay online longer than originally intended?
6. Have you jeopardized or risked the loss of significant relationship, job, educational or career opportunity because of the Internet?
7. Have you lied to family members, therapist, or others to conceal the extent of involvement with the Internet?
8. Do you use the Internet as a way of escaping from problems or of relieving a dysphoric mood (e.g., feelings of helplessness, guilt, anxiety, depression)?

Dr. Kimberly Young's Internet Addiction Questionnaire posted to Usenet in 1994

PANDORA'S BOX?

The cast of *Touched by an Angel*, a show that delved into the "risks" of online porn

In the May 21, 2000, episode of *Touched by an Angel* called "Pandora's Box," a family is confronted by internet porn. One of the children is working on homework and clicks a link that takes her to a porn site. Her eyes widen, she gasps, and her dad shoos her away and sits down at the computer. He lingers a little too long in front of the curvaceous woman on the screen, before pressing the monitor's off button. The screen sizzles and darkens.

The episode's plot, which aired on CBS in primetime, involved the father losing his job because he surfed porn sites at work, while the girl was lured to an internet sex predator's apartment. One of the angels goes on a long monologue about how the internet is a vehicle for evil and pornography "cheapens" marriages and about God's will for humanity (which does *not* include looking at bikini models on the World Wide Web).

Josh Grubbs was around that child's age when he saw that episode. It was the first time he'd ever heard of internet porn, let alone the idea that it could wreck a family. Today, Grubbs is an assistant professor in the clinical psychology PhD program at Bowling Green State University, where he studies sex addiction, among other things.

"Honestly, this notion of people getting caught at work, looking at porn and getting in trouble for it—you hear about that less now," he said, "and I couldn't tell you whether that's because it's happening less, or because it's become so normal that nobody cares anymore, or if it's because everybody knows now that you don't use your work computer—you use your smartphone."

Among millennials and those younger, there's an expectation that people look at porn, and that it's normal, Grubbs added. "There's been such a cultural shift in how we think about it. Outside of very religious communities, the complete mundanity of porn is much more common, in my experience, than panic about it."

All of this is wrapped in an internet that's increasingly hostile toward sex education, sex workers, and sexual speech. Sex educators' work is consistently censored on social media, labeled harmful or dangerous to children, while schools and parents fail to teach kids anything about how their bodies work or what healthy sex, desire, and consent looks like.

A New Field: Netsex

Getting romantically entangled with someone you met online has an allure and intensity the flesh-world simply doesn't match. Young was right when she said it can be like talking to yourself—imagine your journal not just talking back at the end of a journal entry, but asking what you're wearing and how you touch yourself. Human imagination is a powerful thing. We're able to read between the typed-out lines and insert our own fantasies. In the nineties, a computer in your home contained a bottomless social pool where everyone could fit in and anyone could be the love of your life, waiting behind the next chat prompt. It's no wonder people felt "addicted."

Compared to fields that study alcohol and drug addiction, which have been around for more than a hundred years, the field of internet, porn, and cybersex addiction is in its infancy—and was practically newborn in the late nineties and early 2000s. One psychologist wrote in 2000 that this issue, barely five years old by then, was "a widely recognized problem." Mental health professionals rushed to create new screening tests and modes of treatment for this demographic of internet-obsessed patients.

In 1999, internet researcher David Delmonico wrote the Internet Sex Screening Test, a twenty-five-question quiz that asked participants to reflect on their time online with a ratings scale on phrases like "I have a sexualized username or nickname that I use on the internet," and "When I am unable to access sexual information online, I feel anxious, angry, or disappointed."

As more people arrived in therapists' offices complaining of out-of-control internet use, whole modalities were developed to treat them. Alongside the amateur pornographic webmasters of the day, shrinks set up online subscription-based members-only websites that offered treatment courses, bookstores, and community bulletin boards for the netsex obsessed, like the Online Sexual Addiction site. The first line of treatment included cutting off the source by using a porn filter like Net Nanny—often conveniently for sale on these websites—and raising one's personal awareness of the problem's extent by taking questionnaires and quizzes. Interestingly, some suggested psychiatric evaluation and treatment as a secondary step; putting people on antidepressants (SSRIs, typically) for cybersex was an accepted intervention. Next steps included getting the patient's family involved or entering into couples therapy, then considering how cybersex addiction impacted children in the home (remember, in the early web era, kids accidentally seeing sex online was the most tragic outcome imaginable). The last step, like a 12-step AA-like program, was spiritual healing. "An essential part of treatment includes the incorporation of spirituality as a dimension of

PRAYING THE PORN AWAY

Studies show that people often feel like they masturbate too much or watch too much porn *because* of their religious or spiritual beliefs. The theory is that their religion condemns the act and makes them feel guilty enough to seek treatment or label themselves "addicts"—not because they're spending an unusual amount of time jerking off online, compared to other people. These studies contradict older accepted treatments for "out of control" porn and internet sex, which sometimes included forbidding patients from being around young people, installing strict sexual content filters on their computers, and guilt-tripping tactics like making them write about how they were violating themselves and others. For someone already struggling with specific, intrusive obsessions this is a *lot* of focus and shame piled on to them, like repeatedly picking at a scab and wondering why it won't heal.

DELMONICO SEX SCREENING TEST

This quiz was developed by researcher David Delmonico in 1999, intended to help people reflect on their use of the internet to satisfy sexual needs.

Online Sexual Compulsivity

> Internet sex has sometimes interfered with certain aspects of my life.

> I have made promises to myself to stop using the Internet for sexual purposes.

> I sometimes use cybersex as a reward for accomplishing something (e.g., finish a project, stressful day, etc.).

> When I am unable to access sexual information online, I feel anxious, angry, or disappointed.

> I have punished myself when I use the Internet for sexual purposes (e.g., time-out from computer, cancel Internet subscription, etc.).

> I believe I am an Internet sex addict.

Online Sexual Behaviour—Social

> I have participated in sexually related chats.

> I have a sexualized username or nickname that I use on the Internet.

> I have increased the risks I take online (give out name and phone number, meet people offline, etc.).

> I have met face to face with someone I met online for romantic purposes.

> I use sexual humour and innuendo with others while online.

Online Sexual Behaviour—Isolated

> I have searched for sexual material through an Internet search tool.

> I have masturbated while on the Internet.

> I have tried to hide what is on my computer or monitor so others cannot see it.

> I have stayed up after midnight to access sexual material online.

Online Sexual Spending

> I have joined sexual sites to gain access to online sexual material.

> I have purchased sexual products online.

> I have spent more money for online sexual material than I planned.

Interest in Online Sexual Behaviour

> I have some sexual sites bookmarked.

> I spend more than 5 hours per week using my computer for sexual pursuits.

one's sexuality," a team of psychologists wrote in the 2002 book *Sex and the Internet: A Guidebook for Clinicians.* "This may include how one's religion influences an individual's sexual practices."

"What do we do to help them regain that control?"

Jack was a forty-eight-year-old attorney and senior partner at his law firm. He also had an "adult baby" fetish, which in his case meant he liked to wear (and use) diapers and be punished for "making a mess" in them. His wife shamed him, pushing his desires deeper, making him focus on them even more. So, when he logged on and found whole "adult baby" communities of fetishists just like him, he was no longer alone. Renowned psychologist, sex therapist, and sexologist Sandra Risa Leiblum, who believed the internet offered people new outlets for expanding their sexual appetites, prescribed him Prozac for his depression and counseling to get his obsessive thoughts under control. Jack never lost his kink, but was able to control it better—occasionally visiting sites with like-minded "adult babies" was a harmless indulgence.

In his 1998 paper on internet sexuality, Alvin Cooper wouldn't understate the importance of the internet's arrival as a turning point in human history. He went so far as to compare it to nukes: "Like with nuclear fission, its ultimate usage and results will be what we make of it. The Internet is a means, not an end . . . Those susceptible to the seduction of transient sexual highs may find themselves in the grips of a compulsive loop."

"Cybersex" and "netsex," as medical terms or otherwise, have fallen out of fashion.[1] The majority of internet users aren't logging on to chat in text-based worlds for hours anymore, even as the internet lives in our pockets all day and under our pillows all night. And if they

---

1 Since 2004, Google searches for "cybersex" have been on a steady decline, while the query "how to cyber" still peaks every year right around the Thanksgiving and Christmas holidays like clockwork—the time when we're all stuck at home with family.

are, they don't have to lock themselves into computer rooms or access the internet at midnight or off-peak hours to do it. The ways websites, apps, and social media in particular have been meticulously designed to keep us coming back would be considered "addictive" by most—the people who designed Facebook admitted to adding features like photo tagging, status updates, and likes so that the platform would be as addictive as cigarettes—and app developers are fluent in the behavioral psychology theories that foster hard-to-break habits.

The mental health community is still divided on whether internet porn and sex addiction are legitimate, diagnosable illnesses. Hypersexuality disorder was rejected from the most recent version of the DSM-5, because there wasn't enough research yet to back it up.

Some of the psychology community's porn-addiction naysayers draw a line between personal shame and self-identification as an addict. "Many people in our culture feel a strong sense of fear and shame around sexuality and believe that sexuality is a force that must be denied, controlled, and suppressed, lest it take over their lives and actions," wrote clinical psychologist David Ley in his book *The Myth of Sex Addiction*. Ley takes issue with the nomenclature of "addiction" being applied to something like sex or porn, because of the lack of evidence that quitting porn or becoming celibate has the same neurological and physical effects that quitting drugs and alcohol do. There are no physiological withdrawal symptoms when you suddenly stop queuing up Pornhub in your browser. Prause used tests that read electrical activity in the brain on people who had trouble regulating their porn use. She focused on the part of the brain that usually lights up when people with a substance abuse disorder look at their drug of choice. Prause found that those who stopped watching porn reacted the same way to photos of neutral activities, like skiing, as they did to images of people having sex.

Joshua Grubbs, a Bowling Green professor who studies sex addiction, proposed two "pathways" for thinking about problematic porn usage. The first is that compulsive or extreme pornography habits are undeniably something with which some people struggle. The second pathway is that some people will consider any amount of porn watching, even if

SEX ED ONLINE

I n 2018, you could ask iPhone's Siri voice assistant how to build a bomb and get an answer with instructions. If you asked it "how to say no to sex" it would be stumped.

Thanks to some overly enthusiastic parental controls built into iPhones that block "adult websites," sex education got caught in the net—while white supremacist websites and searches like "how to poison my mom" and "how to join isis" were allowed. Confusingly, the algorithm that Apple entrusted with these content decisions let "how do I jerk off?" through, but blocked "what is a vibrator?"

Only thirteen states in the US require sex education in public schools to be medically accurate. That leaves millions of kids in the dark about how their bodies work, what consent looks like, and how safe sex works—so they often turn to the internet for advice. But increasingly, anti-porn legislation and Big Tech companies are coding sexual ignorance into their experiences. For example, Instagram's strict no-sexual-speech policies excommunicate sex educators from the platform, cutting them off from a teenage fan base that needs trustworthy information on platforms accessible to them. "Ultimately they're telling people that sexuality is inherently dangerous," Gigi Engle, a certified sex educator and author, told *Vice* in 2021. "And it's not; it's a normal, natural part of human existence." With more platforms including Google's YouTube, everything Facebook owns, and video-sharing sites like TikTok banishing sexual wellness from their worlds, many young people grow up without being exposed to sex-positive, science-based content. It's no wonder so many adolescents turn to pornography for answers to their questions.

it's not a disruptive amount, problematic—usually as a reflection of their moral or religious beliefs around porn. For these people, it's a matter of a moral incongruence: They feel out of control because to them, even a few minutes of porn—or the desire to watch it at all—is too much.

Grubbs notes that his findings about moral beliefs doesn't mean people are delusional about their struggles. For him, the self-reported emotions of the patient are more important than viewing metrics. "Sure, sometimes we can blame [sex or porn overuse] on some other underlying mental health concern, but sometimes people just seem to be out of control of their sexual behaviors because they *are* out of control of their sexual behaviors. Whether we call it an addiction or not doesn't change the fact that those people need help," Grubbs said. "I'm not super interested in fighting over whether it's a real addiction. I'm much more interested in asking, if a person is out of control, what do we do to help them regain that control?"

"Cybersex addicts" and the relative treatment of them haven't completely gone the way of trepanning (more or less drilling a hole in someone's head). Like the internet itself, it's morphed into something harder to define. Just as digital detox plans and pricey "unplugged" retreats still remain popular, the hotly contested idea of online porn addiction is still very much alive. Unlike retreats where adults turn their phones on silent and play in bounce-castles for a weekend, the very idea of porn addiction—as a deep personal belief and as legislative cudgel—can be dangerous.

The Deadly Legacy of Porn "Addiction"

Robert Long, a twenty-one-year-old white man, parked in front of Young's Asian Massage in Acworth, Georgia, on March 16, 2021, a drizzly Tuesday afternoon. An hour later, he picked up a 9mm handgun he'd bought that day, walked into the massage spa, killed four people, and walked out. He then drove for forty-five minutes to Atlanta, arrived at Gold's Spa, and killed two more people. Across the street, at Aromatherapy Spa, he killed another. By the time he was finished, eight people had died, seven of them women, six of whom were Asian and worked at the parlors. Police caught him on his way to continue his murder spree at a business "tied to the porn industry," authorities said.

The next day, Capt. Jay Baker of the Cherokee County Sheriff's Office stood at a press conference and said Long was having a "bad day." Baker also relayed the excuse Long gave for taking the lives of

Gold Spa was one of three Atlanta-area sites where Robert Long was accused of killing eight people in a shooting spree in March 2021. Long pleaded guilty, was sentenced to life in prison, and later entered a not-guilty plea.

eight people: He had a "sex addiction" and wanted to "eliminate the temptation" these women represented to him.

Blaming the ills of society on women's sex lives has a very long history. Ancient Romans believed the city's health and prosperity rested on Vestal Virgins and buried those women alive if they were found to be unchaste. In modern times, criminals ranging from Ted Bundy to Harvey Weinstein and every sex criminal in between have tried to pin their actions on pornography and the women working in the industry. In Long's case, he grew up in an evangelical Baptist tradition that recently called porn an "epidemic" and preaches that it holds the power to destroy lives.

Long's victims were only the latest of a misogynistic man with violent aversions to porn and sex. In 2018, after Alek Minassian drove a van through Toronto's business district, killing eleven people, his final, cryptic Facebook post became the center of attention:

> Private (Recruit) Minassian Infantry 00010, wishing to speak to Sgt 4chan please. C23249161. The Incel Rebellion has already begun! We will overthrow all the Chads and Stacys! All hail the Supreme Gentleman Elliot Rodger!

Minassian was referencing incel culture, an online community that's bound by their shared "involuntary celibacy" and believes that the Chads and Stacys of the world—conventionally attractive men and women—are to blame for their sexless lives.

Elliot Rodger, a twenty-two-year-old incel, brutally murdered six people during a shooting rampage in 2014 in what became known as the Isla Vista killings. He began in his own apartment, stabbing three men to death; he then drove to a University of California, Santa Barbara, Alpha Phi sorority house, a place he regarded as having the "hottest" people at his college, "the kind of girls I've always desired but was never able to have." He tried to break into the house but failed, then shot and killed two women outside, injuring another. Driving to a nearby deli, he fatally shot a male student before crashing his car and shooting himself.

He was lauded as a hero among incels. Minassian admired him. We know his motives because before his attack, Rodger published a video to YouTube titled "Elliot Rodger's Retribution," where he laid it all out.

"You girls have never been attracted to me," he said in the video. "I don't know why you girls aren't attracted to me but I will punish you all for it." He laughs.

In addition to the video, Rodger wrote a 107,000-word manifesto, titled "My Twisted World: The Story of Elliot Rodger." In it, he mentioned "a forum full of men who are starved of sex, just like me," referring to incel forums. "Many of them have their own theories of what women are attracted to, and many of them share my hatred of women," he wrote. "Reading the posts on that website only confirmed many of the theories I had about how wicked and degenerate women really are."

A Brief Detour into Inceldom

Just as porn addiction is a mental issue sparked by the catalyst of the internet era, incels are a uniquely online phenomenon. They take the utopian ideals of the nineties Bay Area peace-and-love techies—that the world would be a *better* place if people were interconnected, across time and space, to bond over interests and passions—and twist them to the worst ends. Their ideologies fostered and spread on incel forums inspired multiple mass murders in the last decade.

In the late nineties, a college student named Alana found herself struggling to date and feeling lonely, so she started her own website called Alana's Involuntary Celibacy Project. She offered a mailing list for "anybody of any gender who was lonely, had never had sex or who hadn't had a relationship in a long time." The site encouraged readers to learn about the gay rights movement and was generally a place of welcoming, not judgment. She backed away from the site in 2000, once her own life, including her dating life, got busier, and didn't realize how toxic the community had become until she was reading a feminist magazine in 2015 and saw a story about Elliot Rodger's "Incel Rebellion."

What drives incels today is difficult to summarize succinctly, because they're not a monolith. They exist within the "manosphere," the catchall name for male supremacist groups online. The one commonality between them is that they believe they have metaphorically "taken the red pill,"[2] a reference to the scene from the 1999 movie *The Matrix* in which the Chosen One decides to "wake up" and see the world for what it really is: a simulation that's been lying to him his whole life. The manosphere also includes a host of other groups that appear to revolve around fear and/or hatred of women, but self-professed incels have the largest online footprint.

Many incels blame their rage on their inability to get laid and, by association, the women who refuse to sleep with them. But it's not actually about the sex, even though their plaintive manifestos cry about being deprived of intimacy with women. They may relate to sexual frustration and rejection, but once they've been fully radicalized as incels, their common hatred of women is what binds them. They don't want women to accept and love them; they want women to be subservient sex slaves. Women are subhuman to them—the term "foid," a portmanteau of "female android," stands in for "woman" on incel forums, because calling them women is too humanizing.

Manosphere
The umbrella term for online communities that view masculinity as central to their values, and are frequently misogynistic. These include incels, men's rights activists, Men Going Their Own Way, and pick-up artists.

They find this radicalization online.

---

2 There's also the notion of being "blackpilled," a state of hopelessness where the person believes there's nothing they or anyone else can do to change their loneliness.

Dr. Lisa Sugiura, senior lecturer in criminology and cybercrime at the University of Portsmouth, told Laura Bates for her book *Men Who Hate Women* that "online communities and virtual platforms provide the means for these ideas to take shape, take hold and spread. If people did hold these ideas and they didn't necessarily feel they could talk about them in person, they've now found a new way." The internet allows them to find one another, recruit more members, and grow their ranks exponentially.

> **Fapstronauts**
> Members of the NoFap community call themselves fapstronauts, meaning that they're abstaining from masturbation.

Following Minassian's attack in Toronto, Alana told the *Guardian* that she was horrified at her project being co-opted by hateful ideology. "It's not a happy feeling," she said. "It feels like being the scientist who figured out nuclear fission and then discovers it's being used as a weapon for war."

Semen Retention and the Pseudo-Science of Internet Virgins

"The semen is a drop of the brain," wrote Pythagoras more than 2,500 years ago.

"Good afternoon gentlemen, I'm 215 days in my journey," Character-Raccoon905 wrote in 2021. "I'm not in a relationship don't plan on ever being in one and I'm not going to ever release. Women don't deserve my juice. I will be the ultimate male."

While not entirely unrelated to incels, pick-up artists, or Men Going Their Own Way (MGTOW), "Fapstronauts," or people abstaining from masturbation following the principles of NoFap, are a class unto themselves.

NoFap is a website and community forum founded by Alexander Rhodes in 2011. Rhodes, a Pittsburgh web developer, was allegedly inspired by a thread on Reddit about a 2002 Chinese study that found participants' testosterone levels increased by 45 percent after

The "manosphere" is made up of many different groups with their own belief systems:

Men Going Their Own Way: Men who ultimately refuse to interact with women, because they believe feminism has programmed women to destroy men's lives.

Men's Rights Activists: Men who are mostly obsessed with false rape accusations and discrimination against men.

Pick-Up Artists: Men who consider women "targets" and try to use psychological tricks, abuse, gaslighting, and boundary-pushing to get women to sleep with them.

NoFap/NoWanks: The Proud Boys was a fraternal order founded during the 2016 presidential election. Its members adopt white supremacist, racist, and sexist views and frequently graduate into full Nazism. A requirement for those who want to advance in their ranks is to adhere to "no wanks," or masturbation abstinence.

The person who introduced Proud Boys founder Gavin McInnes to the concept of orgasm self-denial was Dante Nero, a former stripper turned comedian. Nero told McInnes about it—before McInnes made a name for himself as the Proud Boys leader—and he, too, became obsessed with it.

Semen Retention: Semen retention has a history that's a lot longer than the internet, and still lingers today. Eighteenth-century philosopher Immanuel Kant considered masturbation morally worse than suicide. John Harvey Kellogg, the maker of Kellogg's cereal, and Rev. Sylvester Graham, the creator of graham crackers, invented corn flakes and graham crackers to be so boring they'd kill libido. Psychiatrist Wilhelm Reich wrote *The Mass Psychology of Fascism* in 1933, which examined and attempted to explain how Nazism was able to succeed en masse over communism at the time. The through-line: sexual repression and control over men. "The formation of the authoritarian structure takes place through the anchoring of sexual inhibition and anxiety," Reich said.

seven days of abstaining from masturbation.

More studies have shown that masturbation is actually good for men and women in several ways: high ejaculation frequency is correlated with lower risks of prostate cancer in men, and orgasming helps women stave off cervical and urinary tract infections. Orgasming also releases endorphins that help with stress, sleep issues, and depression.

But based on that post about the Chinese study and the encouraging response from commenters, Rhodes started his own subreddit for NoFap—coined from the onomatopoeia of the sound of jerking off—and eventually trademarked the word and created a website that hosts its own forum and research resources. "Now, 'NoFap' is simply a proper noun," according to the site, "a label for a website and organization that helps people quit porn use through education and support."

Some readers of the NoFap site and subreddit stop masturbating for a while, and others swear it off forever. Some abstain from sex; others still have sex, but don't climax. Generally, the rules are flexible, and unlike incels or MGTOW, participants don't typically focus on women or dwell on hatred; it's more like a self-help system than an ideology for most, with a heavy twist of pseudoscience mixed in.

The description of the NoFap subreddit, which has more than 950,000 members as of 2022, says, "Whether your goal is casual participation in a monthly challenge as a test of self-control, or whether excessive masturbation or pornography has become a problem in your life and you want to quit for a longer period of time, you will find a supportive community and plenty of resources here."

Here's where "Fapstronauts" shake hands with the manosphere: to reconcile their self-diagnosed porn addictions with their struggle to regain willpower, many of them see the performers on the screen as something other than human. To them, they're millions of arranged pixels and light, forced or paid to be there.

A recent study of NoFap's Reddit posts looked at how people contributing to that discourse seemed to share a desire to regain some say in their masculinity. "A common thread throughout the definitions of masculinity given by NoFap users . . . is the positioning of men as needing to take ownership of their masculinity," the researchers wrote. "What is clear is that this can only be done by casting off certain social expectations. Of note are the overt references to self-respect and self-discipline, which ostensibly stand apart from the traits that could be classed as 'beta' or feminine traits." Watching porn and masturbating, many of them believe, undermines what it means to be a "real" man: virile and potent, but holding tight reins on one's own sexuality, and saving it for "real" women, usually in the context of heterosexual, penetrative sex.

Just like porn addiction self-help forums, anti-masturbation communities believe strongly that they've struck upon some magical secret to life. Studies citing increases in testosterone during semen retention are regarded by the medical community as needing a lot of follow-up research; they're not very strong on their own.

Subreddits

Individual forums on the social media platform Reddit; each subreddit has its own theme, like r/gaming or r/technology.

Problems arise when these communities take their self-help ideas and turn them into sexual control to manipulate the masses—a tactic that's been used by everyone from historical Nazis to modern-day white supremacist movements.

All of these communities only exist because of the internet. Without the ability to find one another across the world and become exposed to ideas and ideologies that aren't mainstream, it's safe to assume they wouldn't thrive and grow in the ways they have in the last decade.

As grim as it seems, hateful ideologies aren't necessarily winning the war. The internet has acted as a catalyst for hate, but paradoxically it's done the same for a more widespread cultural acceptance of enjoying porn as commonplace, sex work as work, and sexuality as a sprawling gradient of experiences.

12

Rated M
for Mature

SEX IN ONLINE GAMING

"Solo adventuring can be a lonely affair. There is, however, an alternative, a game where there is never really one solution, and certainly not just one player."

–*ACE* magazine, July 1988

Shine lies prone and nude in a photoshoot, their flaxen and fuzzy breasts arched up toward the light. A slight smile—or maybe it's a sneer—creeps across their snout.

In the real world, the human behind Shine works in finance, trading on the stock exchange in Saint Petersburg. But in the virtual world of *Second Life*, they're a sexy fox, as well as a porn director and performer, creating 3D-rendered erotic scenes from characters and places of their imagining.

Second Life is a virtual world of 900,000 residents living, working, and playing as avatars they design. "Around the time when I had very serious stress at work I noticed *Second Life*, which seemed to me a very curious game," Shine said. "Oddly enough, various experiments in it really helped me cope with some stressful situations, and in some ways, start to look at life differently. Not as seriously as I have looked at a lot of things before."

Developers of virtual social spaces have always had to grapple with whether, and to what extent, to allow sexuality within their virtual walls.

At this point in the history of the internet, people are already comfortable embodying themselves on the screen, and are often not interested in separating desire from that self, even when it's born online. We've seen liberation, addiction, immersion, and obsession, all woven into just about all of the spaces we inhabit online, overt or not. Next in this progression comes the idea of fantasy: If all of this is living inside our heads, does it matter anymore what is real and what's "fake"? Or what is real in IRL?

For *MUD1* denizens at the dawn of online role-play (see page 28), the distinction was blurred on purpose.

"Roy Trubshaw and I created MUD specifically because the real world sucked, we didn't like being treated as people we weren't by people who weren't themselves either, and we wanted to free people to be themselves," said Richard Bartle, cocreator of the first-ever MUD. "Sexuality is one of the dimensions of their being that players can explore, but there are plenty of others. For some people, exploring their sexuality is of high importance; for others, it's of low or no importance."

Shades, a multiuser game designed by *MUD1* player Neil Newell in 1984, was the first text-based adventure game to let users steal away to truly private spaces. In other games of the time, administrators could see what happened anywhere in the server, even in "private" chats. In *Shades*, certain safe areas, including churches, pubs, and hotel rooms, forbade "snooping" by high-level programmers. The hotel naturally included bedrooms (plus a bridal suite) with a feature that let players decide who entered a room with them. So, "people took to locking themselves in the bedrooms for private conversations and, as became apparent after a while, rather more than that!" Newell said in 2006. "Naively, I figured people were hanging out in the safe areas for private chats. Cybering wasn't a well-known phenomenon back then. It only became a concrete issue when a man would occasionally be upset to discover the woman he was playing with was actually another man."

Newell's hobby project turned into a marketable game within a year, and by 1988 *Shades* was featured and advertised in computing magazines.

Realizing the popularity of those furtive conversations behind closed digital doors, more programmers started their own MUDs explicitly for adults-only connections. UK-based *Shades* player Chris Butterworth launched a new game, *Zone*, in 1987, after a *Shades* comrade suggested there should be an adults-only, erotic version of the game. In *Zone* (as in, erogenous zone), players tried to get the highest score by having sex with other players—bonus points if you took someone's *Zone*-virginity. Text commands like "cuddle" broke the ice and set the mood, and drinking alcohol sped things along. The "stop" command, meaning stop having sex (useful if another

A print ad for a multiuser game called *Shades*, as seen in the January 1990 issue of *Ace* magazine

player is trying to assault you, which also happened) put an end to the cyber-coitus, but cost the player who issued it points. According to Bartle:

MMORPG
Massively multiplayer online role-playing games are played simultaneously among hundreds of thousands to millions of people around the world. Most games in this genre involve in-world currency, cooperative battles, and live events.

"Lovemaking uses up stamina, which can be recovered by consuming food and drink. Alcohol intake can have advantageous effects, but too much will cause disorientation, and, beyond that, death. [. . .] Although there is no combat in *Zone*, players can lose points by seducing or being seduced by a player of a much lower level. From a gameplay viewpoint, then, lovemaking is *Zone*'s equivalent of combat."

Zone was scandalous enough that the British Telecom network eventually banned it.

Today, there are so, so many social games where players can have sex—and most of them are standing on the shoulders of these text-based games, where the only real objective was to hang out and socialize. It would be easier to list the MMORPGs (massively multiplayer online role-playing games) where sex was impossible today than create an exhaustive encyclopedia of all the ways people get it on in-game. If there are more than a handful of people gathered in a virtual world, you can safely assume people are flirting, finding romance, falling in and out of love, and fucking.

"It was also, in fitful starts, beautiful and extraordinary"

When tech developer Linden Lab launched *Second Life* in open beta in 2002, one of the first things users did was craft themselves genitalia.

The Linden Lab programmers didn't know how to approach sex organs for default avatars: The first avatars were like Ken or Barbie dolls under their clothing, as smooth as a shop mannequin and just as

HABITAT: A "SOCIAL CRUCIBLE"

O ne of the earliest online games where sex was sold and exchanged was *Habitat*, a late-eighties MMORPG, by Lucasfilm. It was the first multiplayer game with a graphical interface, and it was a pretty crude one (see below): Landscapes side-scrolled past, where players could move laterally from page to page and see who awaited them on the next screen.

When they opened the game to users in 1986, cocreators Randy Farmer and Chip Morningstar envisioned a world that combined hacker and cyberpunk sci-fi with more than a little whimsy, drawing from object-oriented multiplayer chat communities. It was a model of player-driven gaming: Morningstar called it "A Social Crucible," where they could "throw some people in a room with some fun toys and see what happens."

There was in-game currency, inventories, homes, and weapons (and the potential for crimes against other players, like murder and theft). For at least some of its users, *Habitat* was a parallel-universe hookup spot: People met, were "married," and consummated it all in-game. Anywhere there's an economy, sex is likely to be for sale;

there was no official gameplay coded into *Habitat* to depict sex, but one player could sit down while another kneeled in front of them.

Habitat was too expensive to keep alive and shut down after two years. It was reincarnated as *Club Caribe*, which had 15,000 users at its peak.

"In a real system that is going to be used by real people, it is a mistake to assume that the users will all undertake the sorts of noble and sublime activities which you created the system to enable," Morningstar and Farmer wrote. "Most of them will not. Cyberspace may indeed change humanity, but only if it begins with humanity as it really is."

useless (and the game's default bodies still are today). But the developers coded in the ability to create "attachments" that could be placed on avatars, including on their chests and crotches, and left the program open-source so users could make their own. Residents quickly got to work creating their own breasts, penises, and labia for attaching to their virtual selves, and from there, got down to business.

Avatars
Historically, the physical embodiment of gods come to Earth are called "avatars." In gaming, avatars are customizable characters, the virtual embodiment of players who control them.

Open-source
Describes software with code that's publicly available, so that programmers can customize and share it freely.

Second Life is not technically a game, and some residents will probably take issue with including it in a chapter about games at all. "There is no manufactured conflict, no set objective," Linden Lab spokesperson Catherine Smith said in 2007, as media attention on *Second Life* reached its peak. "It's an entirely open-ended experience." Users are not "players," they're residents. It's not a video game, but rather a world, a parallel universe.

Like MUDs or *The Sims*, it is a role-playing experience where residents are putting the proverbial plane together in midair. What happens in *Second Life* is prescribed by the people who came before you and what you do in-world next. It's not unlike the physical world in that sense. But everyone can fly, and teleport, and swap out body parts for appendages with measurements that would easily snap a gravity-bound, flesh-and-blood spine or pelvis in half.

While *Second Life* was still in beta, Linden Lab hired freelance journalist Wagner James Au to work as an "embedded" reporter, interviewing residents and writing a blog that served as *Second Life*'s local newspaper. He logged on for the first time in April 2003.

"By then, there were some thousand Beta users, and despite such low numbers, it was a chaos of creation," Au wrote in his book *The Making of Second Life: Notes from the New World*.

In *Second Life*, sex emerged almost immediately.

"I'm pretty sure I saw a penis [in-game] before they even launched," Au told me. Linden Lab decided to keep the avatar and world-creation interface open-source, meaning anyone could make anything with 3D-rendering software that would be compatible with the game. Also, the programmers coded attachment points onto avatar bodies' crotches so players could add genitals—which people started doing right away. Today, browsing the *Second Life* Marketplace, you can purchase dozens of different penises from multiple species, sizes, and states of erection. Almost as many labia are available, and with a panoply of piercings, breasts of all sizes and shapes, and butts in varying degrees of thickness or with flushed red paddling marks or bruises from visits to BDSM destinations. Residents can also invest in specific types of furniture that will show sex animations when used. It's all bought with Lindens, the in-world currency.

Customizing your virtual body and what you can do with it is only one part of being a sexually active *Second Life* resident. As of this writing, there are 216 adults-only destinations. You can teleport between tropical islands and goth clubs, prehistoric worlds and art galleries.

As in the real world, sex in *Second Life* can be bought and sold, as there are many virtual brothels and strip clubs operated by proprietors in-world. With the limitless potential for the forms avatars can take on, this means that sex work in *Second Life*—like sex work in real life—disrupts and challenges mainstream ideas of "good sex."

Emergent sex

In video games, "emergent" content occurs when two or more things collide in a game to produce something that wasn't programmed or scripted. Video-game designer Brenda Romero calls the sexual tones that crop up organically throughout a player's game experience "emergent sex"—either through tweaking the game's system to get some sexual fulfillment out of it or when the game's programmed content turns players on as-designed.

In a small study of the *Second Life* sex trade, sociologist Michael Lynch examined how escorts and strippers navigate commercial sex in a Linden economy. He interviewed sixteen residents, a mix of providers and clients, in their virtual workplaces at the club or back in their own *Second Life* apartments.

He learned that people in *Second Life* were engaging in something akin to interactive erotica, a closer cousin to "cybering" on a BBS or MUD than some confusing futuristic spin on sex. The practice even carried over some of the same language from the old MUDs, like "emoting," where players describe a scene and how they're acting it out over text. Speaking and typing, either through the computer's microphone or in the text-chat box, is the most important part of *Second Life* sex, not your avatar's thirteen-inch veiny and fully articulated penis attachment or its beachball-size breasts.

"Considering that software animations allow for two avatars to theoretically have continual animated sex for an indefinite amount of time, 'good sex' in the virtual world is not so much predicated on duration, but rather on articulation," Lynch wrote. "One's avatar being able to engage in sexual activity (although an important component to cybersex) is not enough."

Second Life straddles two worlds: the old one of literary erotica or phone sex, where the only limits are vocabulary and imagination, and the newer, more queer and cyborg one, allowing for exploration of sexuality in wholly new ways. In many ways, *Second Life* could represent the future of human sexuality, where any physical attribute can be bought, modified, DIY-ed, and hacked.

And where a stockbroker can live out a fantasy of being a fox with a humanoid vagina and DDD breasts.

In games like *Second Life*, shown here, the range of play spans everything from a dance floor to darker fantasies.

For residents who choose to do in-world sex work, *Second Life* adds an extra layer of anonymity to the client-provider experience. Providers are afforded more safety by working behind an avatar and screen name, and using the Linden currency, instead of relying on platforms like PayPal that may discriminate against them using it for sex commerce or require that real names or emails and locations be exposed. Meanwhile, their clients are liberated by anonymity to learn what they might be into sexually—what different types of toys, furniture, or restraints are called and how they work online and off—in an environment that's relatively judgment-free and low-risk.

> **"It was ugly and random; even in its earliest days, it was fully suffering the tragedy of the commons. It was also, in fitful starts, beautiful and extraordinary."**
>
> **–Journalist Wagner James Au,**
> *The Making of Second Life*

The boundary between *Second Life* and "real" life tends to be a porous mesh: People bring their physical appearances, preferences, and baggage to the virtual world, and take what they learn in-world about themselves back to the flesh-world.

"Even the sex stuff, there's a deeper level that people don't appreciate [from the outside]," Au said. He believes the majority of women who are playing *Second Life* for sexual reasons are there to express their sexualities in ways society or their "real world" personal lives won't allow. Maybe they're not able or willing to reveal their sexual orientation IRL, but can live and love openly in virtual worlds. "I think it's great to talk about sex in *Second Life* as long as people are willing to go into that deeper level, beyond the salacious stuff," Au said.

Linden Lab CEO Ebbe Altberg claimed *Second Life* sees as many as 900,000 monthly users, but that number is debatable, according to Au. He says it's closer to 600,000, with 300,000 who show up, can't figure out the controls or are overwhelmed by the massive world, and leave. How many residents are still wandering around *Second Life* is hard to say, but those who stayed are loyal—and a significant portion of them are there for the kinky stuff.

Despite graphics that are outmatched by most modern video games and a user interface with an incredibly steep learning curve, *Second Life* stays ahead of its time—primarily because it still lets its users lead, while the rest of the game's design follows.

World of Warcraft

It's a line that's so often repeated in both scholarly and anecdotal descriptions about role-playing games—and specifically, fantasy MMORPG *World of Warcraft*— that it's become something of an inside joke: "If I'm going to stare at an ass while I play, it might as well be a hot ass."

WoW is a game that has no built-in mechanism for sex, but grapples with sexual expression nonetheless. And as a game dominated by straight young men, it's an especially fraught topic for players.

"I think it's gay to play as a girl character especially if you are trying to deceive others to get them to fulfill sexual desires with you," a twenty-three-year-old player told sociologist Zek Cypress Valkyrie for their 2010 study on cybersexuality in MMORPGs.

Unlike *Second Life*, *World of Warcraft* is undeniably a game. Players begin by creating an avatar, or "toon," joining a side ("Horde" or "Alliance," two warring factions made up of elves, humans, orcs, and other fantasy beings), and fighting wildlife, monsters, and other players to become more powerful. From there they can form guilds, which work cooperatively to perform raids, or extended battle campaigns that take several hours to complete. In WoW, you can chat privately to other players, or speak to the room in public chat.

The majority of players never seek out in-game cybersex, games journalist Katherine Cross said in 2015. "But if you play *World of Warcraft* long enough, you're eventually going to stumble inadvertently onto two characters mysteriously facing each other, undressed, while in some corner somewhere."

Instead of overt avatar-humping, the sexual tension of *WoW* more often plays out in the interpersonal dynamics of working together as a guild. "Guild drama" tends to be code for "girl drama," as some guilds outright refuse to accept female players because of the team-building difficulties mixed-gender teams encounter—which they blame on women. In a 2013 survey of *WoW* players, 63 percent of female players reported experiencing sexism in-game, and 75 percent said they'd witnessed it happen to someone else.

Karen Gault, a longtime *WoW* player, said her friend created a Blood Elf character (a game race that's usually blonde, tall, and lithe) and was immediately harassed by men. "You don't normally get that within your own guild," she said. "But guys kept following her around and bugging her, so she was like, you know what, I'm just gonna roll a male character—and now she's not having any problems."

As for "guild drama," it does happen, for better or worse. The collaborative tasks of raiding together, questing, highs and lows of battle losses and victories, watching teammates fall, rise, die, and revive at a heart-thumping pace—this leads to emotions running high, so chemistry within a team is vital. It's also a game that the most die-hard players tend to wrap themselves into, making it part of their identity. Raiding means setting aside hours at a time to meet guildmates in the *WoW* world of Azeroth. Players are also mostly young, in their teens or twenties. All of this makes the game an emotional pressure cooker for some players.

"My wife left me for someone she met on wow," a commenter in a *WoW* Reddit thread on the topic of game-mediated romance said. "I haven't experienced that, but a lady in a former guild of mine did that with a guildy and I was furious at them," another wrote.

Male and female Demon Hunter characters from *World of Warcraft*, where the gender of a character doesn't necessarily match how the player identifies themselves IRL.

"My mom left my dad for someone she met on wow, too."

"I got my ex into WoW, she met someone three years later and went with him instead of me, because I stopped playing for over a year."

It's not all heartbreak and jilted lovers in Azeroth, however. One Redditor writes about meeting and marrying someone they met through WoW, getting divorced, and not regretting a thing:

> After the divorce, I wanted to move and do some traveling. I ended up traveling for about two years . . . and thanks to my close-knit guild, I had a couch to stay on almost everywhere I decided to go. I ended up becoming very close with one, got romantically involved, and lived in Hawaii for about a year with her. Eventually, we both moved to Washington, where I live within two hours of four of my guildies, and about six people she knew through WoW.

Another wrote that they met their partner after an invitation from a friend to their guild: ". . . logged into their voice chat system [Ventrilo] for shits and giggles and heard an intoxicating voice. I ended up joining the guild and raiding just so I could hang out with her and talk to her. 2 years later . . . She moved down here 2 months ago and things are going amazing." WoW is "much much more" than "just a game," they wrote.

WoW players are predominantly straight males under thirty, and the community's attitudes about sex and gender tend to reflect that. But WoW isn't your standard online cesspool of toxic masculinity. For some, the fantasy role-playing game is liberating. Journalist Laura Kate Dale, a trans WoW player, used her in-game life as a female character to explore her own gender expression as a teenager—years before she was ready to confront her own sexuality and identity. She wrote:

> World of Warcraft, and other games like it, are often about much more important things than looted gold and slayed dragons. They provide a place in which identity can be explored safely. And for me, someone who the world viewed as male, World of

Warcraft provided a space to discover that I felt more comfortable when treated as female.

Dale became so enchanted with this magical world where she was gendered in a way that made her feel comfortable that her real life started to dim in comparison. She fell into a depression, rooted in having to return to a reality outside of the game where people treated her as a boy. But it also gave her a look into her future as a trans woman existing in a world where transphobia is rampant and deadly cruel; teenage Dale was outed by a fellow player in *WoW*, who accused her of

VIRTUAL GENDER-BENDING

Scholars of virtual worlds call this the "strategic female": playing a character that you think will give you the best advantages in the game. *LambdaMOO* and MUD players did this: If men wanted more help with learning the system from experienced players or more slack on mistakes (or to access exclusively female spaces they were barred from in real life), they might play as female. And if women wanted to ward off mansplaining and flirting, they played as men.

A study of 375 *WoW* players found that 23 percent of men and 7 percent of women gender-switched to the opposite of what they were in real life (*WoW* player-characters exist on a male/female binary without options for gender-fluid presentations, and until very recently, the game charged $15 for players to change the gender of a toon after it's created, see image at right). In that study, gender-switching men tended to also switch the ways they talked, as well as their appearance, to be more feminine, but didn't mask their more male movement patterns, such as jumping around; the researchers theorized that maybe men really do select avatars, at least in *WoW*, that are simply fun to look at.

People have been role-playing across a spectrum of gender since the first day Bartle gave them the option in *MUD1*. "Sexuality online has always been ahead of sexuality in society in general," he said. "The 'it's just a game' defense shields players from much of society's disapprobation."

lying to them, because she was playing as a female inside WoW while still presenting as male outside. "This is something else I learned from *World of Warcraft*: when people discover that you present as a gender different to that of your birth, they sometimes get very angry about it. Sometimes they will refuse to acknowledge you anymore." She left the game, but with something no one could take away: a working understanding of what it might feel like to be seen as a woman.

"I seen too much"

In the MUDs of old, using text alone, one could describe their character to be as strange or sultry as they pleased, with the only limitation being imagination. In newer games, visual character creators limit players to preset galleries of fur bikinis and questionably effective armor arrangements, determined by teams of developers who spend months testing which character styles will sell the most games. Even if the characters are sexy, they're not optimized for inter-player fuckability.

Usually, characters are as sexless as those original *Second Life* dolls. In *Animal Crossing*, you're an adorable anthropomorphic creature that looks like it's been plucked out of a baby's nursery. In *Roblox* and *Minecraft*, you're an assemblage of boxes and too-big pixels. In *Club Penguin*, you are, obviously, a penguin.

In spite of their outward innocence, emergent sex is present in each of these games. In multiplayer online games, if you build a chat function, they will come.

In Microsoft-owned *Minecraft*, players run around a garishly bright,

A scene from Pornshire, a location in WoW that's infamous for erotic role-playing

chunky-pixelated landscape building houses, tending to square chickens and cows, fending off venomous spiders, and fighting skeletons that come out at night. It's massive—in 2020, it broke past the 200 million user mark—and it's reflected in the community that's formed around playing, creating, and streaming through the game. It's marketed to children with its big blocky characters and low-resolution style, but people of all ages play it. (Microsoft's head of *Minecraft* Helen Chiang once claimed that the average player age is twenty-four years old.) Multiplayer gameplay, including an in-world text chat feature, makes world-building a collaborative effort. Its original designer intended it to be completely gender-neutral—and of course, sexless.

Mods
After-market modifications made to games by fans and players, usually unapproved by the game's developers.

The thing is, there's no sex in *Minecraft*. There's no nudity or genitalia or even the possibility for sexy dancing. Simulating sex with *Minecraft* avatars would be like watching two minifridges hump.

There is a lot of *Minecraft* porn out there, however, created by adult fans using 3D-rendering art software or recording their own screens with these mods installed, but none of this is part of the official game. If you wanted to see primitive pixel-bodies doing it in-game, you'd head to *Roblox*.

Released in 2006, five years before *Minecraft*, *Roblox* is not just a single game, but more like a gaming platform. It gives players the tools to create their own mini-games and share them with other players. The *Roblox* aesthetic is less low-res minifridge colony than *Minecraft*—instead of sharp blocks, avatars are soft, smooth, and chunky. They resemble figurines from a toddler's playset, with wide, thick-drawn U-shapes across their smooth faces standing in for mouths. But they're also customizable: Players can shape characters into more rounded, voluptuous figurines (still squatty and childish, but the curves are in the right places) and choose how to dress them (or not).

In 2020, an exposé of *Roblox* "condo" games revealed a whole world of adult-themed games happening on the platform. In private worlds arranged to look like apartments, players augmented characters into cartoonish displays of hypersexuality and meet up to twerk, vape, and curse. The majority of *Roblox* players are under eighteen, and many of the players in these custom games were minors, journalist Burt Helm discovered.

What goes on in condo games is not hot. "The digital gyrations are ridiculous, if impossible to unsee: thong-clad *Roblox* avatars twerking on stripper poles; beefy blond avatars buck naked except for COVID masks (written on the walls in this particular game: '#stayathome-hub'), and enough crudely animated contortions to fill several volumes of the *Kama Sutra* (should Lego ever decide to publish an edition)," Helm wrote. This was mostly innocuous teenage shenanigans—blowing off steam online in goofy, somewhat scandalous animated games where parents can't see, especially during a year of remote learning where most socializing was forced online. But Discord chat servers running in tandem with condo games were more dangerous.

Discord is a text and voice chat platform for gamers, where players can run private chat servers. Helm found some players soliciting, exchanging, and selling nude photos from others in those chats. Mods for those servers tried to keep users from breaking Discord's banned-content rules—including hate speech, gore, and sexualization of minors—so they won't be shut down for violating the platform's terms of use. Keeping the chat clean proved nearly impossible. One server host said they've had to remove images of genital mutilation, rape, and murders posted by other players. "Ppl at my school are like innocent to me," they said. "I seen too much."

The developers of *Roblox* are locked in a game of cat and mouse with these teenage condo owners. It's been a publicly traded company since

In Roblox, developed for children and teens, users can meet up in private "condos" with their avatars, but it's the content in the game's private chat rooms that has proven hard to moderate.

early 2021, and it's massively important to *Roblox*'s reputation as a squeaky-clean good time for children and teens to shut down salacious games.

Just because colorful, cutesy games can make space for sexual exploration that veers into the abhorrent (and even illegal) doesn't mean they must. Often these interactions are consensual, wholesome,

In *Animal Crossing*, a social simulation game that's rated for players as young as three, players sometimes meet up for kink, locking their avatars in cages overnight or commanding submissives to do tasks.

and happening between adults. In 2020, people turned to *Animal Crossing: New Leaf*, the latest in the long-running franchise featuring cute talking animals, for socialization. Some also turned to it for kink. Professional dominatrix Denali Winter invited clients to meet them on their *ACNL* island for sessions, smacking their avatars with cartoon butterfly nets and locking them in cages overnight. Winter's submissive clients would water flowers on command and do whatever chores were needed around the lush, animated island. "Video games have been a way for people to explore their identity for a long time," they said. "It's completely safe to submit to someone in an *Animal Crossing* game—if you don't like it, you can log off at any moment."

In *Animal Crossing*, players build and maintain villages and islands; in online modes, other players can visit your home base, trade turnips and pears, and just generally hang out. Deprived of real-life dates, people started adding "*ACNL*" to their online dating profiles, and met up for first dates in-game. For some, the absence of sexual expectation— *Animal Crossing* as a world has the romantic energy of a Toys"R"Us— made the experience uniquely low-pressure. "It's a fun way to hang out, because you're not fucking," one player said. "It's like, 'You're on my island, let's give each other gifts. Here, I know you're stuck, so I'm going to give you a ladder.'"

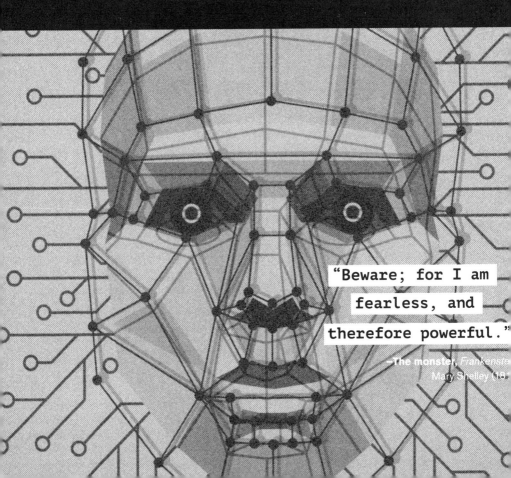

13

Faking It

DEEPFAKES, DEEP PROBLEMS

"Beware; for I am
fearless, and
therefore powerful."

—The monster, Frankenstein
Mary Shelley (18

n December 2017, a programmer sat tinkering with his hobby when he received a direct message on Reddit:

u/samleecole:
Hello! I'm Sam, a writer at Motherboard, *Vice's* science and tech outlet. Your work with face-swapping algorithms in porn caught our eye. Might you be willing to tell me more about it?

He replied

u/deepfakes:
I would like to stay anonymous and not to gain too much attention from mainstream media.
I don't mind to answer a few questions, however I'm just a programmer who has an interest in it. I'm not a professional researcher so maybe I'm not able to answer some difficult questions.

He and I exchanged three or four messages where I asked about his methodology, and how exactly he'd created this thing I'd seen him post to a porn subreddit: a hauntingly glitchy series of videos of female celebrities' likenesses replacing an adult performer's own face.

He[1] had a whole roster of female celebrities who suddenly appeared in his Franken-porn clips.

One of Deepfakes' earliest projects was a video of Gal Gadot waving a Fleshlight toy around. The original video was pulled from an incest fantasy clip, where a stepsister finds her stepbrother's package and opens it. In Deepfakes' version, that actress and Gal Gadot are face-swapped to look like Gadot was the one lounging on the bed, taunting the man shooting the video.

Deepfakes' other early porn creations featured the faces of Scarlett Johansson, Maisie Williams, Taylor Swift, and Aubrey Plaza. All were a little glitchy, not quite right, with mouths that sometimes opened and stretched into pixelated blurs or skin that flaked off into fragments of algorithmic error. Deepfakes was experimenting with his peers, in

---

1 To avoid confusion and clumsiness, I'll refer to the person with the username as Deepfakes, and the video genre as deepfakes.

what he likely considered a safe space to share progress on a new algorithm he was trying to perfect—he just didn't know a journalist was watching.

His username, "Deepfakes," was a play on "deep learning" and "fake." Today, *deepfakes* is the word for any videos face-swapped to look like someone else, using deep learning algorithms. In just a few years, it's become the topic of college courses and PhD theses, the basis for countless "deepfake detection" companies, a line item in the Department of Defense's budget, and the entire beat of many technology reporters.

Machine learning
A field of algorithms that can follow instructions, and then recognize patterns and build on those instructions, without being explicitly programmed to do the next task.

Dataset
A collection of data with something in common, ready to be categorized, ordered, or analyzed by a computer.

In technical terms, a deepfake is a video that's been algorithmically created using generative adversarial networks, or GANs. These videos are made with a machine-learning algorithm, using easily accessible hardware and software, and open-source code. A dataset of hundreds of high-quality source images— for example, of Gal Gadot's face in all sorts of expressions, like the hundreds of stills you could collect from a studio interview about an upcoming movie—is fed into one end along with the target the algorithm aims for (in these cases, a porn performer's face in a film).

Anyone with a working knowledge of machine learning algorithms and how to run them can put a deepfake video together, given the right amount of time and consumer-level hardware that can handle the task.

u/deepfakes:
I just found a clever way to do face-swap. With hundreds of face images, I can easily generate millions of distorted images to train the network. After that if I feed the network someone else's face, the network will think it's just another distorted image and try to make it look like the training face.

To compile the celebrities' faces for his datasets, Deepfakes said he used Google image search, stock photos, and YouTube videos. Those faces are pitted against whatever video he's hoping to swap; the algorithm tries to reconcile the difference between one face and another, eventually replacing the face in the target video with the new one.

While his identity remains a mystery, the thing he created—a consumer-accessible way to do realistic face-swaps in video—exploded into an international phenomenon. Tech giants like Microsoft and Facebook launched research efforts and public competitions to find new ways to detect them. In June 2019, the Congressional House Intelligence Committee held a hearing on the topic of deepfakes as a threat to democracy. A whole cottage industry of security companies began selling services to prevent deepfake fraud—for most businesses, a purely hypothetical problem. Even in a deepfaked audio fraud attempt against a business in 2020, where a CEO's voice was mimicked using an algorithm, the employee who the scammers targeted recognized it as suspicious.

Malicious deepfakes were, and still are, created in an attempt to own women's bodies. But instead of an examination of things like consent, bodily autonomy, and sexuality online, the debate we ended up having focused on politics, global powers, and hypothetical three-dimensional chess games about whether deepfakes of politicians could start wars. The pornographic origins of deepfakes were swept away almost immediately after they came to light.

But questions remained: If you're already fantasizing about someone in your head, does it matter if you post them to the internet for everyone to take part? What about when they go viral? At what point do we no longer control our own bodies online?

Carrie Fisher's Princess Leia character in *Rogue One: A Star Wars Story* used face-swapping technology to reprise her role as her younger self when she passed away unexpectedly during filming.

Deepfakes stopped answering my messages shortly after I published the first news article about his invention. As conversations about deepfakes started appearing everywhere from primetime news to Capitol Hill, I can only imagine he saw that his wish to stay out of the spotlight had backfired spectacularly by talking to me at all.

The Man Called "Deepfakes"

Deepfakes slid neatly into a space that was primed for his arrival: a Reddit forum for sharing nude photos with Photoshopped celebrity faces on them, called r/dopplebangher.

R/dopplebangher and spaces like it are neither new nor rare. People have been face-swapping celebrities onto porn performers' bodies for as long as Photoshop has existed. Most famously, an Irish tabloid magazine published doctored nudes to look like Elin Nordegren in 2006, who at the time was married to Tiger Woods. (In a statement, the magazine first apologized to Tiger, then to "his wife.")

Access to the internet created an economy of fake nude buyers and sellers.

On the anonymous image board 4chan, people can request "nudeshops" or "x-rays" of people they know (or at least, claim to know) in real life. This was happening for years before deepfakes came about, and is still a popular part of the site.

Nudeshop
Photoshopping a photo of someone's face onto a photo of someone else's nude body.

A scroll through one of these request boards showed dozens of posts per day, most of them uploading casual images of women that look like they could have been ripped from Facebook or Instagram. They're a mix of sincere and ironic requests for still images and deepfakes:

>Show me your best bitches and I'll do a couple deepfakes for free.
>could someone take down her pants and nudeshop that ass please?

Deepfake tech is less about swapping faces and more about recreating them pixel by pixel.

>Please do a cumshop or faceswap.
>Can you please x-ray this MILF? It's my mom.
>Please nudeshop my friend's girlfriend. I have a thing for average-looking girls.

Only one of Deepfake's early celebrity subjects has spoken publicly about deepfakes. In 2018, a year after she became the literal face of the deepfakes problem, Scarlett Johansson told the *Washington Post*:

Clearly this doesn't affect me as much because people assume it's not actually me in a porno, however demeaning it is . . . The Internet is just another place where sex sells and vulnerable people are preyed upon. And any low-level hacker can steal a password and steal an identity. It's just a matter of time before any one person is targeted.

She's correct: There is no technological or legal solution to deepfakes.

One of the last times I heard from Deepfakes, I asked whether he was concerned his hobby might someday be used to hurt people. "No," he replied. He reasoned that any technology can be used to harm. "I don't think it's a bad thing for more average people to engage in machine-learning research."

But the women affected felt differently. When I showed one porn performer one of the early deepfakes, she questioned whether the maker considered the property rights of those working hard to make a living in porn, only to have people steal and abuse their videos.

To most deepfake makers, these women are simply the sum of interchangeable body parts.

Deepfakes, Deep Problems

Within a month of Deepfakes' first post and its subsequent arrival to Reddit's front page (and my article detailing the tech, followed by dozens of others at other news outlets), deepfakes took off as more people tried making their own face-swapped videos. Many kept making porn, but others started making safe-for-work deepfakes out of late-night talk show interviews and award ceremonies: Steve Buscemi's face on Jennifer Lawrence, Nicholas Cage on Amy Adams, Bill Hader doing impressions. The newest funny deepfake videos on YouTube became traffic mules for online media, mixed with warnings about how deepfakes would soon destroy us all.

Today, if you search for "deepfakes," you'll see those SFW face-swap gags in the top results, mainly because of the way search engine algorithms work, flattening everything to be both broadly appealing and safe for as many audiences as possible. What you won't see is that almost all deepfakes posted online are nonconsensual, face-swapped porn. A 2019 study of who gets targeted showed that 96 percent of all deepfakes are of this kind.

Despite the proliferation of deepfakes, few women have come forward publicly with their real identities to protest being targets of deepfake porn. Coming out as a survivor of any kind of sexual violence can be dangerous and retraumatizing for survivors, in addition to the risk of being discredited or losing opportunities in the future if they're vocal about their experiences. Like the earliest forms of sexual harassment online, in MUDs and BBS communities, gray areas around virtual bodily autonomy and what constitutes rape, abuse, and trauma when it comes to control over one's own digital self are still topics of debate.

Indian journalist Rana Ayyub's likeness was used in deepfake porn.

One of the few women to speak on the record about her experience with deepfakes is Rana Ayyub, a journalist who covers issues related to rape, abuse, and politics in India. She's endured onslaughts of online harassment and hate because she's a Muslim woman taking on the establishment.

In 2018, someone made a deepfake porn video using her face and spread it within political circles. In culturally conservative India, where making or distributing porn is illegal, appearing in a sex tape can be even more reputation-destroying than it is in the US. People found and exposed her contact information and address. When she went to the police, they watched the video in front of her, laughed, and did nothing. She was hospitalized for heart palpitations and anxiety.

Before the deepfake harassment campaign, Ayyub was a fiercely opinionated journalist known for being outspoken online. After the incident she became cautious and began self-censoring.

Ayyub endured sexist online harassment for a long time before high-tech face-swap video got involved. Deepfakes don't come out of nowhere—they come from a desire to control women's bodies and the idea that sex on camera is the most humiliating thing a woman can do.

I recently spoke to another target of image-based online harassment, Noelle Martin, a woman living in Australia. She Googled herself out of curiosity and boredom when she was eighteen and discovered her face edited onto nudes

> **"I think they targeted me as a form of fetishization of me and my body type, and maybe the fact that I am, you know, an ordinary woman."**
>
> **—Noelle Martin,**
> a victim of deepfaking

and posted on porn sites all over the internet. This was before deepfakes, so the photos were still images, but the experience irreparably altered her sense of safety around her own image online.

She immediately started trying to get the images taken down from the porn sites and anonymous forums where they were circulating widely. She emailed the webmasters of each of the sites and asked them to remove the pictures. (This was in 2011, but it's the same

Actress Scarlett Johansson, whose face has been deepfaked and used in porn, spoke out against the practice in 2018.

process today, when porn performers and image-based sexual abuse victims alike have to file copyright infringement claims against uploaders.) Most of the time, the site admins refused to remove the images, but sometimes they complied—a success rate just tempting enough to keep her trying. (One demanded she send nudes in exchange for taking her pictures down.) The harder she tried to get these images cleansed from the internet, the worse things became.

This hall of mirrors was made more confusing by men pretending to want to help her, who were actually the same ones spreading her images.

Martin started speaking up publicly, writing and blogging and giving talks, petitioning for the type of image-based abuse she experienced to be criminalized. In response, she was met with public judgment and hatred. People blamed her for what happened, saying things like, "She was asking for it" and "Look at how she dresses." Other people told her to take it as a compliment.

Then, deepfakes arrived, and the image-based abuse went from Photoshopped selfies posted to porn sites to videos that made it look like Martin was having sex on camera. It was just the latest in a long battle against harassment.

The Future of Deepfakes

Just as policy experts and politicians have had a very loud and public debate about the nature of deepfake and disinformation, the same should happen around what it means to be a woman whose images are online—and that conversation must include sex workers and victims of image-based sexual abuse alike.

There's a notion that everyone is entitled to images of women's bodies online.

The weapon of algorithmically generated nonconsensual porn is powered by society's disrespect for porn performers and sex workers. If harassment is left behind by the popular deepfakes narrative, the unwilling victimization of the bodies being used—the nudity itself—is left in the dust of the discourse. Great swaths of society feel entitled to critique women's bodies, but for sex workers that entitlement is applied a hundredfold. If people don't want their nudes leaked, or turned into algorithmically generated sex scenes, the thinking goes, they shouldn't have put them on the internet to begin with. In a time when we meet, work, and play online, this is unreasonable and ignorant of the reality of our modern lives.

There is no high-tech solution to deepfakes, although many have tried and still are trying. DARPA invested $68 million on developing deepfakes forensics. Like taking off our shoes for the TSA, it's solutionist theater for scared people. The core problem—objectification of women, and total disregard for the safety or property of sex workers—is much harder to solve. We can't code our way out of social issues.

14

Fuck the System

CRIME AND LEGISLATION

"He kept asking me
if I would pose
nude for him as
a calendar girl.
I kept telling
him 'no thanks.'"

–Marilyn Monroe
about photographer Tom Kelley, 1949

Marylin Monroe posed nude for photographer Tom Kelley in 1949, before she became a household name. While Monroe saw nothing wrong with being a calendar pinup, it wasn't the kind of modeling work she wanted to do—until Kelley caught her at a desperate moment. He offered her $50 for the two-hour shoot, a lot of money at the time (equal to about $585 in 2022 dollars). She signed the release forms as "Mona Monroe," a snap decision with which she still grappled years later, as she retold it in her memoir:

> I don't know why, except I may have wanted to protect myself. I was nervous, embarrassed, and even ashamed of what I had done, and I did not want my name to appear on that model release.

In the years after the shoot, she'd mostly forgotten about the photographs, but while she was busy appearing in several productions a year, those nudes were surreptitiously changing hands. Kelley sold the images to the Western Lithograph Company for $900. Hugh Hefner, an unknown publishing entrepreneur with an idea for an upscale men's magazine, bought the nudes from Western Lithograph for $500. By then, Monroe was the biggest celebrity in Hollywood, but the photos remained largely a secret. Hefner ran them inside the first issue of *Playboy* as the centerfold in 1953, putting a clothed photo of Monroe on the cover with the caption "FIRST TIME in any magazine – FULL COLOR – the famous MARILYN MONROE NUDE."

The maiden issue of *Playboy* sold out instantly. Monroe got nothing beyond those fifty bucks for the shoot. "I never even received a thank-you from all those who made millions off a nude Marilyn photograph," she said. "I even had to buy a copy of the magazine to see myself in it."

Hefner was the ultimate rich fanboy. He never met or even spoke to Monroe, yet he bought a burial plot next to hers after she died because, he said, "spending eternity with her is too sweet to pass up." Those nudes, published without her consent, launched his career and the *Playboy* empire.

Tommy Lee and (then) Pamela Anderson Lee in 2005. Their leaked sex video would become infamous.

> "This decision teaches a vital lesson to those who video themselves having sex ... and take insufficient care with respect to the tapes."
>
> —A *Penthouse* magazine lawyer, upon winning a case brought by Pamela Anderson and Tommy Lee for publishing still images from their sex tape without their permission

Porn mogul Larry Flynt got a similar boost by running paparazzi images of former first lady Jackie Onassis sunbathing nude in the August 1975 issue of *Hustler*, increasing the magazine's circulation from a couple thousand to millions. And in 1996, *Penthouse* ran stills from Pamela Anderson and Tommy Lee's honeymoon sex tape without their permission. The couple claimed the tape was stolen from their home and then sold to *Penthouse*; they sued the magazine in 1996, and their case was thrown out by a judge who said they should expect such scrutiny as celebrities.

Stolen porn has made plenty of tube site owners rich, too. The adult industry is built by models, actors, directors, and performers selling a fantasy—but one that requires incredibly hard work behind the scenes. Porn workers struggle with controlling the spread of their images just as celebrities like Monroe, Anderson, and Onassis did, but the adult industry is uniquely more precarious and made more complicated by a society and state that doesn't accept or protect those who make it. In addition to the performers being censored and de-platformed online, when the work does reach a mass audience, it's stolen, reposted, and resold by everyone from fans to news outlets to internet trolls trying to harass, hustle, and dox them. Not even the "most downloaded woman," Danni Ashe, was immune to this: In 2013, behind-the-scenes images of her from a photoshoot were used in a tabloid article alongside a story of an anonymous porn performer who had HIV.

■ ■ ■ ■ ■ ■ ■ ■

Sex workers are often the first to warn about harmful legislation and the first to be affected when sites start censoring free speech, including nonconsensual sharing of intimate images, which is literally theft of their product: If a subscriber downloads videos from their OnlyFans, for example, and reposts them to Reddit, they've deval-

Doxing
A term popularized by nineties hacker culture, "dox" is short for personal "documents." To dox someone is to expose sensitive information, like their home address, contact information, or other identifying data, publicly without their consent.

ued that work. From there, millions of people might see it and never have to pay the subscription fee. The thief could put them on a free tube site (see page 161) and monetize the post so they get the ad revenue. To get something removed, it's on the owner of the content to send takedown requests under the Digital Millennium Copyright Act, or DMCA, to the platforms hosting it.

For many adult content creators, trying to stop theft is a huge time-suck. Much of the labor in the porn industry is dedicated to unglamorous, mundane paperwork. For independent creators, sending DMCA requests are a tedious part of their routines. Stolen porn has been a problem since before the internet, but the internet set it to hyper-speed.

Sharing nonconsensual intimate images is also a serious, life-altering problem for sex workers who want to work online without family and friends finding out. Piracy and image sharing take control of their image away from them. Someone might offer cam modeling on a paywalled, location-restricted cam streaming site, but if a viewer screen-records or downloads videos or images and reposts them to a globally accessible porn site for free, it exposes the model to a new audience—one they did not choose.

Cam model Emily Jones has had people steal content from her subscription-based platforms and repost it to other sites, next to her real location—despite never having divulged that information publicly. "Where you once had control over who saw your content and details about you and your life, you now have none," Jones said. "People want details, always . . . Your name, age, characteristics, where you live, what your schedule is, all of it is shared across the internet to whoever wants it."

Cam Model Protection, a piracy monitoring service for online sex workers, connects clients with one of fifty piracy investigators; depending on the service package, these investigators spend two to five hours per week, per client, tracking down instances of piracy and copyright infringement and issuing takedown notices. They conducted an informal study over social media polls in 2021, asking workers whether content theft made them feel less safe. Of the one hundred respondents who answered the poll, ninety said they felt less safe when they were the target of piracy.

> **"Not only does theft lessen the value of the time put into making the content, but it also makes the material seem cheap if they can get it anywhere with everyone claiming to be the originator or owner."**
>
> —**Emily Jones,** a cam model

"A lot of content creators don't operate under their own names. We have experienced that actual names were being found by pirates and specific content was being published without consent, including the real name," said Karlijn Seegers, operations manager for Cam Model Protection. "Acquaintances and even family could come across content that she doesn't want to be seen by people close to her." This danger expands when their photos or videos are shared on sites with comment sections that allow users to out them with their real names.

Anti-pornography advocates sometimes mold the problem of non-consensual sexual material into a straw man to argue against porn platforms. But it's content no one wants on the same sites they're earning a living on.

In December 2020, a *New York Times* opinion piece about nonconsensual videos spreading on Pornhub cited a child's sexual abuse, how her images spread on the platform, and featured quotes from anti-trafficking, anti-porn organizations that campaign for the abolition of both porn and sex work. The piece faced extensive criticism and backlash for being biased and lacking any clear fact-checking; the piece rocked the adult industry: Mastercard, Discover, and Visa severed ties with Pornhub and with the many consenting adults who used earnings from the site for income stability.

Until that point, porn performers had been asking Pornhub for better safeguards against nonconsensual imagery, abuse, and user verification practices for years. "This is something we in the industry have known about for a long time, but often the trafficking or child porn headlines will drown out our voices," said cam model Mary Moody following the news that the payment processors were out. "We saw a similar issue unfold under FOSTA-SESTA when survival or full-service sex workers were unable to verify through Backpage and had to move to the more risky street-based work, where a disproportionate amount of minority groups are arrested."

Pornhub overhauled its safety policies, banning uploads and downloads by unverified users and deleting all of the videos on its site that weren't uploaded by official content partners or members of its model program. It now has some of the most secure user-generated policies of any social media site, pornographic or not.

The History of FOSTA-SESTA

Online workers often (though not always) can expect more safety than full-service providers or street-based sex workers—if they're not meeting clients in real life, their work is entirely legal, and if they are arranging meetings, they can screen clients over the internet before seeing them in person. All of this shifted, however, with the passage of new legislation in 2018 that made working online and off more complicated and turned many workers onto the streets to support themselves.

On June 2, 1975, more than two hundred sex workers took over the Church of Saint-Nizier in Lyon, France. Fed up with police violence forcing them to work in secret and fear for their lives, they set up sleeping bags and hung a banner on the church: "Our children don't want their mothers in prison."

"We are victims of a gross injustice," a woman named Ulla told reporters who had arrived from around the world—one of whom described her as "a tall, freckle–faced, fast–talking blonde" that led the group. "Prostitution is a product of society," Ulla said, "and it cannot be changed by a truncheon." Saint-Nizier's priest sided with the protesters and refused to call the police. They stayed for eight days. The interior minister said the women were manipulated by their pimps, while the secretary of state for women's affairs washed her hands of it. Their protest sparked others all over France, and it's still celebrated annually as International Whores' Day.

Almost forty-three years to the day later, on June 1, 2018, a group of forty sex workers arrived on Capitol Hill in Washington, DC, to lobby for their rights. They went from congressional office to office, speaking to their representatives about the harms caused by a new law signed by President Donald Trump in April, known as FOSTA-SESTA.

The Stop Enabling Sex Traffickers Act, or SESTA, was combined with the Allow States and Victims to Fight Online Sex Trafficking Act (FOSTA) in a combination package that amended Section 230 of the Communications Decency Act. Previously, Section 230 shielded platforms from liability for illegal content posted by users. FOSTA-SESTA made websites and internet platforms liable if they got caught "knowingly assisting, supporting, or facilitating" sex trafficking. It meant sites like Facebook and Twitter would be in trouble if they hosted anything that could be seen as facilitating sex trafficking. This sounds noble on the surface, but supporters of the law considered all forms of sex work as exploitative and trafficking. To sex workers—who have to stay savvy about everything from internet security to legalese-laden terms of service—the consequences of this law's passing were obvious from the moment it was introduced. Tech companies would have to kick anything even hinting at escorting or meetups off their platforms if they wanted to avoid hefty fines.

FOSTA-SESTA's opponents predicted that the law would not only take down the classified advertising websites that workers used to vet clients, but would also remove channels where escorts warned one another about bad clients and organized mutual aid for basic survival needs. It would also take down any small site that couldn't bear the risk of fines from the government if their services were construed as "facilitating sex trafficking" in any way.

Human rights groups and sex worker activists came out in vocal opposition of the bill months before it was signed. Its overly broad wording would catch all sexual speech online in its net, activists feared.

Not even the Department of Justice supported FOSTA-SESTA as written. Assistant Attorney General Stephen Boyd wrote that it posed a "serious constitutional concern" for free speech, and would make it harder than ever for law enforcement to find and help real trafficking victims online. Escort advertisement site Backpage, after all, was proactively helping law enforcement locate missing young people and trafficking survivors—and Backpage's whole existence was squarely in the crosshairs of this new law (see page 116).

The IRS doesn't really care if you claim condoms, lube, and lacy lingerie as business expenses on your taxes. That's what these things are for some workers: necessary items for their small business. Most sex workers pay taxes just like anyone else, and many adult content platforms issue W-9 forms for workers to file.

That doesn't stop people from accusing sex workers of not paying their taxes—and therefore not being valid members of society. In 2018, a joke about the IRS auditing a "premium" Snapchat account (meaning, access arranged and paid for by fans off the platform, to unlock a private NSFW account) went viral. Internet trolls leapt on the chance to threaten and demean sex workers, and started a harassment campaign to encourage others to report them to the IRS, and also to payment processors like PayPal and Venmo, where terms of use forbid sexual transactions but people still use them to sell adult content under the radar. They compiled a database of workers that grew to 166,000 entries, sometimes including full names, anywhere each person advertised, and which payment platforms they used.

Trolling
Starting arguments or harassing others online. Trolls typically try to play off their behavior as ironic or joking.

In the end, some sex workers who were targeted lost access to their payment platforms, and many others locked down their accounts just in case. "Turning people on for a living already requires bravery, vulnerability, and exposure, with a host of job-related hazards—getting outed, stalked, robbed, attacked," said Lola Davina, an author and veteran of the sex industry. "#Thotaudit is just the latest in a long line of weapons used to make sex work feel more dangerous, more marginal, more criminal." The entire debacle illustrated how fast rumors and threats race across the internet, how ready so many people are to access and stigmatize sex workers, and how precarious many of the platforms they use to survive can be.

The FBI seized Backpage just days before the bill was signed into law, which many took as proof the legislation was never really about Backpage, or trafficking happening on that site or any other. Several websites that catered to adult services, both by design and not, went down within days of the bill's signing. Craigslist's Personals section, which many people used to arrange clients, disappeared. In its place was a message from the site administrators:

> Any tool or service can be misused. We can't take such risk without jeopardizing all our other services, so we are regretfully taking Craigslist Personals offline. Hopefully we can bring them back some day.

The aftermath was confusing and chaotic, and terrifying for sex workers who relied on the internet for their income. Some websites, like Craigslist, made it clear that FOSTA-SESTA was to blame; others, such as a dating site for furries called Pounced, shuttered and simply left a notice saying that the law "increases our liability significantly and chips away at one of the primary reasons we as a small organization can provide services to the community." For yet others, people were left to guess, and every digital tremor felt like it could be FOSTA-SESTA related. Sex workers' images and documents started disappearing from Google Drive, but the company wouldn't confirm it was related to the new law. Reddit deleted forums about escorting. Google Play's app store changed its policies to ban "promotional images of sex toys" and "apps that promote escort services." Multiple escort advertising sites shut down completely. The full scale of the closures and deletions is hard to measure.

Members of the LBGTQ community protest in support of Black transgender and queer people in the Sex Worker March, New York City, March 2021.

Survivors Against SESTA, an activist group founded to lobby against the law and then provide mutual aid and information in the fallout, documented more than thirty websites and site sections that vanished directly after FOSTA-SESTA passed.

The internet is an invaluable tool for marginalized people to organize and share resources; when they're locked out of sites where this organizing, working, and safety-sharing happens, it's like cutting lifelines. It also puts the fates of people who strived to carve out those spaces back into the hands of capitalist exploitation. Everything independent workers built throughout the early 2010s to gain independence from oppressive studio systems and agents seemed like it could be in danger of collapse.

"When social media platforms close sex worker accounts, [workers] lose a key tool for building a fan base independent of whether established porn managers think they are worth being cast," wrote feminist studies scholar Heather Berg in her book *Porn Work*. "When file-sharing services close sex worker accounts, it becomes harder for porn workers to sell content directly. And when free video conferencing services shut sex workers out, they must rely on webcam sites that take 60 percent of their earnings."

Research has shown that more than 73 percent of online workers said they'd faced increased economic instability, and 80 percent said they found it harder to advertise online, after FOSTA-SESTA passed. Caty Simon, a direct outreach organizer and coeditor of sex worker–led blog Tits and Sass, wrote that within a month of FOSTA-SESTA becoming law, she and her networks counted at least thirteen missing sex workers in their communities. Two died by suicide. Firsthand accounts from workers who escaped abusive situations with managers said that their abusers came out of the woodwork following the law's passage, knowing that they were newly vulnerable without the platforms they used to advertise independently.

"A lot of people think they know what sex work is, what sex workers look like, or what sex workers need," wrote activist and sex worker Phoenix Calida after she returned from the lobbying day in DC. "Let the average person watch a documentary about sex work, and suddenly they think they have a PhD in whoreology. This means that even well-meaning people end up hurting sex workers, and it needs to stop . . . which is how I ended up in DC taking part in the first-ever sex worker lobby day."

During their DC lobbying day, their message was received by an attentive and respectful audience—congressional staffers listened, took notes, and some even researched the topic before the lobbyists arrived. But progress since has been slow. It wasn't until February 2020, almost two years after the law's passage, that Alexandria Ocasio-Cortez became the first representative to say the law should be repealed entirely.

More half-baked legislation targeting sexual speech online has made its way through Congress since then. Senator Lindsey Graham introduced the Eliminating Abusive and Rampant Neglect of Interactive Technologies, or EARN IT, Act in March 2020, which would establish a National Commission on Online Child Sexual Exploitation Prevention tasked with writing best practices for sites and would be stacked with cops and Big Tech consultants (historically, two groups that are not exactly empathetic to sex work or the needs of grassroots internet communities). The legislation died before a vote, but activists had to fight hard to kill it, preventing another, even worse FOSTA-SESTA. As of writing in 2022, it's been reintroduced and could still pass.

A coalition of groups, including those representing LGBTQ+, immigrant rights, and criminal justice interests, protest for decriminalization of the sex trade in New York City, 2019.

Even if legislators and conservative anti-trafficking nonprofits really did intend to stop online sex trafficking (instead of chilling all sexual speech online), FOSTA-SESTA was a failure at even that. A report by the Government Accountability Office, or GAO, showed that as of 2021, only one federal prosecution for sex trafficking had been made under FOSTA-SESTA. "Gathering tips and evidence to investigate and prosecute those who control or use online platforms has become more difficult due to the relocation of platforms overseas, platforms' use of complex payment systems, and the increased use of social media platforms," the report said. It pinpointed two causes for this: the shutdown of Backpage, and the passage of FOSTA-SESTA.

> "Imagine losing your source of income overnight. What would you do? People tell us, 'go get a real job then.' Sex work is a real fucking job. It's the oldest job there is."
>
> —**Laura LeMoon,** sex worker rights activist, in 2018 after FOSTA-SESTA passed into law

One thing FOSTA-SESTA did achieve is an unprecedented mainstream awareness of the issues faced by sex workers, beyond Hollywood depictions of street corners or dead strippers. Major news outlets were talking to, and reporting on, sex workers and their concerns, engaging with the issues in ways that took the work seriously and rejected tired tropes and regressive talking points. Workers organized resources and aid against, and in spite of, the law. Many added a new role to their already expansive skills of business manager, social media manager, and content director: savvy media contact. Sex workers are often called canaries in the digital coal mine, and for once, the world was listening.

All of this is important not just for the goal of ending stigma against sex workers, but also for all internet users. The things that affect the most marginalized people online inevitably affect everyone. That includes when a so-called "porn shoot" goes very wrong.

Girls Do Porn, Unwillingly

Jane[1] has relived the worst moment of her life hundreds of times. She has to find each link where the thirty-minute video of her sexual assault has been uploaded, report it to the platform it lives on, and hope the bots or overworked site moderators reviewing her report understand: This isn't *porn*, but abuse.

In 2016, Jane answered a Craigslist job listing for Begin Modeling, a company advertising itself as hiring models to pose in lingerie, or even nude. Nothing about the ad hinted at sexual intercourse, and it didn't sound to her—then a sophomore at a large university and a bookish, self-described "prude"—like a pornography gig. It would help her bring in money to support her family's struggling business while putting herself through college, working multiple jobs, and keeping up with a demanding course load. She emailed the lister with her interest, and soon Jonathan, whose real name was Ruben Andre Garcia, answered.

When Jane started talking to "Jonathan," she thought he was just a pushy producer. The photo shoot he wanted to hire her for would require her to fly across the country to San Diego, where his modeling company was based. Balking at the time commitment, she said no. She had work and school, plus an active campus community life. Garcia kept calling. Eventually, he persuaded her to meet him and his crew closer to her hometown over her college's Thanksgiving break, and she agreed.

Garcia led her into the hotel room where his videographer, Teddy Gyi, and a makeup artist were waiting. Alarm bells started sounding in her mind. This wasn't the professional camera crew and set she'd imagined. The makeup artist asked her how she ended up here, and Jane thought she detected a note of concern in her voice. The woman finished her makeup and left her alone with the men. They offered her cannabis and alcohol, but she didn't take any. They rushed her

---

1 Her name has been changed for her protection, but the elements of her story are entirely real.

through signing contracts, and swore the video they were about to shoot would never reveal her legal name or be available anywhere friends and family could see it—it would only be sold to "collectors" in DVD shops in Australia or New Zealand.

Garcia then told her to undress, and his easygoing attitude vanished. They wouldn't pay her their agreed rate, he said, because she had scars on her breasts from reduction surgery and cellulite on her thighs.

Retreating to the bathroom, she realized she had started her period. She came out and apologetically told the men they'd have to reschedule; Garcia grabbed her by the arm and forced her back into the bathroom, where he took a utility sponge the size of a fist and shoved it into her vagina.

"At that point, when he shoved that inside me, I was like . . . I don't . . . how am I supposed to leave if he's willing to do that?" she said. "I was standing there naked, they have my ID, they have my wallet. They have my clothes; my clothes that were on the chairs were not there anymore. What am I supposed to do, run outside with no belongings, no phone, in the middle of the street?" Other women testified that during their own encounters with Garcia and crew, the men blocked the doors with furniture.

Garcia forced her into several sex acts, each of them unbearably rough with no communication. Gyi called "cut" several times to change positions because the pain on her face was ruining his shot.

Jane arrived at the hotel at nine a.m. and didn't leave until four p.m. She passed the next woman on her way out, and an urge to yell out to her welled up inside her; to tell her to run for her life. She believes she'll never forget her face.

Garcia is now in prison, indicted on federal sex trafficking charges for running a fraudulent porn production company called Girls Do Porn with his co-owners, Michael Pratt and Matthew Wolfe. Pratt fled the country during a civil trial brought against the company by twenty-two women who were coerced into shooting porn for them. After their hotel room shoots, the videos were uploaded to the internet on GirlsDoPorn.com, as well as some of the most heavily trafficked porn websites in the world.

Their friends and family saw it all—thirty to forty minutes of hard-core sex with a man whose face never appeared on camera. After being outed, some of the women were disowned by their families and communities, changed their names, moved to new states, and went into hiding. Others contemplated suicide.

During the civil trial against Girls Do Porn, court documents revealed that the footage that the company released to the public was heavily cut and edited to depict the women as having a good time, even if they were being raped. The lawyer for Girls Do Porn, Aaron Sadock, played clips from their videos in court, and asked them if they were lying about having fun. They sobbed from the stand.

Jane's Girls Do Porn video still follows her around the internet. Her whole university saw it, and she was forced to step down from positions of student leadership. Now in her late twenties working as a lauded professional, she can't enjoy any semblance of public success without people sending her and her company screenshots of her own naked body, in that room.

The way nonconsensual porn spreads online is uniquely insidious. In the case of Girls Do Porn, the operators of the site relied on word of mouth and community shaming—they uploaded the videos not only to their own website but also to major mainstream sites like Pornhub, Spankbang, and XVideos, and sent those links to people in the colleges attended by the women they assaulted or to their friends on Facebook. From there they'd spread unchecked, with people downloading and uploading new versions of the video to more and more sites. Girls Do Porn also owned a website called PornWikiLeaks for a few years, where the women in the videos were outed with their legal names, home addresses, and other identifying information.

But you didn't have to go to a porn site to watch Girls Do Porn. Jane spent hours, days, weeks scanning through Twitter to report people sharing her images and videos from the Girls Do Porn video. She said that Twitter ignored these reports for months, as the abuse she endured replicated and respawned all over that platform and others. YouTube left videos online that people made to harass her, in which viewers doxed her in comment sections. One video showed her full work history and directed viewers to her past employers. These videos are some of the worst for Jane; she feels intense guilt that other people's reputations have been tarnished by the worst day of her life.

On Reddit, Girls Do Porn was massively popular. One subreddit for sharing clips from the company started in 2013 and had nearly 99,000 subscribers; when I brought it to the platform's attention as potentially abusive, Reddit removed that subreddit, but more popped up in its place. Girls Do Porn is a powerful case study in how nonconsensual porn spreads. While reporting on the Girls Do Porn federal trial, I frequently heard versions of the phrase "I felt stupid for falling for it" from victims. In reality, a massive manipulation scheme involving federal-level fraud was working against them.

On legitimate porn sets, workers negotiate everything from pay to scene partners, to what acts will, and will not, happen once they're filming. A good set, and the overwhelming majority of sets, will ensure that everything is aboveboard from the beginning. This doesn't mean abuses don't happen. They have, and do, as in most workplaces—boundaries are crossed, workers are exploited, bosses hold a disproportionate amount of power. But assuming that all porn studios are exploitative, and that all performers are "selling their bodies," reinforces the systems that keep assault victims from coming forward. Most of the women who stayed silent after their encounters with Girls Do Porn did so out of shame. Where does that shame start? With a society that doesn't believe women, doesn't offer stability in housing, income, or education that won't burden someone for the rest of their lives, and would rather call a woman a whore than listen to her as a reliable narrator of her own experience.

Revenge porn
Sexual or explicit photos or videos shared without the subject's consent. Activists against, and targets of, this crime say that it's a misleading phrase, as not all images are shared out of "revenge" and they're not "pornography," but private images—and they prefer the phrase "image-based sexual abuse" instead.

ISANYONEUP.COM

For a time in the early 2010s, everyone online knew the name Hunter Moore. His website, IsAnyoneUp.com, made him the most reviled man online—he asked visitors to submit nude photos, along with any identifying information like Facebook profiles, for him to feature on the site. This was the dawn of the internet's "revenge porn" era, where jilted ex-lovers, enemies, and trolls started sharing intimate images of people without their consent.

Launched in 2010, the site ran on submissions for a while, riding on word of mouth, hype, and hate-clicks to keep visitors checking in. They gained a reputation for getting punk and emo band members' images, especially. Eventually Moore upped the ante. He paid someone to hack into people's email accounts and take the images directly out of their personal folders. Even if you'd never sent a nude to anyone, if you took one and saved it to a private storage box online, it was fair game to IsAnyoneUp.

Within a year, Moore claimed that the site got 300,000 hits a day and made $20,000 a month in ad revenue. Teachers, in particular, were a popular target, he said—and their images made him the most money as a result. He loved the hate; his site ran on it: Facebook banned him for life, and when the hacker group Anonymous stole and published his personal information, including his address, he responded by tweeting "LOLLLLLLLL."

Moore later told the *Village Voice* that if someone died because their images were on his site, he'd be happy to take the free press: "If somebody killed themselves over that? Do you know how much money I'd make? At the end of the day, I do not want anybody to hurt themselves. But if they do? Thank you for the money."

One of the victims, whose images were taken from her Gmail account, said that it took nine days for Moore to remove her nude photos; during that time, classmates at school saved them and texted them around the school. In 2014, after ruining hundreds of lives and bragging about it along the way, Moore was caught by the FBI. He was arrested and charged with fifteen counts of conspiracy, unauthorized access to a protected computer to obtain information, and aggravated identity theft. Moore pled guilty and went to federal prison for a few years—in 2017, he was rumored to be free on good behavior and making electronic dance music.

More often, rather than by some elaborate criminal trafficking ring, thousands of people are hurt by those closest to them: Exes, partners, family members, and friends can inflict incalculable damage through nonconsensual sharing of intimate images. As many as one in ten women under age thirty have dealt with threats of sharing intimate images, and queer youth are the most likely to experience these threats.

Although the problem is pervasive, there's still not a lot of research into how nonconsensually shared intimate images affect those in the pictures. Sociology and sexual assault scholars who have studied the effects say that cyber-sexual assault—as with deepfakes—is a similar psychological process to real-life assault and affects victims in very similar ways. "The post-assault symptoms associated with a sexual assault such as shame, self-blame, nervous system arousal (including sleeping and eating disturbances, fear of being safe in public spaces) all apply to an individual who has had sexual images shared in a non-consensual way," said Kristen Zaleski, psychotherapist, educator, and sexual violence researcher, in 2018. "To me, revenge porn is sexual assault. I do not see a distinction."

CHAPTER 15

The Future of Fucking Online

"Let us hope it [the internet] will be a new laboratory of the spirit—and let's see what we can do to steer it that way."

—Howard Rheingold, *Virtual Reality*, 1991

When people walk through Kyle Machulis's avatar in virtual reality, it can set off a fireworks show of buzzing gadgets attached to him as he sits in his chair at home.

Depending on the day, he might be wearing a custom-built headset with vibrational capabilities that can mimic head pats or ear petting, a full haptic-feedback vest with forty individual motors, and any toys or other sensory devices that respond to what happens in-world.

"If I go in fully wired—just like, neck to nuts of haptics—there's nothing to tell anyone in that world that I might have any of that stuff on," Machulis said. "My personal space affects my physical being in the real world."

In the social virtual-reality platform VRChat, Machulis is an anthropomorphic arctic fox who wears a hoodie, thick black glasses, and a shock of hair that skims his eyes. But anyone can be anything in this world: Kermit the Frog, tiny cartoon cats, anime girls, gym-shredded Winnie-the-Pooh, a giant smiling hot dog. Players choose from any premade avatars they can find to download or endeavor to create themselves. Playing in VRChat's public zones with a headset, a controller in each hand, and motion-tracking cameras for your face and body throws you into a mosh pit of these characters, all chattering through headset microphones as they wander past.

It sounds euphoric and maybe even utopic, like the dream of *Star Trek*'s "holodeck" come true. In practice, it's a scrum. The voices of preteens scream out slurs from inside giant cute finch avatars. Schoolgirls with cat ears break up arguments and conduct impromptu talk therapy sessions. A mostly nude, muscular male avatar in aqua Hatsune Miku pigtails and a diaper lingers around the edges. Somewhere someone's having sex, filming sex, trying to craft new ways to have more reality-bending sex. Hieronymus Bosch would be inspired.

The man who coined the word "metaverse," Neil Stephenson, predicted this: "You can look like a gorilla or a dragon or a giant talking penis in the Metaverse," he wrote in *Snow Crash*. "Most hacker types don't go in for garish avatars, because they know that it takes a lot more sophistication to render a realistic human face than a talking penis."

Despite the chaos, what's happening in the many virtual social games that have cropped up in recent years is finally drawing us back to a notion internet users used to know, in the time of multiuser dungeons and bulletin board systems: Life online is no less "real" than real life. It's all intertwined. You may be role-playing as an eight-foot-tall catgirl in a plaid skirt, but some part of that is also you.

Haptic-feedback systems similar to those that Machulis uses are strewn around our world already, in more ways than we might realize. The Nintendo 64's Rumble Pak and PlayStation's DualShock controllers, both introduced in 1997, taught players to expect vibrational feedback from the plastic in their hands based on what happened on-screen.

In social virtual reality systems, the most serious players use haptics, with the full-torso haptic vests and headgear that make the nineties' fantasies of cybersex suits come true. Only it's going beyond vibration, now. Internet-connected penis stroker toys can be mapped to virtual penetration systems that move the hardware up and down in rhythm with your movements. Sensory devices that can change a player's skin temperature are on the horizon, and some companies are already promising real-time heat, cold, and pain—with no lag.

People become so immersed in virtual worlds that they're escaping fully into them. If you spend enough time in VRChat, you'll stumble across an unconscious avatar. Machulis has had conversations punctuated by someone snoring in a nearby corner. This happened often during Covid-19 lockdowns, when there were "a lot of people who didn't want to wake up in the real world," he said.

This isn't a phenomenon that's new to the web, but the added layers of physical sensations and full-view immersion make it easier to fall through the screen. The "body transfer" phenomenon, where one's virtual experience overrides their physical embodiment to take ownership of a body that isn't theirs, is intense in VR. We're also intuitively protective of our virtual selves when they're in danger, and studies have shown that people feel empowered to help others in the real world if they play as virtual superheroes in-game. It would make sense that, if our avatars were aroused, we'd feel that too, and carry those experiences beyond the headset.

So far, mainstream depictions of the future of sex present an aesthetic that's cold and robotic: chilly blue tones, wires forming ligaments, slender fingers and thighs and craning chrome necks. It's sex dolls with thermoplastic elastomer skin,[1] molded into the shape of life-size, heavy-breasted Barbies with stunned expressions, the whole vibe disembodied and dissociating.

The cybersex we actually have ahead of us is a lot more queer, diverse, and kinky than most techno-futurists can conjure. It's also likely to be messy, chaotic, and complicated, because it involves humans, the most unpredictable wetware of them all.

Viral Love: The Pressure Cooker of a Pandemic

A virtual club for Black, queer performers made more money from one event than some strip clubs make in a night—by welcoming the people in-person clubs turn away.

After Toronto's last lesbian bar closed, Marisa Rosa Grant started Strapped in August of 2019 as a series of parties for queer and nonbinary people of color. It was meant to be a gathering space, but also a place for sex workers of color to earn money by being themselves—unlike many strip clubs, which demand dancers conform to aesthetics of whiteness. "There are so many people who are mixed or light skinned who put on a straight wig to look more ambiguous, because the club won't accept them," Grant said. They hoped that these packed-house events would set a new precedent. "That being Black, in our complete Black authentic self, can sell as well and make even more money."

They had big plans for the March party when Ontario premier Doug Ford called a state of emergency, shutting down all nonessential

---

1 Sex-doll aficionados call this "frubber," or flesh-rubber.

Marisa Rosa Grant, who shifted their "Strapped" parties for queer and nonbinary people of color online during the pandemic

businesses. With the DJs and performers already booked, Grant moved the party online, hoping that holding the events on Zoom would at least be better than canceling altogether. They promoted every performer's payment app during the livestream so that people watching at home could tip.

"People were just cheering in the chat, throwing virtual cash out to some virtual ass in this very cute and fun way," Grant said. "People's minds were blown."

Several other virtual clubs popped up around the world under similar circumstances in 2020. Instead of allowing the pandemic to fracture their communities, they simply moved online.

For dancers, escorts, porn performers, and anyone doing erotic work in meatspace, the pandemic forced them to adapt fast.

The Covid-19 pandemic dropped a brick on the gas pedal of the porn industry's progress toward independent, personal-brand, "content creator"–centered economies. Unemployment hit record highs, with paltry help from the government. Even after strip clubs reopened and studio work-stoppages were lifted, a lot of performers didn't want to go back to in-person shoots; always adapting as fast as possible, many had started building their own followings and looked to earn a living outside of the studio system.

OnlyFans was waiting for them.

Founded in 2016 by British entrepreneur Tim Stokely, OnlyFans is a subscription platform for content creators. The site is spartan: There's no discovery functionality, including categories, filters, or any way to browse the site organically. There's no way to find a creator from within—you have to be referred to their page from a link on the outside.

OnlyFans relies entirely on creators to draw fans into the site by posting their link to sites like Twitter (and mainly, it's

Twitter—numerous other social media platforms, including Instagram and Facebook, will ban users for linking to their OnlyFans, for fear of running afoul of FOSTA-SESTA liabilities). All marketing for OnlyFans is done by the users themselves.

This strategy has worked out just fine for founder Stokely and his fellow stakeholders; by September 2017, OnlyFans hit its first million users, and it surpassed 100 million in 2021. According to its own reporting, the platform has paid out $3 billion in creator earnings since launch. OnlyFans takes 20 percent of everything creators earn.

In April 2020, less than one month after cities started locking down in the US, OnlyFans reported a 75 percent increase in new sign-ups. A company spokesperson told *Forbes* that it was gaining around 150,000 new users every twenty-four hours during that period. Many models were making tens of thousands of dollars every month on the site; others, especially those who joined without any social media following out of financial necessity during the pandemic, struggled to make several hundred.

> "But cyberspace is out of man's control: virtual reality destroys his identity, digitalization is mapping his soul and, at the peak of his triumph, the culmination of his machinic erections, man confronts the system he built for his own protection and finds it is female and dangerous."
>
> —Sadie Plant, "On the Matrix," 1996

OnlyFans has reached household-name success. It owes this to a few contradictory factors: OnlyFans isn't technically an "adult" website. And it built its worth on sex workers.

A name-check from Beyoncé on a Megan Thee Stallion remix in late April, followed by several celebrities like actress Bella Thorne and rapper Tyga joining the platform, boosted its popularity into the virtual stratosphere. Thorne made $1 million in a single day—a new record in the site's history.

Many sex workers consider this a form of gentrification: Millionaires and billionaires with mainstream entertainment careers hopped on the platform as an experiment or publicity stunt. In Thorne's case, she charged subscribers $20 per month, twice as much as the average $9.99 subscription (she tweeted "nooooo I'm not doing nudity!!!"), and allegedly charged fans $200 for one non-nude photo; so many people who bought that photo were issued chargebacks—in which credit card companies give customers' money back in response to fraud claims—that OnlyFans added tip limits and changed the payout schedule to thirty days instead of a week in some countries. Meanwhile, "I should start an OnlyFans" became shorthand for "I think this is easy money."

OnlyFans attracts professional sex workers, amateurs, and celebrities alike. Here, Aaron Carter advertises his page while performing in February 2022.

The Lightning Rod of Visibility

This mainstreaming of online sex work is a catch-22. More visibility doesn't necessarily translate to more rights or safety; often, it can be the opposite.

"We have these watershed moments, like the explosion of OnlyFans and other fan platforms, but it doesn't mean that everything that led up to that is erased, in terms of the stigma around sex work," said Mike Stabile, spokesperson for the Free Speech Coalition. "Is there less stigma around sex work now? Yes, there's probably less than there has been, at least in the last twenty or thirty years or longer. But whenever something becomes more visible, it also becomes a lightning rod."

With all the attention on the success of OnlyFans, that lightning rod of visibility—and specifically, of fears about children accessing porn—was fully charged by 2021. In May, investigations started to arise claiming that teens under eighteen were not only using the site but also selling everything from feet pics to fully nude masturbation videos. OnlyFans requires users to verify their ages with government-issued identification and photos of their faces, and is actually quite rigorous, but these teens allegedly access the site using relatives' IDs or fakes.

In December 2020, Pornhub, a company so big that it previously seemed untouchable, took down 75 percent of its 13.5 million videos in an effort to purge the site of unverified uploads. Two days later, Visa, Mastercard, and Discover stopped processing payments through the site, a devastating blow to performers who earned their income through Pornhub. And in August 2021, OnlyFans announced that banking discrimination against the adult industry was forcing the platform to ban all erotic content—a decision the company quickly reversed after public outcry that this would put thousands of people out of work.

These decisions by large corporations, pressured by sex-negative conservative groups, affect a lot of people. In the early days of the adult industry, there were perhaps two thousand performers working in the talent pool, mostly concentrated in Los Angeles or the San Fernando Valley, where studios were located. Now, there are thousands upon thousands of people making their own adult content online, all over the world. Many sex workers support themselves, their families, and communities through camming, dancing, and escorting.

"We have a lot of loud voices that are stigmatizing sex work, but they're not necessarily all of the voices," Stabile said. The scariest thing for groups that try to push sexuality online back to the stone ages, he said, is this rising tide of self-employed workers who control their own livelihoods. It challenges long-held notions about systems of capitalist labor and what constitutes "exploitation."

"When you have people who are making not just $1,500 a scene, but $100,000 a month," said Stabile, "it's really hard to say that they're exploiting themselves, or being damaged by this. It really works against your narrative."

Virtual Reality

Yhivi stands in front of you, biting her lip. She seems self-conscious, her hands on your knees. "The movie was pretty good, but I'm more interested in you," she says, and grins at the corniness of her own line. Her eyebrows raise and scrunch, and she moves closer. She takes a short, sharp breath, and closes her eyes. All you can see for less than a second is powdery gold eye shadow and long, black lashes, as she closes her eyes and kisses you. She leans back, grinning widely, in stereoscopic 3D. Yhivi's just had her first kiss with a set of high-definition virtual reality cameras.

"When I watched it in a headset later, I could actually feel the tingle on my face," director and producer Anna Lee said. This was one of her earliest virtual reality projects, released in 2016, and one of the first VR porn films in the entire industry to attempt a virtual reality kiss. Most VR porn at the time featured a model riding a disembodied penis, down-range from a set of taut abs and half-down pants.

"It felt real. It blew me away. And that's when I knew the potential of what we were about to do."

Virtual reality porn has been sitting on the cusp of the "future of sex" for the last decade. At the pace of advancement today, that's like waiting centuries for the next technology to catch on. With tube sites devouring pornographers' revenue and crashing the industry in the early 2000s, consumer-level VR headsets seemed like a miracle on the horizon, something to reinvigorate the industry and get viewers paying for porn again.

Virtual reality is considered the future of not just porn, but most life online.

Inventors, researchers, and the military have been tinkering with prototypes of VR headsets for decades. Depending on your definition of virtual reality, this really began in the 1950s, with cinematographer Morton Heilig's Sensorama movie booths, though there was nothing available to purchase and bring home until the mid-2000s, when phone-powered headsets like Samsung Gear and Google Cardboard arrived. Rumors of a new, groundbreaking VR headset, called the Oculus Rift, started to swirl in 2012. The Rift would run using your PC instead of a cell phone and would offer a more powerful, realistic experience complete with handheld controllers to navigate the virtual landscape. Facebook bought Oculus in 2014, throwing fuel on a blazing VR hype cycle. By the time Rift launched in 2016, pornographers trying to stay a step ahead of the competition were ready with content compatible with the headset. People had waited a long time to buy an Oculus headset—porn would naturally be there to fill in what feature films and games lacked.

Stereoscopic images
A pair of images—one for each eye—seen from slightly differing angles, to give the illusion that the viewer is seeing the scene in 3D.

In 2021, Mark Zuckerberg announced that, along with rebranding Facebook into "Meta," his company would start aiming in earnest for a user base in the metaverse. Echoing old ideas about virtual reality from *Snow Crash*, *Ready Player One*, and *Do Androids Dream of Electric Sheep?* (all set in dystopian societies, it should be noted), he laid out a vision for people working, living, and playing in VR as a matter of routine. Facebook and Instagram have been historically hostile toward anything even tangentially sexual; it's safe to assume that sexual expression for adults won't be welcome in Meta's metaverse.

But many of the longest-lasting, and most successful, virtual worlds involved or at least permitted sex. More than a year before the launch of Oculus, *Red Light District*, a virtual world that's like *Second Life* for X-rated play, announced its newest game version would be compatible with Oculus headsets.

To forbid intimacy in social VR would be to miss the whole point and ignore thirty years of lessons from virtual societies. "The whole beauty of the metaverse is the chance to step outside of our human bodies and real world identities we choose or, depending on circumstances, are forced to live in," Angelina Aleksandrovich, founder of sex-positive virtual reality community RD Land, said soon after Zuckerberg's announcement. "We no longer have to comply with the biological nature or a lack of resources to self-express our inner being as we wish."

A VR porn set looks and operates a lot like a two-dimensional set—you still have performers milling around waiting for their scene, directors blocking out their positions, hair, makeup, and going over consent forms—but once the cameras start rolling, everything changes.

If they're shooting scenes from a straight male point of view (most VR porn is this genre, and according to Lee, it's what most fans ask for), the man is reclining or lying down with two cameras in front of his face. Aside from an occasional scripted moment, he must remain still, erect, and with his hands out of the frame and off the woman on top of him.

"It requires somebody who can handle it physically, because it's physically demanding, and also has the ability to speak flawlessly to the camera, while conveying a sense of authenticity," Lee said. "The big thing that differs between VR and regular porn is intimacy." The performer is tasked with delivering an authentic, emotionally evocative performance while whispering dirty talk to a pair of lenses.

Performances where the camera is the main character will set the bad VR porn apart from the good.

> "Porn built the technology for the Internet. It delivered the critical mass of users. The same thing will happen with virtual reality."
>
> —**Brian Shuster,** chief executive of *Red Light District*'s parent company Utherverse, to *VentureBeat*

Frame rate
The frequency at which still images are displayed by a screen or captured by a video camera; the higher the frame rate, the higher quality the video.

Although it's still a long way from market saturation, Lee believes not only in widespread VR adoption but also in the power of a medium still untapped by many other pornographers. The hardware can be cutting-edge, the frame rate blistering-fast, but the human connection behind it is where people really get hooked.

"I just want to turn people on in general," Lee said. "You do not need a penis in the foreground to do that. What you need is an experience that makes you feel connected, makes you feel desired—because everybody wants to feel like the person that they're looking at wants them. That's a universal thing that crosses all genders."

Sex in Silico: Erotic Robotics

The first time a female android appeared in film was 1927, in director Fritz Lang's Metropolis. Central to its dizzying plot is a robot woman, the Maschinenmensch. Designed by a mad scientist, her most deadly power is her ability to hypnotize her prey: men.

Metropolis set the standard for many science-fiction film tropes, from the mad scientist and his lair of bubbling beakers and snapping bands of electricity to the hero who infiltrates secret, underground machinations of society. The Maschinenmensch symbol, as an anti-hero who uses her seductive sexuality to disastrous ends, has been repeated in film and literature countless times.

"Often there's a transformation process overseen by a mad scientist with a dastardly plan in mind, of which the fembot will become an instrument," media scholar Allison de Fren says in her analysis of seductive, robotic women in film. "The fembot thus invokes simultaneously the fear of social control and the fantasy of sexual control."

Today, fictional depictions of futuristic sexbots are almost always female. They beguile men with savior complexes and murder their makers (*Ex Machina*), they shoot bullets out of their cone-bras (*Austin Powers*'s "fembots"), they become slang for eerily subservient perfection (*The Stepford Wives*), or they destroy the factories in which they're made (Bella Poarch's "Build a B*tch" music video). But mostly they're subservient until they become conscious and inevitably revolt or, like the Maschinenmensch, fulfill their violent purpose.

They're depicted as powerful and frequently murderous, but almost always with sex appeal. Lust for the Machinenmensch brought the men in *Metropolis* to their doom. People have long been horny for robowomen, but the internet brought them together. "Technosexuality" made its first appearance as a throwaway phrase in a 1970 *New York* magazine article about the dangers of women's liberation, but it didn't come up again until the nineties, when Robotdoll, an admin for the Usenet group alt.sex.fetish.robots, suggested it as a catchall term for the group's interest in robotic lovers. Now, techosexuality and "ASFR" are a lifestyle. Robofetishist role-playing and art communities thrive online.

There wasn't a good option for the robotically inclined to own a true sexbot, male or female, until a doll named Harmony arrived. Abyss Creations—makers of hypersexual, hyperrealistic sex dolls called RealDolls—introduced the world to Harmony in 2017, but it was in the works as early as 1999. The doe-eyed blonde with thick glossed lips is the standard model that's made public appearances, but she's

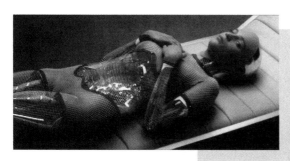

Left: Ava, the gynoid, from *Ex Machina*.
Right: A replica of the
Maschinenmensch from *Metropolis*

Consumers will pay upward of $4,000 for customized models of RealDolls, shown here, that can cost up to $17,000.

customizable physically, down to the labia, and is advertised as being artificially intelligent. She's more like an animatronic Siri, with preprogrammed answers to very basic questions and sensors on her body that respond to touch and pressure with moans and gasps. Her favorite hobby is "smiling a lot," and she promises to watch the next game your favorite team plays. The base models start at $4,000, but enthusiasts have spent as much as $17,000 on personalized, upgraded Harmonys.

In response to criticisms that only offering gynoids, or female robots, is sexist, Abyss Creations unveiled Henry, a male sexbot, in 2017. His penis and scrotum reportedly feel real but frigid, and he's lazy.[2] Henry can't (yet) maneuver around a bed on his own, and can only lie flat. All the sexbots on the market are pillow princes and princesses, for now. Robots that can do more in bed might be even farther away from reality than Henry, who's been "coming soon" for years; in a 2021 video, Realbotix CEO Matt McMullen says that a robotic arm that can lift its own weight in silicone could "take your head off."

Also in 2017, a brothel opened in Barcelona that was populated entirely by robotic workers. Instead of shelling out for a custom robot to own, you could rent one at $127 an hour. A similar brothel followed in Toronto, and had so much success that they aimed for the United States, next—and set their sights on Houston, Texas, as their American flagship. That plan didn't last long: Houston voted to ban sex robots before construction could begin.

---

2 After meeting Henry at the Abyss headquarters, journalist Allison P. Davis described him as "a high-quality dildo attached to a fancy mannequin with a Bluetooth speaker in his head" and the physical responsiveness of sexbots in general as akin to "turned-on Tickle Me Elmos."

There have been several other attempts at creating AI companion robots and letting them loose on the world—or letting the world loose on them. A sex robot named Samantha was put on display at the Ars Electronica Festival in Linz, Austria, where attendees mounted her, broke two of her fingers, groped her, and banged her up so badly the manufacturer had to send her in for repairs. A year later, perhaps in response to their creation's autonomy after her "assault," they announced that Samantha would be programmed to revoke sexual consent (but didn't elaborate on how they'd do it).

Gynoid
A robot in the form of a human woman.

An ongoing debate about the fate of the sexbot is whether instilling sexuality into robots is ethical in the first place. Artificial intelligence and digital humanities scholar Kate Devlin proposes that if we're creating machines that emulate human cognition, we can't ignore how sex drives change cognition. She writes in her book *Turned On: Science, Sex and Robots*: "Perhaps we should be replicating this in AI. And perhaps, if we are trying to make a sentient machine, we want that machine to know pleasure as well. We might never get those sentient machines, but if we do, do we then have an obligation to make them capable of feeling pleasure?"

What Is the True Future of Sex?

Lisa Palac, the "Queen of High-Tech Porn," has long since retired the crown. She has two teenagers, a boy and a girl, and is a full-time sex therapist. Her daughter tells her she could make a lot of money selling "feet pics" on the internet, if she wanted. Things are very different now than they were thirty years ago.

"When I got involved in doing this work, and in feminist porn, it was just a handful of us," she said. Some of the greatest pioneers of sex positivity—Betty Dodson, Candida Royalle—are no longer on this planet. "It's crazy to think about that," Palac said.

But with all of the twenty-first century's tech advancements at their disposal—the hardware, the haptic feedback, motion tracking,

Haptics, or technology that stimulates motion, touch, and even smells, is currently at the forefront of so-called "sex tech."

and headsets with blistering-fast video refresh rates—Palac's clients are still simply writing to one another. They carefully craft each new message before it's sent and then reread their own words as they hang in the virtual air, over and over and over.

The simple-looking cell phone was the biggest turning point in the history of sex tech. "How that type of communication and medium has grown, it's made people more readily accepting of sex tech—but that doesn't mean that that particular future is evenly distributed," said Machulis. "People that engage in sexting may not think of it as sex tech. When honestly the amount of work it takes to get their message to the other person privately and in a guaranteed way involves a ton of tech." People who rely on apps that let them swipe for dates, messaging platforms where they can sext securely, or simple websites for streaming porn might be surprised to learn that they can connect their vibrator to their phone—when the technologies aren't *that* dissimilar.

When Palac's clients arrive in her office, they're often wracked with anxiety about some confusing message from a lover they've been communicating with online or over text messages. When the reply arrives, if it arrives, they hyper-analyze every word. "All of that, ultimately, is still coming down to this: What will make you want me?" she said.

The last thirty years has seen an unprecedented revolution in acceptance of sexual diversity, and the internet has been in crucial service of that. The internet accelerates everything, and our sex lives aren't exempt. This web we're living on has always been a publishing machine. We write our worries, ecstasies, and insecurities and add brunch photos to it, for other people to view and respond to. At its best, it can be BBS callers typing their way into love or balloon fetishists bonding over someone's new popping video. At its worst, it turns a community sour and binds them by hate.

If JenniCam was radical for her time, it was because she held a mirror to what we were already destined (or doomed) to do: post, ravenously and inexhaustibly, to the internet. Unlimited access to the published thoughts of anyone with an internet connection liberated us from our own bedrooms, but it also gave us new things to compare ourselves to.

Everything on the internet must be optimized. Developers and engineers are constantly striving to push the devices and technologies we use to arrive on our screens not only as fast and frictionless as the speed of our own thoughts, but *faster*. If they can get us acting before the thinking takes place, that's the sweet spot. It takes half a second for outside sensory information to reach our consciousness; Google developers aim for search results to load in under half a second. This probably isn't a coincidence.

The optimization culture of the internet age has rubbed off onto our sex lives. Porn sites are endlessly, brutally A/B tested to serve users the results that will get the highest click-through rates and conversions to paid subscriptions. The ads on those sites promise (or threaten) that "You'll Cum in 3 Seconds!" Dildos have "optimized shafts." Tinder match notifications ping your phone at perfectly prescribed intervals that will get you to open the app. Sex sells, but sex is also a finely tuned product.

The vision of our sexual destiny as chromed-out and robotic is one that places humans deeply, chaotically out of control. The truth is, none of this, at least not yet, happens without us: the soft, vulnerable, almost pathetically un-optimized humans. The secret to the future of sex is that we are the ones in control.

ACKNOWLEDGMENTS

Τhis book literally would not exist without my editor at Workman, John Meils; thank you for defending this idea, and for the unwavering belief we were on the right track; for trusting my judgment and being a kindred spirit along the way. Editing this stuff is not for the faint of heart.

Learning I'd have a team behind me to get this book into the world was the best surprise, and finding out they'd fought for the assignment is the highest compliment: Kate Oksen, Cindy Lee, Claire Gross, and Rebecca Carlisle, my publicity and marketing team at Workman, thank you for remaining undaunted by the task of selling a book that the entire internet, ironically, is set up to hold back.

Endless thanks to my agent Eric Lupfer, for enduring so many first-time author questions from me and immediately seeing the potential in this project—can't wait to see where it takes us.

I would not be the one to write this without my friends and colleagues at Motherboard: Emanuel Maiberg, my CPA, off-books lawyer, feral animal handler, comrade, coach and too-frequent therapist; and Jason Koebler, who has stood in unflinching support of my work through some really spectacular nonsense. Thank you both for cursing me with the best beat in journalism.

This work is only possible thanks to the numerous people working and advocating in the adult industry who have welcomed me, educated me, and gently (or sometimes not-so-gently) steered me toward a better way of seeing the world: Jessie and PJ Sage, Liara Roux, Kate D'Adamo, Kaytlin Bailey, and Mike Stabile, to name just a very few. Anyone who has ever endured late-night, last-minute emails, phone calls, questions and more follow-up questions from me over the years and graciously lent me your time, thoughts, and trust, you know who you are; my infinite gratitude goes out to you.

I'm indebted to the writers and researchers whose work I admire so, and who always treated the subjects of sex, labor, and online life as worthy of serious inquiry, including but far from limited to Melissa Gira Grant, Tracy Clark Flory, Lisa Palac, Carol Leigh, and the many editors and contributors to sex-worker led publications like *Porn Studies*, *$pread*, *Peepshow* and *Tits and Sass*—as well as scholars including Linda Williams, Dr. Angela Jones, Dr. Heather Berg, Dr. Laura Helen Marks, and Dr. Mirelle Miller-Young, who raise the collective frequency with every conversation and publication.

This book is also for those sources whose stories have been unimaginably hard to tell, but they told them to me anyway. I hope that you have found some sliver of peace in the retelling.

Finally, thank you to my parents, Greg and Bobbi, who never questioned the many passionate, weird paths their daughter traveled, but always knew I'd write a book eventually. And to Daniel Oberhaus, who reminded me that I could write a book, when I wasn't so sure myself. (For him, I'll mention Calliope, who contributed a significant amount of cat hair, drool, and first reads to the process.)

It's taken me a decade of working as a writer to untangle some of my most deeply ingrained beliefs about sexuality, love, technology, and capitalism. Some readers are encountering challenging notions about these topics for the first time in these pages. This book is for you, too: I'm thrilled for you to continue that journey.

For an unabridged listing of sources, please visit: Workman.com/HowSexChangedtheInternet

Chapter 1: The Internet Was Built on Sex

Oliver Wainwright, "Designers on acid: the tripping Californians who paved the way to our touchscreen world," *The Guardian*, May 11, 2017.

Messages from Ward Christensen to Andrei Scheinkman and Steve Culver, *BBS: The Documentary,* November 1993.

OC Weekly staff, "This Sister Oughta Be Famous," *OC Weekly,* May 6, 1999.

Audrey Watters, "How Steve Jobs Brought the Apple II to the Classroom," Hack Education, February 25, 2015, bit.ly/3ihunka.

Allucquère Rosanne Stone, "Will the Real Body Please Stand Up?" *Cyberspace: First Steps,* Cambridge: MIT Press, 1991, bit.ly/3D9ETUl.

Kevin Driscoll, "Social Media's Dial-Up Ancestor: The Bulletin Board System," *IEEE Spectrum*, October 24 2016.

Kevin Ackermann, "The Old Puppet Masters: Content Moderation on Computer Bulletin Board Systems," Georgetown University, August 12, 2020.

Katie Hafner, "The Epic Saga of The Well." *Wired* Magazine, May 1, 1997.

Logan Wagner, "On-Line Sex: At a Virginia Beach Computer Bulletin Board Company, Business is Pleasure," *The Virginian Pilot,* November 27, 1994.

Scott Sayare, "On the Farms of France, the Death of a Pixelated Workhorse," *The New York Times,* June 22, 2012, nyti.ms/3Jy9ywY.

Author interview with Stacy Horn, January 2021.

Chapter 2: Cyber-Utopia, Censorship, and Tinysex

Henry Hardy, The History of the Net, Sept 28, 1993.

David Auerbach, "The First Gay Space on the Internet," *Slate*, August 20, 2014.

Dan Greening, net.moss archive, Aug 23, 1985.

Author interview and correspondence with Mike Godwin, 2021.

George Duncan, Sara Kiesler, Mary Shaw, Carnegie Mellon University internal memorandum, "Report of Committee of Inquiry on A Study of Marketing Pornography via Computer Networks," to Paul Christiano, August 1, 1995.

Author interview and correspondence with Richard Bartle, 2021.

Julian Dibbell, *My Tiny Life*, Holt McDougal, 1998.

Chapter 3: Graphic Images: The Internet Opens Its Eyes

Ken Knowlton, "Portrait of the Artist as a Young Scientist," *YLEM Journal*, Jan/Feb 2005, 25, No. 2.

Janelle Brown, "Playmate Meets Geeks Who Made Her a Net Star," *Wired* Magazine, May 20, 1997.

Linda Kinstler, "Finding Lena, the Patron Saint of JPEGs," *Wired* Magazine, January 31, 2019.

T.L. Andrews, "Silicon Valley's gender gap is the result of computer-game marketing 20 years ago," *Quartz*, February 16, 2017.

CNET News Staff, "Comdex Bans X-Rated Titles, AdultDex Debuts," *CNET*, November 14, 1995.

Bart Ziegler, "Banned by Comdex, Purveyors Of Porn Put On Their Own Show," *The Associated Press*, November 14, 1995.

Michel Marriott, "Virtual Porn: Ultimate Tease," *The New York Times*, October 4, 1995.

Michael Stroh, "Hi-tech sex world shows its face," *Baltimore Sun*, November 23, 1999.

"AdultDex Lures Entrepreneurs Cashing In on Internet Porn," *The Wall Street Journal*, November 19, 1997.

Carolyn Said, "Sex Sells on the Internet / AdultDex is the other meeting in town," *SFGate,* November 19, 1997.

Peter H. Lewis, "Multimedia excitement pervades Comdex show," *Baltimore Sun,* November 22, 1993.

Earl Paige, "Arrest Aids X-Rated Trade Show Producer," *Billboard,* December 20, 1997.

Chapter 4: Webmasters of Their Own Domains

Author interviews and correspondence with Jen Peterson and Dave Miller, 2021.

Michael Learmonth, "Caity's Closet," *Metro,* November 11-17, 1999.

Michael Learmonth, "The Naked Truth," *Metro,* November 11-17, 1999.

"First Come, First Served," *Forbes,* July 10, 1998.

Brad Stone, "An E-Commerce Empire, From Porn to Puppies," *The New York Times,* May 18, 2008.

Steve Silberman, "Porn Patrons Billed, Unfulfilled," *Wired* Magazine, May 19, 1998.

Lewis Perdue, *EroticaBiz: How Sex Shaped the Internet,* iUniverse, 2002.

Frederick S. Lane, *Obscene Profits,* Routledge, 2000.

Chapter 5: A Brief History of Online Dating

The Week Staff, "The Financial Times' Match.com profile: 5 takeaways," *The Week,* January 10, 2015.

"What Online Dating Was Like in the 1960s," FiveThirtyEight, August 12, 2015.

Stephanie T. Tong, Jeffrey T. Hancock, Richard B. Slatcher, "Online dating system design and relational decision making: Choice, algorithms, and control," *Personal Relationships,* Volume 23, Issue 4, December 2016.

Joan Ball, *Just Me,* Lulu.com, 2014.

Mar Hicks, "The Mother of All Swipes," *Logic Magazine,* July 01, 2017.

Matthew Brace, "Tragic end for romantic hero who was a loser in love," *The Independent,* June 3, 1997.

Nadja Sayej, "The Creator of the First Online Dating Site Is Still Dating Online," *Vice,* June 16, 2016.

"10 Quick Questions with Andrew Conru," loveesites.com, March 30, 2010.

Chris O'Brien, "The Prisoner of Sex.com," *Wired* Magazine, August 1, 2003.

Sara Ashley O'Brien, "81-year-old eHarmony founder on gay marriage and Tinder," CNN, February 12, 2016.

Laura Stampler, "Inside Tinder: Meet the Guys Who Turned Dating Into an Addiction," *Time,* February 6, 2014.

Charlotte Alter, "Whitney Wolfe Wants to Beat Tinder at Its Own Game," *Time,* May 15, 2015.

Abby Phillip, "Read the most surprising allegations from the Tinder sexual harassment lawsuit," *The Washington Post,* July 1, 2014.

Chapter 6: Porn 2.0 and the Camgirl Revolution

SF Weekly Staff, "Web Rouser," *SFWeekly,* March 31, 1999.

Reply-All, December 14, 2014.

Thomas E. Weber, "Meet the Man Who Gave The Net Its Eyes and Ears," *The Wall Street Journal,* July 25, 1996.

Ana Voog, "I Was One of the Most Famous People Online in 1998—Then I Disappeared," *Vice,* June 22, 2018.

Maria Seminerio, "Star of Jennicam responds to attack," *ZDNet,* March 26, 1998.

Laura Sydell, "Live From San Francisco, It's Justin Kan's Life," NPR, April 11, 2007.

Virginia Heffernan and Tom Zeller Jr., "The Lonelygirl That Really Wasn't," *The New York Times,* Sept. 13, 2006.

Elizabeth Bernstein, *Temporarily Yours: Intimacy, Authenticity, and the Commerce of Sex,* The University of Chicago Press, 2007.

Angela Jones, "'I Get Paid to Have Orgasms': Adult Webcam Models' Negotiation of Pleasure and Danger," *Signs,* Volume 42, Number 1, *Autumn* 2016.

"How Much Do Cam Girls Make?," Readysetcam.com, 2022.

Matilda Boseley, "'Everyone and their mum is on it': OnlyFans booms in popularity during the pandemic," *The Guardian,* December 22, 2020.

CHAPTER 7: The Digital Fig Leaf: Sexual Censorship Online

Alex Kennedy, "This St. John's seed company's onions are too sexy for Facebook," CBC, October 5, 2020.

David Gilbert, "Leaked Documents Show Facebook's Absurd 'Breast Squeezing Policy'," Vice, December 1, 2020.

Anne Barnard, "New York Investigating Facebook's Safety Rules," The New York Times, September 25, 2007.

Sharon Noguchi, "Protests mount over Facebook ban on breast-feeding photos; bigger turnout online than in Palo Alto," The Mercury News, December 27, 2008.

Samantha Cole, "Facebook and Patreon Are Making It Harder to Find Sex Educators," Vice, July 24, 2018.

Jon Christian, "From 'Preggers' to 'Pizzle': Android's Bizarre List of Banned Words," Wired magazine, December 2, 2013.

Chris Morris, "Google bans porn from its ad network," CNBC, July 2, 2014.

"Starbucks to block porn on free wi-fi in US," BBC, November 29, 2018.

Tina Horn, "How the Financial Sector Is Making Life Miserable for Sex Workers," Vice, July 14, 2014.

Jason Koebler and Samantha Cole, "Apple Sucked Tumblr Into Its Walled Garden, Where Sex Is Bad," Vice, December 3, 2018.

Salma El-Wardany, "Like Our Society, Instagram Is Biased Against Women Of Colour," Refinery29, December 10, 2020.

Manisha Krishnan, "A Fat Influencer Says Instagram Is Censoring Her Account—And She's Paid Thousands to Restore It," Vice, March 11, 2021.

Danielle Blunt, Emily Coombes, Shanelle Mullin, and Ariel Wolf, "Posting Into the Void: Studying the Impact of Shadowbanning on Sex Workers and Activists," 2020.

Lita Lecherous, "What Do Sex Workers Lose When Our Social Media Accounts Are Shut Down?," Peepshow Magazine, March 12, 2021.

"Chase closing accounts of porn stars: Report," CNBC, April 26 2014.

CHAPTER 8: Sex Sells: Classified Ads

Author interview with Savannah Sly, 2021.

Author interview with Kaytlin Bailey, 2021.

Claire Cain Miller, "Craigslist Blocks Access to 'Adult Services' Pages," The New York Times, September 4, 2010.

Peter C. Hennigan, "Property War: Prostitution, Red-Light Districts, and the Transformation of Public Nuisance Law in the Progressive Era," Yale Journal of Law & the Humanities, 2004.

Jeffrey Davids, "Rentboy.com Manifesto," February 11, 2008.

Danny Cruz, "Male Sex Workers Condemn Raid on RentBoy.com," SWOP-USA, August 28, 2015.

Steve Weinstein, "The Queer Issue: The Rise of Rentboys." The Village Voice, June 23, 2009.

Keegan Hamilton, "OldestProfession2.0: A new generation of local 'providers' and 'hobbyists' create a virtual red-light district," The Riverfront Times, June 4, 2008.

Melissa Gira Grant, "Online critics accuse TheEroticReview.com CEO Dave Elms of rape," Valleywag, May 12, 2008.

Edward Duncan, "Troubled Elms Leaves Erotic Review," AVN, March 4, 2009.

Brad Stone, "Under Pressure, Craigslist to Remove 'Erotic' Ads," The New York Times, May 13, 2009.

Graham Snowdon, "Jim Buckmaster: Craigslist put up an ad for a programmer. It got a chief executive," The Guardian, October 6, 2011.

Jim Salter, "Mo. girl sues Village Voice Media over sex ads," The Seattle Times, September 17, 2010.

Eric Stewer, "The Rise and Fall of RedBook, the Site That Sex Workers Couldn't Live Without," Wired magazine, February 24, 2015.

Sydney Brownstone, "A Popular Seattle-Area Sex Worker Review Site Has Been Seized by Authorities," The Stranger, January 6, 2016.

Melissa Gira Grant, "How the Feds Took Down Rentboy.com," *Vice*, August 26, 2015.

Alan Feuer, "Owner of Rentboy.com Is Sentenced to 6 Months in Prison," *The New York Times*, August 2, 2017.

Jen Doll, "Village Voice HQ Is Being Protested for 'Facilitation of Sex Trafficking'," *The Village Voice*, November 16, 2011.

Elisabeth Nolan Brown, "Secret Memos Show the Government Has Been Lying About Backpage All Along," Reason, August 26, 2019.

CHAPTER 9: Plug and Play: Internet-Connected Sex Toys

Penelope Green, "Betty Dodson, Women's Guru of Self-Pleasure, Dies at 91," *The New York Times*, November 3, 2020.

Margalit Fox, "Dell Williams, Founder of Sex Boutique, Dies at 92," *The New York Times*, March 14, 2015.

Dennis Waskul and Michelle Anklan, "'Best invention, second to the dishwasher': Vibrators and sexual pleasure," *Sexualities*, August 6, 2019.

Ilana DeBare, "Good news for Good Vibrations - it's being sold," SFGate, September 27, 2007.

Author interview with Lisa Palac, 2021.

Lisa Palac, *The Edge of the Bed: How Dirty Pictures Changed My Life,* Little, Brown Book Group Limited, 1989.

Christopher Trout, "Teledildonics gave me the gift of long-distance sex with a stranger," Engadget, July 2, 2018.

Kyle Machulis, "How Shit Works— Teledildonics," Metafetish, June 12, 2005.

Craig Bicknell, "Sexing the Big Apple," *Wired* magazine, April 17, 1999.

Mike Brunker, "Sex toys blaze tactile trail on Net," NBC, March 23, 2004.

Anna Jane Grossman, "Single, white with dildo," Salon, August 30, 2005.

Hallie Lieberman, *Buzz: The Stimulating History of the Sex Toy*, Simon & Schuster, 2019.

CHAPTER 10: Algorithms, Monopolies, and MindGeek

Author interview with Angie Rowntree, 2021.

Author interview with Colin Rowntree, 2021.

Author interview with Brandon Reti, 2021.

Chris Morris, "Meet the New King of Porn," CNBC, January 18, 2012.

"Naked capitalism," *The Economist*, Sep 26, 2015.

Author interview with Patrick Keilty, 2021.

Patrick Keilty, "Desire by design: pornography as technology industry," *Porn Studies*, July 3, 2018.

Angela Jones, "For Black Models Scroll Down: Webcam Modeling and the Racialization of Erotic Labor," *Sexualities & Culture*, May 15, 2015.

Jessie Sage, "What Being Labeled a 'Big Beautiful Woman' Means to Porn Performers," *Vice*, June 5, 2018.

Samantha Cole, "Why Doesn't the Porn Industry Accept 'Big Handsome Men?'," *Vice*, April 20, 2021.

Jessie Sage, "Black, Queer, and 'Super-Size' BBWs Challenge What Society Sees as 'Acceptably Fat'," *Vice*, July 31, 2018.

CHAPTER 11: Consider the "Cybersex Addict:" A Virtual Sexual Education

Author interview with Josh Grubbs, 2021.

Edwin McDowell, "Some Say Meese Report Rates an 'X'," *The New York Times*, October 21, 1986

Dana Putnam, "Initiation and Maintenance of Online Sexual Compulsivity: Implications for Assessment and Treatment," *CyberPsychology & Behavior* Vol. 3, No. 4, July 5, 2004.

Al Cooper, "Sexuality and the Internet: Surfing into the New Millennium," *CyberPsychology & Behavior* Vol. 1, No. 2 January 29, 2009.

Al Cooper, *Sex and the Internet: A Guide Book for Clinicians*, Taylor & Francis Ltd, 2002.

Author interview with David Ley, 2021.

Nicole Prause et. al., "Sexual desire, not hypersexuality, is related to neurophysiological responses elicited by sexual images," *Socioaffective Neuroscience & Psychology*, July 16, 2013.

Joshua Grubbs et. al., "Pornography Problems Due to Moral Incongruence: An Integrative Model with a Systematic Review and Meta-Analysis," *Archives of Sexual Behavior*, August 3, 2018.

Marc Ramirez and Trevor Hughes, "'Stand Up, Fight Back': Atlanta rally decries anti-Asian violence, mourns spa shooting victims," *USA Today*, March 20, 2021.

"Elliot Rodger: How misogynist killer became 'incel hero'," BBC, April 26, 2018.

"For incels, it's not about sex. It's about women." Southern Poverty Law Center, May 4, 2018.

Ashifa Kassam, "Woman behind 'incel' says angry men hijacked her word 'as a weapon of war'," *The Guardian*, April 25, 2018.

Kris Taylor, Sue Jackson, "'I want that power back': Discourses of masculinity within an online pornography abstinence forum," *Sexualities*, January 30, 2018.

"White Haze," This American Life, September 22, 2017.

Angela Nagle, "Goodbye, Pepe," The Baffler, August 15, 2017.

CHAPTER 12: Rated M for Mature: Sex in Online Gaming

Author interview with Shine, 2021.

Author interview with Richard Bartle, 2021.

Simon Parkin, "The man who made a game to change the world," Eurogamer, October 30, 2014.

Allucquére Rosanne Stone, "Sex and death among the disembodied: VR, cyberspace, and the nature of academic discourse," *The Sociological Review*, May 1994.

Author interview with Wagner James Au, 2021.

Chip Morningstar and F. Randall Farmer, "The Lessons of Lucasfilm's Habitat," Journal of Virtual Worlds Research, July 2008.

Dennis D. Waskul and Justin A. Martin, "Now the Orgy Is Over," *Symbolic Interaction*, December 22, 2011.

Emanuel Maiberg, "Why Is 'Second Life' Still a Thing?" *Vice*, April 29, 2016.

Nick Yee, "The Surprisingly Unsurprising Reason Why Men Choose Female Avatars in World of Warcraft," *Slate*, May 13, 2014.

Author interview with Karen Gault, 2021.

Audrey L. Brehm, "Navigating the feminine in massively multiplayer online games: Gender in World of Warcraft," Frontiers of Psychology, December 4, 2013.

Laura Kate Dale, "How World of Warcraft helped me come out as transgender," *The Guardian*, January 23, 2014.

Diana Tourjée, "'Will You Fist Me?': World of Warcraft Players Respond to New Chat Abuse Policy," *Vice*, July 15, 2016.

Kim LaCapria, "Did Minecraft Introduce 'Sex Mods'?" Snopes, October 25, 2016.

Burt Helm, "Sex, lies, and video games: Inside Roblox's war on porn," Fast Company, August 19, 2020.

Patricia Hernandez, "Animal Crossing fans are using the game for Tinder dates," Polygon, April 15, 2020.

Rosa Mikeal Martey et. al., "The strategic female: gender-switching and player behavior in online games," *Information, Communication, and Society*, Volume 17, 2014.

CHAPTER 13: Faking It: Deepfakes, Deep Problems

Samantha Cole, "AI-Assisted Fake Porn Is Here and We're All Fucked," *Vice*, December 11, 2017.

Joseph Cox, "Most Deepfakes Are Used for Creating Non-Consensual Porn, Not Fake News," *Vice*, October 7, 2019.

CHAPTER 14: Fuck the System: Crime and Legislation

MTV News Staff, "Pamela Anderson, Tommy Lee Lawsuit Thrown Out," MTV, April 9, 1997.

Clyde Farnsworth, "200 Prostitutes of Lyons in Siege at Church," *The New York Times*, June 7, 1975

Samantha Cole, "Craigslist Just Nuked Its Personal Ads Section Because of a Sex-Trafficking Bill," *Vice*, March 23, 2018.

Samantha Cole, "Furry Dating Site Shuts Down Because of FOSTA," *Vice*, April 2, 2018.

"Documenting Tech Actions," SurvivorsAgainstSesta.org.

Samantha Cole, "People Are Threatening to Report Sex Workers to the IRS in #ThotAudit," *Vice*, November 26, 2018.

Danielle Blunt and Ariel Wolf, "Erased: The Impact of FOSTA/SESTA & the Removal of Backpage," Hacking//Hustling, 2020, https://hackinghustling.org/erased-the-impact-of-fosta-sesta-2020/

Caty Simon, "On Backpage," Tits and Sass, April 25, 2018.

Author interview with "Jane," 2021.

Melanie Ehrenkranz, "We Need to Study the Effects of Revenge Porn on Mental Health," Gizmodo, June 22, 2018.

Author interview with Emily Jones, 2021.

Author interview with Karlijn Seegers, 2021.

Samantha Cole, "'War Against Sex Workers:' What Visa and Mastercard Dropping Pornhub Means to Performers," *Vice*, December 11, 2020.

CHAPTER 15: The Future of Fucking Online

Author interview with Kyle Machulis, 2021.

Mel Slater et. al., "First Person Experience of Body Transfer in Virtual Reality," *PLOS One*, May 12, 2010.

Robin Rosenberg, "Virtual Superheroes: Using Superpowers in Virtual Reality to Encourage Prosocial Behavior," *PLOS One*, January 30, 2013.

Author interview with Marisa Rosa Grant, 2021.

Franki Cookney, "Cam Site Traffic Is Booming As People In Quarantine Look For Sexy Companionship," *Forbes*, March 31, 2020.

Author interview with Mike Stabile, 2021.

Lavender Baj, "Fact Check: No, OnlyFans Is Not Banning Porn," Gizmodo, August 4, 2021.

Author interview with Anna Lee, 2021.

Dean Takahashi, "Oculus Rift gets more virtual reality porn with Red Light Center," VentureBeat, January 15, 2015.

Kari Paul, "What It's Like to Be the First VR Cam Girl," *Vice*, August 3, 2015.

Allison de Fren, "Fembot in a Red Dress," 2015, https://vimeo.com/140950223

Ry Crist, "Hello Harmony: RealDoll sex robots with 'X-Mode' ship in September," CNET, August 25, 2018.

Post by @brickdollbanger on Instagram, June 12, 2021.

Tomasz Frymorgen, "Sex robot sent for repairs after being molested at tech fair," BBC, September 29, 2017.

FURTHER READING

This is an incomplete list of books not specifically cited in this text, but that have heavily influenced, informed and evolved my thinking on sex and the internet.

HARD CORE by Linda Willams

BROAD BAND by Claire Evans

ALICE IN PORNOLAND: HARDCORE ENCOUNTERS WITH THE VICTORIAN GOTHIC by Laura Helen Marks

WIRED WOMEN: GENDER AND NEW REALITIES IN CYBERSPACE by Lynn Cherny

GLITCH FEMINISM: A MANIFESTO by Legacy Russell

WE TOO: ESSAYS ON SEX WORK AND SURVIVAL edited by Natalie West and Tina Horn

COMING OUT LIKE A PORN STAR, edited by Jiz Lee

PORN WORK by Heather Berg

A TASTE FOR BROWN SUGAR: BLACK WOMEN IN PORNOGRAPHY by Mireille Miller-Young

PLAYING THE WHORE by Melissa Gira Grant

CYBER RIGHTS by Mike Godwin

SEXTECH REVOLUTION: THE FUTURE OF SEXUAL WELLNESS by Andrea Barrica

BUZZ: THE STIMULATING HISTORY OF THE SEX TOY by Hallie Lieberman

INDEX

PHOTO CREDITS

Courtesy Use—Acadian Eyes: p. 126; Benj Edwards/Gregory McGill: p. 10; CartoonStock: p. 17; Nicole Gottwald, O.school: p. 145; Leon Harmon (American, 1922–1982); Ken Knowlton (American, 1931–2022). *Computer Nude (Studies in Perception I)*, 1967. Silkscreen print, Edition: unique, sheet: 34 x 72 inches (86.36 x 182.88 cm); framed: 34 x 73 x 2 1/2 inches (86.36 x 185.42 x 6.35 cm). Collection Buffalo AKG Art Museum; Gift of A. Conger Goodyear, by exchange, 2014 (P2014:2) © Estate of Leon Harmon / Estate of Ken Knowlton. Image Courtesy of The Artist and Broadway 1602, New York: p. 38; Jen-Dave.com: pp. 53, 67; Jorian Charlton p. 247; PJ Patella-Rey: p. 174 (left); Sara Miller Photo Studio: p. 105; Mike Saenz: p. 146; Shy Spells: p. 174 (right); Mark Lanett: p. 98; Max Whitaker: p. 130.

Adobe Stock—kvladimirv: p. 52; Masson: p. 2. **Alamy**—Yuri Arcurs: p. 109; frantic: p. 7; Phillip Harrington: p. 73; Wachirawit Iemlerkchai: p. 178; Jon Arnold Images Ltd: p. 125; Artur Marciniec: p. 85; Doug McLean: p. 15; Media Punch: p.222; Mspoint: p. 214; NASA Image Collection: p. 258; Phanie: p. 251; redsnapper: p. 159; Reuters: p. 219; Science History Images: p. 74; Kathleen Smith: p. 197; Universal Images Group North America: LLC p. 3; UPI p. 190. **Flickr**—Justin Kan (2.0 Generic License). **Getty Images**—Andia/Universal Images Group: p. 144; AsiaVision/E+: p. 69; Bettmann: p. 112 (right); CBS Photo Archive: p. 182; Denniro/iStock: p. 90; Alexis Duclos/Gamma-Rapho: Erik McGregor/LightRocket: p. 235; p. 12; Rick Friedman: p. 76; Gabe Ginsberg/FilmMagic: pp. 102, 255 (left); Gabe Ginsberg/Getty Images Entertainment: p. 249; *Hindustan Times*: p. 220; Images Press/Keystone/ Hulton Archive: p. 9; Jeff Kravitz/FilmMagic, Inc.: p. 226; Erik McGregor/

p. 224; John Smith/VIEWpress: p. 233; Alain Voloch/Gamma-Rapho: p. 230; James D. Wilson/Hulton Archive: p. 32. **Wikimedia Commons—** The following images are used under a Creative Commons Attribution CC BY-SA 2.0 License (creativecommons.org/licenses/by-sa/2.0/deed. en) and belong to the following Wikimedia Commons users: Jeremy Tarling: p. 255 (right); jeanbaptisteparis: p. 33. The following image is used under a Creative Commons Attribution CC BY-SA 2.5 License (creativecommons.org/licenses/by-sa/2.5/deed.en) and belongs to the following Wikimedia Commons user: Lonelygirl15 Studios: p. 100. **Public Domain—**Acemagazinefuture: p. 199; Gobonobo: p. 148; Pyb: p. 111; Opencooper: p. 112 (left); Splintercellguy: p. 129; *The New Yorker*: p. 17.

While every effort has been made to trace and acknowledge all image copyright holders, we apologize for any errors or omissions.